EP First Reader

EP Reader Series

Volume 1

Second Edition

CONTENTS

ACKNOWLEDGEMENTS

Thank you to my faithful friends who support me and Easy Peasy each and every day.

Thank you to Abigail Baia for the use of her beautiful cover image.

Welcome to Easy Peasy All-in-One Homeschool's First Reader

This is Easy Peasy's offline version of its assignments for Reading 1. The novels and poetry included are found in the public domain and have been gathered here along with each day's assignment directions. Online activities from Easy Peasy's website have been replaced with offline activities found in this book.

The transition to chapter books can be hard. Your child should be able to read these books, but the size of the reading may feel like too much. If your child isn't feeling up to reading the chapter, have him or her read aloud a sentence, and then you read aloud a sentence. When you feel ready, move to reading a paragraph aloud at a time. Then you could read the first half of the story and your child can finish it. Then move to letting your child read the whole thing alone. It would be good for your child to read aloud to someone for the reading assignments until your child is feeling fluent and competent reading novels.

The child is instructed to tell someone about what happened in the chapter. It is normal at this age to have to ask leading questions. Ask, "Who was the chapter about?" "Where was he?" "What did he do?" "What happened when he did that?" "How did he feel about it?" etc.

Day 1

1. Read chapter 1 of *The Tale of Jolly Robin*.
2. Write the title and author of the book.
3. What does the Roman numeral for number 1 look like? If you can't remember, look for the letter or letters after where it says "chapter," right before the title of the chapter.
4. Tell what happened in the story to a parent or older sibling.
5. Why did Jolly's father stop bringing food to him and make him get out of the nest to get it himself? (Answers)

THE TALE OF JOLLY ROBIN   BY ARTHUR SCOTT BAILEY

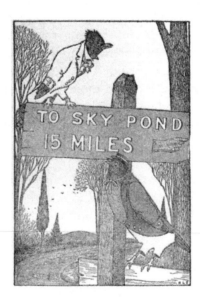

Chapter I NESTLINGS

Of course, there was a time, once, when Jolly Robin was just a nestling himself. With two brothers and one sister--all of them, like him, much spotted with black--he lived in a house in one of Farmer Green's apple trees.

The house was made of grass and leaves, plastered on the inside with mud, and lined with softer, finer grass, which his mother had chosen with the greatest care.

But Jolly never paid much attention to his first home. What interested him more than anything else was food. From dawn till dark, he was always cheeping for something to eat. And since the other children were just as hungry as he was, those four growing babies kept their parents busy finding food for them. It was then that Jolly Robin learned to like angleworms. And though he ate greedily of insects and bugs, as well as wild berries, he liked angleworms best.

Jolly and his sister and his brothers could always tell when their father or their mother brought home some dainty, because the moment the parent lighted upon the limb where the nest was built they could feel their home sink slightly, from the added weight upon the branch.

Then the youngsters would set up a loud squalling, with a great craning of necks and stretching of orange-colored mouths.

Sometimes, when the dainty was specially big, Mr. or Mrs. Robin would say, "Cuck! cuck!" That meant "Open wide!" But they seldom found it necessary to give that order.

Somehow, Jolly Robin managed to eat more than the rest of the nestlings. And so he grew faster than the others. He soon learned a few tricks, too. For instance, if Mrs. Robin happened to be sitting on the nest, to keep her family warm, when Mr. Robin returned with a lunch for the children, Jolly had a trick that he played on his mother, in case she didn't move off the nest fast enough to suit him.

He would whisper to the rest of the children. And then they would jostle their fond parent, lifting her up above them, and sometimes almost upsetting her, so that she had hard work to keep from falling off the nest.

Mrs. Robin did not like that trick very well. But she knew that Jolly would not annoy her with it long. Indeed, he was only eleven days old when he left his birthplace and went out into the wide world.

You see, the young folk grew so fast that they soon more than filled the house. So there was nothing their parents could do but persuade them to leave home and learn to fly.

One day, therefore, Mr. Robin did not bring his children's food to the edge of the nest and drop it into their mouths. Instead, he stood on the limb a little distance away from them and showed them a plump angleworm.

The sight of that dainty was more than Jolly Robin could resist. He scrambled boldly out of the nest; and tottering up to his father on his wobbling legs, he snatched the tempting morsel out of his proud parent's bill.

Jolly never went back to the nest after that. The next day Mrs. Robin coaxed the other children from home in the same fashion. And though it may seem a heartless act, it was really the best thing that could have happened to Jolly and his sister and his brothers.

You see, they had to learn to fly. And so long as they stayed in the nest they could never learn a difficult feat like flying.

Day 2

1. Read chapter 2 of *The Tale of Jolly Robin*.
2. What does the Roman numeral for number 2 look like? (Look at the chapter heading.)
3. Tell what happened in the chapter to a parent or older sibling. (It is normal at this age to have to ask leading questions. Ask, "Who was the chapter about?" "Where was he?" "What did he do?" "What happened when he did that?" "How did he feel about it?")
4. What were Jolly and his parents afraid of? (Answers)

Chapter II LEARNING TO FLY

After Jolly Robin had gulped down the fat angleworm with which his father had coaxed him to leave the nest, he clung desperately to the limb. With no food in sight he had plenty of time to look about him and to be alarmed.

The day was not gone before he had a great fright. He tumbled out of the apple tree and fell squawking and fluttering upon the ground.

Luckily, his mother happened to be at home. She went to Jolly at once and told him not to be afraid.

"Nothing will hurt you," she said, "if you'll only keep still. But if you squall like that, the cat will find you."

It may seem strange, but his mother's words frightened Jolly all the more. They scared him so thoroughly that he stopped making a noise, anyhow. And that was how he learned never to talk when he was on the ground near a house where a cat might live.

"Now," said Jolly's mother, as soon as he was still, "I'll teach you a new game. Just watch me!" And spreading her wings, she flapped them, and sprang into the air.

Soon Jolly was trying to imitate her. And it was not long before he found himself gliding a short distance, skimming along just off the ground.

But in spite of all his efforts, he couldn't help falling again. Though his mother tried to show him how to fly into a tree-top, Jolly Robin seemed unable to learn the trick.

At last Mr. Robin said to his wife: "I'll teach him the rest. You've made a good beginning. But he must learn more at once. There's no telling when the cat may come into the orchard to hunt for field-mice. And you know what would happen then."

His wife shuddered. But Mr. Robin told her not to worry.

"I'll soon have this youngster so he can fly as well as anybody," he declared.

So he went and hopped about on the ground with Jolly for a little while, showing him how to find worms beneath the grass carpet of the orchard.

And then, in a loud voice, Mr. Robin suddenly cried: "The cat! The cat!" And he flew into an old tree near-by.

Jolly Robin had never seen Farmer Green's cat. But he had heard that she was a dreadful, fierce creature. And when his father shouted her name Jolly was so startled that he forgot he didn't quite know how to fly. Before he knew what he was doing, he followed his father right up into the old apple tree and perched himself on a low branch.

That was the way he learned to fly, for he never had the least trouble about it afterward. And as soon as he realized that he had actually flown from the ground to the bough he was so pleased that he began to laugh merrily.

As for the cat, she was not in the orchard at all. Indeed, Jolly's father had not said that she was. You see, he had played a joke on his son.

Now, up to that time Jolly Robin had not been named. You must remember that he was not two weeks old. And having three other children of the same age, his parents had not been able to think of names for all of them.

But this big youngster laughed so heartily that his father named him "Jolly," on the spot. And "Jolly" he remained ever afterward.

Day 3

1. Read chapter 3 of *The Tale of Jolly Robin*.
2. What does the Roman numeral for number 3 look like?
3. Tell what happened in the chapter to a parent or older sibling.

Chapter III THE WIDE, WIDE WORLD

After he learned to fly, Jolly Robin's father took him into the woods to spend each night in a roost where there were many other young robins, whose fathers had likewise brought them there.

Jolly learned a great deal from being with so many new friends. It was not long before he could find plenty of food for himself, without help from anyone.

He discovered, too, that there was safety in numbers. For example, if Jasper Jay made too great a nuisance of himself by bullying a young robin, a mob of robins could easily put Jasper to flight.

"Always help other people!" That was a motto that all the youngsters had to learn. And another was this: "Follow your father's lead!"

Later in the season, in October, when the robin cousins and uncles and aunts and sisters and brothers and all the rest of the relations made their long journey to their winter homes in the South, Jolly found that there was a good reason for such rules. If he hadn't followed his father then he might have lost his way, because--since it was the first time he had ever been out of Pleasant Valley--he knew nothing whatever about travelling.

He looked forward with much interest to the journey, for as the days grew shorter he heard a great deal of talk about the trip among his elders. And while he was waiting for the day when they should leave he became acquainted with many new and delicious morsels to eat. He roamed about picking wild grapes, mulberries and elderberries. And he did not scorn a large, green katydid when he chanced to find one.

There was always some new dainty to be sampled; though as the weather grew colder Jolly began to understand that in winter Pleasant Valley would not be so fine a place to live.

However, he managed to find food enough so that he continued to grow rapidly. The night after he found a mountain ash on a hillside, full of bright red berries, his father said that he seemed much taller than he had been that morning.

"You must have eaten a great many of those berries," said Mr. Robin.

"Well, I notice one thing," Jolly observed. "My waistcoat is fast losing its black spots. And it's redder than it was. The red berries certainly colored it in some way."

Mr. Robin replied that he had never heard of such a thing happening. He looked curiously at his son's waistcoat.

"It does seem to look different," he said. "It's brighter than it was."

Really, that was only because Jolly was fast growing up. But neither he nor his father stopped to think of that. And since Jolly had learned that motto, "Follow your father's lead," he thought his waistcoat ought to be just as red as old Mr. Robin's was.

So Jolly visited the mountain ash each day and fairly stuffed himself with the bright red fruit. It did him no harm, anyhow. And he enjoyed eating it.

And the next spring, when Jolly Robin returned to Pleasant Valley, after spending the winter in the South, there was not a redder waistcoat than his in all the neighborhood.

Day 4

1. Read chapter 4 of *The Tale of Jolly Robin*.
2. What does the Roman numeral for number 4 look like?
3. Tell what happened in the chapter to a parent or older sibling. (Another way to help your child talk about the chapter is to ask about the title of the chapter and what it means.)

Chapter IV WHAT JOLLY DID BEST

Jolly Robin had something on his mind. For several days he had been turning a certain matter over in his head. But in spite of all his thinking, he seemed unable to find any answer to the question that was troubling him. So at last he decided he would have to ask somebody to help him.

And that was why Jolly stopped Jimmy Rabbit near the garden one day.

"I want your advice," he told Jimmy Rabbit.

"Certainly!" that young gentleman replied. And he sat himself down upon his wheelbarrow and looked very earnest. "If it's anything about gardening," he said, "I should advise you to raise cabbages, by all means."

But Jolly Robin said he wasn't thinking of planting a garden.

"In fact," he explained, "the trouble is, I don't know what to do. I'd like to have some regular work, you know. And since you've had a good deal of experience, having run a tooth-pulling parlor, a barber-shop, and a shoe-store, I thought you might be able to tell me what would be a good business for me to take up."

For a few minutes Jimmy Rabbit did not speak. But he nodded his head wisely.

"Let me see!" he said at last. "What's the thing you do best?"

Jolly Robin replied at once that he thought he could fly better than he could do anything else. And he felt so happy, because he was sure Jimmy Rabbit was going to help him, that he began to laugh gaily. And he couldn't help singing a snatch of a new song he had heard that morning. And then he laughed again.

"You're mistaken," Jimmy Rabbit said to him. "You fly well enough, I dare say. But there are others who can beat you at flying.... No!" he declared. "What you can do better than anybody I know is to laugh. And if I were you I should make laughing my regular business."

That idea struck Jolly Robin as being so funny that he laughed harder than ever. And Jimmy Rabbit nodded his head again, as if to say, "I'm right and I know it!"

At last Jolly Robin stopped laughing long enough to ask Jimmy to explain how anyone could make a business of laughing. "I don't see how it could be done," said Jolly Robin.

"Why--it's simple enough!" Jimmy told him. "All you need do is to find somebody who will hire you to laugh for him. There are people, you know, who find it very difficult to laugh. I should think they'd be glad to pay somebody to do their laughing for them."

"Name someone!" Jolly Robin urged him.

And Jimmy Rabbit did. "There's old Mr. Crow!" he said. "You know how solemn he is. It's positively painful to hear him try to laugh at a joke. I'm sure he would be delighted with this idea. And if I were you I'd see him before somebody else does."

Jolly Robin looked puzzled. "Who would ever think of such a thing but you?" he asked.

"Nobody!" Jimmy Rabbit replied. "But I like the scheme so well that I almost wish I hadn't mentioned it. And unless you make your bargain with old Mr. Crow at once I may decide to go into the laughing business myself.... My advice to you," he said, "is to hurry!"

13

So Jolly Robin thanked him. And then he flew away to find old Mr. Crow. Of course, he went to the cornfield first.

Day 5

1. Read chapter 5 of *The Tale of Jolly Robin*.
2. What does the Roman numeral for number 5 look like?
3. Tell what happened in the chapter to a parent or older sibling.

Chapter V LAUGHING FOR MR. CROW

Sure enough! old Mr. Crow was in the cornfield. And though he was feeling somewhat peevish that morning, because a coon had disturbed his rest the night before, he listened to what Jolly Robin had to say.

"I've come to ask you a question," Jolly told him. "I've decided to go into business--the laughing business. And I want to inquire if you wouldn't like to engage me to do your laughing for you."

Well, that struck old Mr. Crow as being very funny. He forgot all about his loss of sleep. And his eye twinkled quite merrily. He tried to laugh, too; but it was a pitiful attempt--no more than a hoarse cackle, which was, as Jimmy Rabbit had said, positively painful. Old Mr. Crow seemed to realize that he was making a very queer sound. He hastily turned his laugh into a cough and pretended that he had a kernel of corn stuck in his throat.

"What are your prices?" he asked Jolly Robin. "Are you going to charge by the day or by the laugh?"

"Just as you prefer!" Jolly answered.

"Well, I'll have to think about it," old Mr. Crow told him. "It's a question that I wouldn't care to decide in a hurry. If I paid you by the day you might not laugh at all. And if I paid you by the laugh you might laugh all the time.... It would be pretty expensive, either way. And I don't believe I'd like that."

"I'll tell you what I'll do," said Jolly Robin then. "I'll stay with you one day for nothing. And we'll see how the arrangement suits us."

That suggestion pleased Mr. Crow.

"Agreed!" he said quickly. "And now," he added, "you may laugh for me, because I am quite delighted."

So Jolly Robin laughed happily. And old Mr. Crow remarked that it was a fair laugh, though not so loud as he would have liked.

"I'll do better next time," Jolly assured him.

"Good!" said Mr. Crow. "And now, since I've finished my breakfast, we'll go over to the woods and see what's going on there this morning."

The first person they saw in the woods was Peter Mink. He was fishing for trout in Broad Brook. And old Mr. Crow, as soon as he spied him, sang out: "How many of Farmer Green's fish have you eaten this morning?"

Peter Mink was just crawling out of the water, with a fish in his mouth. When he heard Mr. Crow calling to him, he dropped his trout upon a rock and looked up quickly.

"How much of Farmer Green's corn have you stolen for your breakfast?" he cried. At that Jolly Robin began to laugh. But Mr. Crow stopped him quickly.

"Don't laugh!" the old gentleman squawked. "There's nothing to laugh at, so far as I can see."

So Jolly managed to smother his laughter, for he noticed that Mr. Crow was angry.

"You'll have to be careful," Mr. Crow warned him. "You mustn't laugh at the wrong time, you know."

"I'll do my best," Jolly Robin promised. And he could see already that old Mr. Crow was going to be hard to please.

Day 6

1. Read chapter 6 of *The Tale of Jolly Robin*.
2. What does the Roman numeral for number 6 look like?
3. Tell what happened in the chapter to a parent or older sibling.

Chapter VI TICKLING A NOSE

Old Mr. Crow did not want to stay near the brook to talk with Peter Mink. Calling to Jolly Robin to follow him, he flapped his way to the edge of the woods and sat in a tree overlooking the pasture.

"Here comes Tommy Fox!" Mr. Crow exclaimed. "We ought to have some fun with him. So when it's time for you to laugh for me, don't forget to laugh loudly."

"I'll remember," Jolly promised him. And just by way of practice he chirruped so merrily that Tommy Fox pricked up his ears and came bounding up to the tree where Jolly and Mr. Crow were sitting.

"Good morning!" Mr. Crow cried to Tommy. "Is that a hen's feather that's stuck behind your ear?" he asked very solemnly.

"No!" said Tommy Fox. "It's a crow's; and I certainly had a fine breakfast."

Now, Jolly Robin wasn't quite sure whether he ought to laugh or not. And then Tommy winked at him. So Jolly thought there must be a joke somewhere and he began to chirrup as loudly as he could.

"For pity's sake, keep still!" old Mr. Crow snapped.

"But you wanted me to laugh louder," Jolly reminded him.

"Yes," said Mr. Crow--"when there's anything to laugh at."

"But didn't Tommy Fox make a joke?" Jolly Robin asked.

"A very poor one!" old Mr. Crow replied. "A very poor joke, indeed!... I see," he added, "I see you've not had much experience laughing for people. And here's where you make a mistake. You laugh at other people's jokes, which is all wrong. After this you must laugh at my jokes--do you understand?"

Jolly Robin said he understood. And Mr. Crow remarked that he was glad there would be no more trouble.

"And now," the old fellow said, "now we'll go over to the swamp, where Uncle Sammy Coon lives. We ought to have some fun with him."

So over to the swamp they flew, where they found Uncle Sammy Coon sunning himself in the top of a tall hemlock.

"Howdy do!" said Mr. Crow.

But Uncle Sammy Coon did not answer.

"We're in luck!" Mr. Crow said with a chuckle. "I declare, I believe the old beggar's asleep. Just watch me play a practical joke on him!"

So Mr. Crow lighted on a branch near Uncle Sammy Coon and began tickling his nose.

Pretty soon Uncle Sammy Coon sneezed. And when that happened, Mr. Crow jumped back quickly. But Uncle Sammy didn't awake--at least, he didn't open his eyes. So Mr. Crow tickled his nose again.

Now, old Mr. Crow was so amused that he glanced at Jolly Robin, to see if he was watching. And in that instant when Mr. Crow looked away, Uncle Sammy Coon leaped at him. He caught Mr. Crow by the tail, too.

The old gentleman set up a great din. He squawked, "Help! help!" at the top of his voice and flapped his broad wings.

The struggle was over in a moment. By a great effort Mr. Crow broke away, leaving one of his tail-feathers with Uncle Sammy Coon, and flew into another tree near-by.

Then Jolly Robin laughed as if he would never stop. He thought that it must be the proper time to laugh, because Mr. Crow had said he was going to play a joke on Uncle Sammy.

Mr. Crow, however, seemed to think differently about the matter.

"Do keep quiet!" he cried. "There's nothing to laugh at, so far as I can see."

"But you said you were going to play a joke on Uncle Sammy Coon, didn't you?" Jolly inquired.

"Yes!" Mr. Crow replied. "But it's no joke to lose a tail-feather. And I wouldn't think of laughing at what just happened.... Besides," he continued, "your laughter is altogether wrong. What you must try to do is to laugh very sadly. In fact," he added, "I wouldn't mind if you shed a few tears, because I feel quite upset over this unfortunate accident."

Well, Jolly Robin saw at once that it was impossible for him to please Mr. Crow.

"My laughter," he said, "is always merry. I couldn't laugh sadly, no matter how hard I might try. And as for shedding tears, I couldn't weep for you even if you lost all your tail-feathers, Mr. Crow."

"Then you may leave at once!" Mr. Crow cried, just as if Farmer Green's pasture belonged to him.

"Yes!" Jolly Robin answered. "I may--and then again, I may not!"

And since he stayed right there and laughed, old Mr. Crow himself flew away. It was a long while, too, before he could bear to hear people laugh. For he thought they must be laughing at him, because he had lost a tail-feather.

And perhaps that was what amused Jolly Robin, though I never thought of that before.

Day 7

1. Read chapter 7 of *The Tale of Jolly Robin*.
2. What does the Roman numeral for number 7 look like?
3. Tell what happened in the chapter to a parent or older sibling.

Chapter VII A NEW WAY TO TRAVEL

The time had come when Jolly Robin was ready to begin his long journey to the South, for it was growing quite cold. On some days there was no sun at all. And even when the weather was fair the sun rose late and went to bed early. It was exactly the sort of weather Jolly Robin did not like.

"No doubt you'll be leaving us soon," Jasper Jay remarked to Jolly one day, when the two chanced to meet in Farmer Green's woods, where the beeches grew.

"I expect to start to-morrow," Jolly Robin answered with a short laugh. The mere thought of his warm, light-flooded winter home in the Southland made him feel glad.

"Well, well!" Jasper Jay exclaimed. "I'm glad I happened to see you, for I know of a new way to travel."

And Jolly Robin wanted to know all about it. "If it's a better way than the old, I'll be pleased to try it," he said.

"Oh! it's much better," Jasper told him. "If I hadn't made up my mind to spend the winter in Pleasant Valley, I'd go the new way myself. But the beechnut crop is good this fall. So I shall stay right here to enjoy it."

"Tell me how we're to go, if you please!" Jolly Robin urged him.

"We?" said Jasper. "You don't mean to say you are going with a crowd, do you?"

"Why, yes!" Jolly Robin replied. "All the Robins are leaving tomorrow. And I had intended to go with them."

Jasper Jay shook his head. "Take my advice and don't do any such thing," he said. "You'll find it quieter travelling alone. And though you may not know it, it's the fashionable thing to do."

Jolly Robin laughed when Jasper said that. "But I'm not a fashionable person!" he exclaimed.

"Then you should become one," Jasper told him. "Besides, the new way is easier, as well as more stylish. But if you're afraid to try something new, of course I wouldn't think of urging you."

"I'm not afraid!" Jolly Robin cried. "And if you'll only tell me what I'm to do, I promise you I'll do it!"

"Good!" said Jasper Jay. "Meet me here day after to-morrow and I'll start you on your journey. I can't explain anything now, because I must hurry over to the woods at once, where my cousin, Mr. Crow, is waiting for me." Then he flew away, screaming a loud good-by as he went.

So Jolly Robin hastened back to the orchard, to find his wife and tell her what he had decided to do.

He had no difficulty at all in finding her. But he had no end of trouble trying to persuade her to travel with him the new way, instead of going along with the crowd in the good, old-fashioned style. In fact, she raised so many objections, saying how lonely it would be and how dangerous it was to travel in a small party and that she didn't want to be fashionable--she raised so many objections that at last Jolly Robin said very well! she might do as she pleased. But as for him, he was going to meet Jasper Jay just as he had promised. And since the new way was easier, he expected to reach their winter home long before she arrived, even if he did start a day later.

But he was disappointed, all the same. And he kept up such a constant laughing and joking all the rest of that day that his wife knew he must be feeling quite out of sorts. For that was a way Jolly Robin had. The worse he felt, the happier he always acted. And it was not a bad way, either.

Day 8

1. Read *The Tale of Jolly Robin*, chapter 8.
2. What does the Roman numeral for number 8 look like?
3. Tell what happened in the chapter to a parent or older sibling.

Chapter VIII JOLLY IS LEFT BEHIND

All of Jolly Robin's friends and relations were greatly surprised when they saw him bidding his wife and children good-by, on the day the Robin family started from Pleasant Valley for their winter home in the South.

"What's this?" they cried. "Aren't you coming with us?"

And Jolly Robin laughed and said to them gaily: "Not today! But you'll find me waiting for you when you reach your journey's end."

His wife, however, shook her head.

"It's one of his queer notions--his and Jasper Jay's," she explained.

"Tut, tut!" her husband said. And he chucked her under the chin—and winked at his friends.

There was no time to say anything more, for everyone was eager to start. So the travellers called good-by to Jolly, while he waved a farewell to them.

It was not many minutes before he was the only member of the Robin family left in Pleasant Valley. He felt very lonely, all at once. And he wanted to hurry after the others. But he knew what Jasper Jay would say, if he did. Jasper would be sure to tell people that Jolly Robin was afraid to travel a new way.... Of course, Jolly didn't want that to be said about him. So he looked as cheerful as he could; and he whistled the merriest tune he knew. Nobody--except his wife, maybe--would have guessed that he wasn't perfectly happy.

Jolly spent a very lonely night. When he went to the roost where the whole Robin family had been sleeping for several weeks, he found it distressingly silent, after the gay chatter that he had grown accustomed to hearing there. And try as he would, he could not keep just a hint of sadness out of his good-night song.

But in the morning he felt better. And he welcomed the dawn with a carol that was joyous enough for anybody. For this was the day when Jasper Jay was going to show him the new way to travel. Yes! he, too, would soon be hurrying southwards, where the sun was warm.

It was no wonder that he sang, "Cheerily-cheerup, cheerily-cheerup," right merrily.

As soon as he had eaten his breakfast, Jolly went to the place where the beeches grew, to find Jasper Jay. And Jasper was there, just finishing his own breakfast. But he was too busy, he said, to bother with Jolly Robin just then.

"You meet me in the orchard this afternoon," he said, "when the sun's over the mountain, and I'll start you on your journey."

So Jolly Robin had to wait all the long day, while Jasper Jay did a hundred silly things, such as mocking Farmer Green's cat, and teasing a sleepy young owl, and making the woods echo with his hoarse screams.

Jasper was late, too, in keeping his appointment in the orchard. Jolly Robin waited for him until almost sunset before Jasper Jay appeared.

But Jolly was so glad to see Jasper that he never once thought of being angry with him.

"Come along!" said the blue-coated rascal. "Follow me and you'll soon learn the new way to the South. And if it isn't a good one I hope I'll never eat another beechnut."

Jolly Robin laughed. He was sure, then, that he had nothing to worry about.

For everybody knew that Jasper Jay was especially fond of beechnuts.

Day 9

1. Read *The Tale of Jolly Robin*, chapter 9.
2. What does the Roman numeral for number 9 look like?
3. Tell what happened in the chapter to a parent or older sibling.

Chapter IX JOLLY'S MISTAKE

With Jolly Robin following close behind him, Jasper Jay flew directly to the crossroads, almost half-way to the village. Once there, he perched himself upon the sign-post at the four corners. And Jolly Robin seated himself upon one of the boards that were nailed to the post. "Here we are!" said Jasper Jay. "You see how easy it is."

"When will the post begin to move?" Jolly Robin inquired, a bit anxiously. He had waited a whole day to begin his long journey to the South, so it was only natural that he should want to start at once.

"What's that you say?" asked Jasper Jay. And when Jolly repeated his question, Jasper began to scream with laughter. "Well, that's a good one!" he said at last. "So you thought the post was going to pull itself out of the ground and fly away with you, did you?"

"Why, yes!" Jolly Robin replied. "Aren't these wings?" he asked, looking down at the boards. "They're already spread," he observed.

It was some minutes before Jasper Jay could answer him, for he was laughing again. But finally he managed to speak. "Those aren't wings!" he cried. "They're sign-boards, to tell you which road to take. Of course, you can't expect to read a sign when you're sitting on it. Just go over to the fence across the road and you can see the sign that you're on now."

So Jolly Robin fluttered over to the fence. And from there he could see the sign-board plainly. This is what it looked like: TO SKY POND, 15 MILES.

"There!" Jasper Jay cried, when Jolly had read the sign aloud. "You see how easy it is. All you need do is to follow this road to which the hand points."

"Then I shall have to fly, after all," Jolly Robin said. He had expected to have a ride. And naturally he was disappointed. Then he read the sign once more. "Sky Pond!" he exclaimed. "I don't want to go to Sky Pond. I want to go to the South!"

"Well, Sky Pond's south of Pleasant Valley," Jasper Jay explained. "It's right on your way to your winter home. And all you have to do when you reach Sky Pond will be to find another sign, which ought to say something like this: 'To the South, one thousand miles.' You see how simple it is," Jasper Jay remarked. "With a sign-board to guide you, you can't go wrong."

But it seemed to Jolly that the new way of travelling was far more difficult than the old. He said as much to Jasper Jay, too. "I wish----" he added--"I wish I had started yesterday, with the others."

At that Jasper Jay said, "Nonsense!" And he muttered something about dunces, and mollycoddles, and--yes! 'fraid-cats!

Perhaps Jasper hadn't intended that Jolly Robin should hear those words--and perhaps he had. Anyhow, he was sorry afterward that he had spoken so loud. For the first thing he knew, Jolly Robin flew straight at him with shrill chirps of rage. And Jasper was so surprised—and frightened, too--that he flew off as fast as he could go, following the road that led to Sky Pond, fifteen miles away, with Jolly Robin after him.

Jolly chased him for a long time, until at last Jasper Jay swerved to one side and turned toward home.

But Jolly Robin followed him no longer. He kept straight on, and on, and on. And he flew so fast and so far before he stopped that he overtook the party that had started a whole day ahead of him.

So he travelled to his winter home in the old-fashioned way, after all. And though Jolly Robin laughed when he told his friends about Jasper Jay's new style of travelling, there was one thing over which he could not smile, even then.

You see, "'fraid-cat" was a name he couldn't abide.

Day 10

1. Read *The Tale of Jolly Robin*, chapter 10.
2. What does the Roman numeral for number 10 look like?
3. Tell what happened in the chapter to a parent or older sibling.
4. Do you know what the "white giant" is? What do you think?

Chapter X THE WHITE GIANT

It was a raw March day when Jolly Robin returned to Pleasant Valley one spring. There had just been a heavy fall of snow--big, wet flakes which Farmer Green called "sugar-snow," though it was no sweeter than any other. Johnnie Green liked that kind of snow because it made the best snowballs. And he had had a fine time playing in the orchard near the farmhouse, not long before Jolly Robin appeared there.

Now, the orchard was the place where Jolly Robin and his wife had had their nest the summer before. So it was natural that he should want to go there at once and look about a bit.

He perched himself on a bare limb, where he sang "Cheerily-cheerup" a few times, in spite of the snow and the cold, whistling wind. He knew that the weather would grow warmer soon; and he was glad to be in Pleasant Valley once more, though he had to confess to himself that he liked the orchard better when the grass was green and the trees were gay with apple-blossoms.

"It's really a beautiful place for a home," he told himself. "I don't wonder that Farmer Green likes to live near the orchard. And now I'll just go over to the house and see if I can't get a peep at him and his wife and his boy, Johnnie--and the hired-man, too."

So Jolly Robin jumped off the bough and started through the frosty air toward the farmhouse. But all at once he saw a sight that sent him darting into a tree. He hid there for a while and something made him shiver--something besides the cold wind.

Yes! Jolly Robin was the least bit frightened. For he had caught a glimpse of a strange man. It was neither Farmer Green nor his hired-man, for this was a giant. He had big, black eyes and a great lump of a nose, which stuck out queerly from his pale moon-face. He was dressed all in white, except for a battered, old, black hat, which he wore tipped over one eye. In one hand he held a stick. And it seemed to Jolly Robin that the queer man was just about to hurl it at something.

In spite of his uneasiness, Jolly peeped around his tree and watched the stranger. But he did not throw the stick. He stood quite still and seemed to be waiting. And Jolly Robin waited, too, and stared at him.

"Maybe there's a squirrel hiding behind a tree," he said to himself. "Perhaps this man in white is going to throw the stick as soon as the squirrel shows himself."

But no squirrel appeared. And Jolly Robin was just about to start for the farmhouse again when he saw somebody pop out of the woodshed door and come running toward the orchard. "Here's Johnnie Green!" Jolly exclaimed.

He knew Johnnie at once, because neither Farmer Green nor the hired-man ever went hopping and skipping about like that.

Pretty soon Jolly saw Johnnie Green stop and make an armful of snowballs. And then he went straight toward the stranger in white. Though Johnnie began to shout, the man in white did not even turn his head. And then Johnnie Green shied a snowball at him.

The snowball sailed through the air and struck the stranger's battered hat, knocking it off into the snow. And, of course, Jolly Robin couldn't help laughing. He was more surprised than ever, too, because the moon-faced man did not move even then. Anyone else would have wheeled about and chased Johnnie Green. But this odd gentleman didn't seem to know that his hat had been knocked off.

"That's queer!" said Jolly Robin to himself. "He must be asleep. But I should think he would wake up."

While Jolly was wondering, Johnnie Green threw another snowball. And when it struck the stranger a very peculiar thing happened.

And Jolly Robin did not laugh. He was too frightened to do anything but gasp.

Day 11

1. Read *The Tale of Jolly Robin*, chapter 11.
2. What does the Roman numeral for number 11 look like?
3. Tell what happened in the chapter to a parent or older sibling.

Chapter XI WHAT A SNOWBALL DID

Jolly Robin was too frightened to laugh when he saw Johnnie Green's second snowball strike the moon-faced stranger in the orchard. You see, the snowball hit one of the stranger's arms. And to Jolly's amazement, the arm at once dropped off and dashed upon the ground, breaking into a dozen pieces.

That alone was enough to startle Jolly Robin. But the moon-faced man paid not the slightest attention to the accident. There was something ghostly in the way he stood there, all in white, never moving, never once saying a word.

But Johnnie Green did not seem frightened at all. He set up a great shouting and began to let fly his snowballs as fast as he could throw them.

They did not all find the mark. But the very last one struck the silent stranger squarely upon his left ear. And to Jolly Robin's horror, his head toppled off and fell horridly at his feet.

Jolly Robin fully expected the man in white to turn and chase Johnnie Green then--or at least to hurl his stick at Johnnie. But nothing of the sort happened. And Jolly did not wait for anything more. He felt that he had seen quite enough. So he flew away to the shelter of the woods, to find somebody to whom he could talk and tell of the strange thing that had happened in the orchard.

Over in the woods Jolly was lucky enough to meet Jimmy Rabbit, who was always very friendly toward him. And as soon as he had inquired about Jimmy Rabbit's health (they had not seen each other since the previous fall, you know), Jolly related how he had seen Johnnie Green knock off the head of the man in the orchard.

"And the man never paid the slightest heed to what happened," said Jolly Robin. "He had a stick in his hand; but he didn't throw it."

"There's nothing queer about that," Jimmy Rabbit remarked. "How could he see where to throw his stick, when he had no head?"

But Jolly Robin could not answer that question. And he looked more puzzled than ever. "I don't understand it," he said with a shake of his own head. "The whole affair was very odd. I'm afraid I shall not care to live in the orchard this summer, especially if there's a headless man there! For how can he ever see to leave the orchard?"

It was Jimmy Rabbit's turn to look puzzled, for that was a question that he couldn't answer.

"Maybe there is something queer about this case," he said. "I'll go over to the orchard to-morrow and take a look at that headless stranger and see what I think about him. If you'll meet me here we can go together."

Now, Jolly Robin had almost decided that he would never go near the orchard again. But he felt that if he went with Jimmy Rabbit there ought not to be much danger. So he agreed to Jimmy's suggestion.

"I'll be here before the morning's gone," he promised.

Day 12

1. Read *The Tale of Jolly Robin*, chapter 12.
2. What does the Roman numeral for number 12 look like?
3. Tell what happened in the chapter to a parent or older sibling.
4. What was the white giant? (Answers)

Chapter XII JOLLY FEELS BETTER

Jolly Robin awoke at dawn. And he knew at once that the day was going to be a fine one. Though the sun had not yet peeped above the rim of the eastern hills, Jolly Robin was sure that there would be plenty of sunshine a little later. He had many ways of his own for telling the weather; and he never made a mistake about it.

Now, it had grown quite warm by the time Jolly Robin went to the woods late in the morning to meet Jimmy Rabbit. And the snow had melted away as if by magic.

"Summer's coming! Summer's coming!" Jolly called joyfully as soon as Jimmy Rabbit came hopping into sight. "The apple-blossoms will burst out before we know it."

"Yes--and the cabbages, too," Jimmy Rabbit replied. "I'm glad the white giant in the orchard lost his head," he added, "because there's no telling what he would have done to the cabbages later, if he had wandered into the garden. He might have eaten every one of them. And I shouldn't have liked that very well."

Then they started off together toward the orchard to look at the headless stranger who had given Jolly Robin such a fright the day before. Jimmy Rabbit went bounding along with great leaps, while Jolly Robin flew above him and tried not to go too fast for his long-eared friend.

Once in the orchard, Jolly led Jimmy to the spot where he had seen Johnnie Green knock off the giant's head with the snowball.

"Here he is!" Jolly Robin whispered--for he was still somewhat afraid of the giant, in spite of his having lost his head. "He doesn't seem as big as he was yesterday. And he has dropped the stick that he carried."

Jimmy Rabbit stopped short in his tracks and stared at the still figure under the apple tree. For a few moments he did not speak.

"That looks to me like snow," he said at last. And he crept up to what was left of the giant and sniffed at him. "It is snow!" he declared.

When he heard that, Jolly Robin flew to a low branch just above the giant.

"I don't understand it," he said. "There's his head on the ground, with the big, black eyes. They certainly aren't made of snow."

"No!" Jimmy Rabbit agreed, as he sniffed at the terrible eyes. "They're butternuts--that's what they are!"

29

Well, Jolly Robin was so surprised that he all but tumbled off his perch.

"There's his hat--" he continued, as he clung to the limb--"that's a real hat. It's not made of snow--or butternuts, either."

"Yes!" Jimmy Rabbit said. "It's a sure-enough hat. Farmer Green wore it on Sundays for a good many years. I've often seen him starting for the meeting-house over the hill with this very hat on his head."

"Then the giant stole it from him!" Jolly Robin cried in great excitement.

But Jimmy Rabbit thought differently.

"It's my opinion--" he said--"it's my opinion that Johnnie Green took this old hat and put it on the giant's head, after he had made him."

"Made him!" Jolly Robin repeated. "You don't mean to say that Johnnie Green could make a giant, do you?"

"Well, he knows how to make a snow-man--so I've been told," Jimmy Rabbit replied. "And though I've never seen one before, it's plain that that's what this creature is."

Jolly Robin had listened with growing wonder. Spending his winters in the South, as he did, he had never even heard of a snow-man.

"Are they dangerous--these snow-men?" he inquired anxiously.

"This one certainly isn't," Jimmy Rabbit told him. "With his head off, he can't do any harm. And with the sun shining so warm I should say that by to-morrow he'll be gone for good. It looks to me as if he might be the last snow-man of the winter, for I don't believe there'll be any more snow until next fall."

"Good!" Jolly Robin cried. "I shall come back to the orchard to live, after all, just as I had intended." And he felt so happy that he began to sing.

"I'm glad I brought you here to see the snow giant," he told Jimmy Rabbit, when he had finished his song. "But when my wife and I start to build our summer-house a little later in the spring, I hope you'll say nothing to her about this affair. It might upset her, you know, if she knew that a giant lost his head in the orchard--even if he was made of snow."

"I understand!" said Jimmy Rabbit. "And I won't mention the matter to her. You're afraid she might lose her head, I suppose, if she heard about it."

Having made a joke, Jimmy Rabbit thought it was a good time for him to be leaving. So he said good-by and hopped briskly away.

And Jolly Robin's wife never knew that her husband and Jimmy Rabbit had a secret that they did not tell her.

Of course, if they had told her it would have been no secret at all.

Day 13

1. Read *The Tale of Jolly Robin*, chapter 13.
2. What does the Roman numeral for number 13 look like?
3. Tell what happened in the chapter to a parent or older sibling.

Chapter XIII THE HERMIT

Though Jolly Robin was quite bold for his size, he had a cousin who was actually shy. This timid relation of Jolly's belonged to the Hermit Thrush family; and Jolly Robin always spoke of him as "The Hermit," which was a good name for him, because he never strayed from the depths of the swamp near Black Creek. At least, he stayed there all summer long, until the time came for him to go South.

If Jolly Robin wanted to see this shy cousin, he had to go into the swamp. For the Hermit never repaid any of Jolly's calls. He was afraid of Farmer Green and the other people that lived in the farmhouse. Apple orchards, and gardens and open fields he considered good places to avoid, because he thought them dangerous.

"There's no place to live that's quite as safe and pleasant as a swamp," he often remarked. "I have one brother who prefers an evergreen thicket, which doesn't make a bad home. And another brother of mine lives in some bushes near a road. But how he can like such a dwelling-place as that is more than I can understand."

Now, there were two things for which this cousin of Jolly Robin's was noted. He was an exquisite singer; and he always wore a fine, spotted waistcoat.

Jolly always admired the Hermit's singing. But he didn't like his spotted waistcoat at all.

"That cousin of mine is too much of a dandy," Jolly remarked to his wife one day. "I'm going to pay him a visit this afternoon. And I shall speak to him about that waistcoat he's so fond of wearing. It's well enough for city birds to dress in such finery. But it's a foppish thing for anybody to wear way up here in the country."

Jolly's wife told him plainly that he had better mind his own business.

"It's no affair of yours," she said. "And you ought not to mention the matter to your cousin."

Jolly Robin did not answer her. He thought there was no use arguing with his wife. And since the Hermit was his own cousin, he saw no reason why he shouldn't tell his relation exactly what he thought.

The Hermit appeared glad to see Jolly Robin when he came to the swamp that afternoon. At least, the Hermit said he was much pleased. He had very polished manners for a person that lived in a swamp. Beside him, Jolly Robin seemed somewhat awkward and clownish. But then, Jolly always claimed that he was just a plain, rough-and-ready countryman.

"I never put on any airs," he often said. "Farmer Green and I are a good deal alike in that respect."

After the Hermit had inquired about Jolly's health, and that of his wife as well, he smoothed down his spotted vest, flicked a bit of moss off his tail, and said that if Jolly cared to hear him he would sing one of his best songs.

"I'd like to hear you sing!" Jolly told him.

So the Hermit sang a very sweet and tender melody, which was quite different from Jolly's cheery carols.

It was a great pleasure to hear such a beautiful song. And Jolly Robin was so delighted that he began to laugh heartily the moment his cousin had finished the final note.

"I wouldn't laugh, if I were you," the Hermit reproved him mildly. "That's a sad song.... If you care to weep, I'd be more than gratified," he said. And he shuddered slightly, because Jolly's boisterous laughter grated upon his sensitive nerves.

You can see, just from that, that the Hermit was a very different person from his merry cousin, Jolly Robin.

Day 14

1. Read *The Tale of Jolly Robin*, chapter 14.
2. What does the Roman numeral for number 14 look like?
3. Tell what happened in the chapter to a parent or older sibling.

Chapter XIV ONE OR TWO BLUNDERS

Jolly Robin's cousin, the Hermit, seemed much disappointed because Jolly did not weep after hearing the beautiful, sad song. But no matter how mournful a song might be, Jolly Robin could no more have shed tears over it than a fish could have. Naturally, a fish never weeps, because it would be a silly thing to do. Surrounded by water as he is, a fish could never see his own tears. And so all the weeping he might do would be merely wasted. Not wanting to hurt his cousin's feelings, Jolly Robin said that he would try to weep after he went home. And that made the Hermit feel happier once more.

"Perhaps you'd like to see our eggs?" he suggested. And since Jolly Robin said he would be delighted to look at them, if the Hermit's wife had no objection, his cousin led him further into the swamp. And there, in a nest of moss and leaves, lined with pine needles, the Hermit proudly pointed to three greenish blue eggs, somewhat smaller than those in Jolly's own nest in Farmer Green's orchard.

Jolly Robin stared at the nest in amazement. And pretty soon the Hermit grew quite uncomfortable. "What's the matter?" he asked. "You seem surprised."

"I certainly am!" Jolly Robin cried. "How do you dare do it?"

"Do what?" his cousin inquired uneasily.

"Why, you and your wife have built your nest on the ground!"

"Well, why shouldn't we?" the Hermit asked. And he looked the least bit angry.

"But everybody knows that the best place for a nest is in a tree," Jolly Robin told him. His cousin shook his head at that.

"It's a matter of taste," he said. "Our families have always preferred to build their nests on the ground. And as for me, I shall continue to follow their example.... It suits me very well," he added.

Jolly Robin couldn't help laughing, the sight struck him as being such an odd one.

"It's a wonder--" he remarked--"it's a wonder your wife doesn't bury her eggs in the sand beside the creek, like old Mrs. Turtle."

"I'd thank you," said the Hermit, stiffly, "not to say such things about my wife." And though he spoke politely enough, his manner was quite cold. It was clear that he felt terribly insulted.

Jolly Robin saw that he had blundered. And wishing to change the subject, he said hastily: "Won't you sing another song?"

So the Hermit cleared his throat and began to sing again.

Although this song was not so sad as the first one, Jolly Robin did not like it half so well. The chorus, especially, he considered quite offensive. And it is not surprising, perhaps, that it displeased him, for this is the way it went:

"Any old vest
May do for the rest;
But I like a spotted one best!"

If it hadn't been for that song, Jolly Robin would not have remembered that he had intended to speak to his cousin about his spotted waistcoat. Jolly had been so interested in the nest on the ground that the matter of the waistcoat had slipped out of his mind. But now he suddenly recalled the reason why he had come to see the Hermit. And he disliked his cousin's spotted finery more than ever.

Thereupon, he resolved that he would speak about it, too.

Day 15

1. Read *The Tale of Jolly Robin*, chapter 15.
2. What does the Roman numeral for number 15 look like?
3. Tell what happened in the chapter to a parent or older sibling.

Chapter XV LOST--A COUSIN!

When the Hermit Thrush had finished his song about the spotted vest, he looked at his cousin Jolly Robin out of the corner of his eye.

"How do you like that one?" he inquired. He noticed that Jolly was not laughing.

"That seems to me to be a very silly song," Jolly Robin said. "But I'm glad you sang it, because it has reminded me that I was going to speak to you about that spotted waistcoat you're so fond of wearing."

"What's the matter with my waistcoat?" the Hermit asked quickly. "I'm sure it's a very handsome one."

"I don't like it!" Jolly told him. "I wouldn't be caught with it on me for anything. Everybody says that you're a great dandy because you wear it. And since you're my cousin, I think I ought to tell you what people are saying about you."

"I don't care what people say!" the Hermit exclaimed. "Those that don't like my beautiful waistcoat can look the other way when I'm around. And if my style of dress doesn't please you, I'd suggest that you keep out of this swamp."

"Now, don't get angry!" Jolly Robin begged.

He gave his cousin a smile, hoping that it might make him feel pleasanter. "I was only trying to help you. I was only going to advise you to wear a red waistcoat, like mine."

Now, the mere thought of wearing a red waistcoat made the Hermit feel faint. Some people say that all great singers are like that. If they don't like a thing, they can't bear even to think about it. And it was a fact that the words "red waistcoat" had always made Jolly Robin's cousin shudder.

Maybe one reason why he never went to visit Jolly was because he couldn't endure the sight of his bright red vest.

Of course, Jolly Robin knew nothing about all this.

"Red would be very becoming to you," he continued. "And it's certainly a cheerful color, too. You need brightening up. I don't believe it's good for you, living in this damp swamp and singing sad songs. What you ought to do is to get some clothes like mine and bring your wife over to Farmer Green's orchard and build a nest in an apple tree....We could have some gay times together," he said smilingly.

Like many other people Jolly Robin thought his own ways were the best. And since the Hermit was just as sure that nobody else knew how to dress, or how to sing, or how to build a house as well as he did, it is quite plain that the two cousins never could agree.

"Just tell your wife about my plan when she comes home," said Jolly Robin. "And I'll fly over tomorrow and show you the way to the orchard."

"I'll tell her," his cousin promised.

"Good!" said Jolly Robin. And he gave his delicate cousin a hearty slap on the back, which made the poor fellow wince--for it hurt him not a little. "Good-by!" Jolly cried. And chirping loudly, he flew back home.

Now, Jolly noticed, as he left, that his cousin called "Farewell!" in a melancholy tone. But he thought no more about it at the time. He told his wife the good news as soon as he reached the orchard; for Jolly was sure that his cousin the Hermit was going to follow his advice.

But the next day Jolly met with a great surprise. When he went to the swamp near Black Creek he couldn't find his cousin anywhere--nor his cousin's wife, either. Even their three eggs had disappeared from the nest on the ground.

"I hope Fatty Coon hasn't eaten the eggs," said Jolly Robin, as he gazed into the empty nest. "But it's no more than anybody could expect who's so foolish as to build a nest on the ground." He grew quite uneasy. And he was puzzled, too.

Later, when Jolly Robin met old Mr. Crow, he learned that his cousin, the Hermit Thrush, and his wife had moved away from the swamp the evening before.

"They've left for parts unknown," old Mr. Crow explained. "I saw them when they started. And when I asked your cousin where they were going, he said that they didn't know, but they were hoping to find some peaceful neighborhood where they had no relations."

"That's strange!" Jolly Robin exclaimed. "We are very fond of each other--my cousin and I. By the way," he added, "did you happen to notice what sort of waistcoat he was wearing?"

Mr. Crow said he had noticed; and that it was a light-colored one with dark spots.

"Dear me!" said Jolly Robin. "I was hoping he had put on a red one. But since he moved in such a hurry, perhaps he hadn't time to change."

Whether that was the case, Jolly Robin never learned. For he never saw his cousin the Hermit again.

Day 16

1. Read *The Tale of Jolly Robin*, chapter 16.
2. What does the Roman numeral for number 16 look like?
3. Tell what happened in the chapter to a parent or older sibling.

Chapter XVI JEALOUS JASPER JAY

The feathered folk in Pleasant Valley were all aflutter. They had heard a strange tale--the oddest tale, almost, that had ever been told in their neighborhood.

It was Jolly Robin who had started the story. And since he was not in the habit of playing jokes on people, everybody believed what he said--at least, everybody except Jasper Jay. He declared from the first that Jolly Robin's tale was a hoax.

"I claim that there's not a word of truth in it!" Jasper Jay said.

Now, there was a reason why Jasper spoke in that disagreeable way. He didn't want the story to be true. And, somehow, he felt that if he said it was a hoax, it would really prove to be one.

"I know well enough," said Jasper, "that there's no golden bird in Pleasant Valley--and nowhere else, either!"

You see, Jolly Robin had hurried to the woods one day and told everyone he met that a wonderful golden bird had come to Pleasant Valley.

"He's not just yellow, like a goldfinch. He's solid gold all over, from the tip of his bill to the tip of his tail. Even his feet are golden. And he glistens in the sunshine as if he were afire!" That was the way Jolly Robin described the marvellous newcomer. "He's the handsomest bird that ever was seen," he added.

Perhaps Jasper Jay was jealous. You know he was a great dandy, being very proud of his blue suit, which was really quite beautiful. Anyhow, Jasper Jay began to sulk as soon as he heard the news.

"Where is this magnificent person?" he asked Jolly Robin with a sneer. "Do let me see him! And if he wants to fight, I'll soon spoil his finery for him. He won't look so elegant after I've pulled out his tail-feathers."

But Jolly Robin wouldn't tell anybody where he had seen the wonderful bird. He said the golden bird was three times as big as Jasper Jay. And he didn't want Jasper to get hurt, even if he was so disagreeable.

Anyone can see, just from that, that Jolly Robin was very kind.

"You'd better be careful, or I'll fight you, too!" Jasper warned him.

But Jolly was not afraid. He knew that Jasper was something of a braggart and a bully. He had chased Jasper once. And he thought he could do it again, if he had to.

"My cousin will tell me where to find this yellow fellow," said Jasper Jay at last. "There's not much that happens in Pleasant Valley that my cousin doesn't know about." So he flew off to find old Mr. Crow—for he was the cousin of whom Jasper was speaking.

Jasper found Mr. Crow in his favorite tree in the pine woods. And sure enough! the old gentleman seemed to know all about the golden bird. But like Jolly Robin, he refused to say where he had seen him. To tell the truth, Mr. Crow had never set eyes on the strange bird. But he did not like to admit it. "He's a great credit to the neighborhood," said old Mr. Crow. "And you'd better let him alone, if you should happen to find him, because he's solid gold, you know. And if you flew at him and tried to peck him, just as likely as not you'd break your bill on him, he's so hard." Old Mr. Crow's warning, however, had no effect at all upon Jasper Jay.

"I'm going to search every corner in the valley until I find this fop. And I'll teach him that he'd better get out of our neighborhood with his fine airs."

When he heard that, old Mr. Crow shook his head.

"You're going to have trouble!" he told Jasper. And then he hurried away to tell Jolly Robin that he ought to advise the golden bird to leave Pleasant Valley.

But Jolly Robin said he had not spoken with the stranger. And never having talked with a golden bird, he felt a bit shy about saying anything to him.

"Then there'll be a terrible fight, I'm afraid," said Mr. Crow.

"I'm afraid so," Jolly Robin agreed. And strange as it may seem, they both said that if there was going to be a fight they didn't want to miss seeing it.

Day 17

1. Read *The Tale of Jolly Robin*, chapter 17.
2. What does the Roman numeral for number 17 look like?
3. Tell what happened in the chapter to a parent or older sibling.

Chapter XVII ONLY A ROOSTER

Jasper Jay spent several days looking for the great golden bird that Jolly Robin had described. But Jasper couldn't find the wonderful creature anywhere. And he was wondering if it wasn't just a hoax after all, as he had claimed. He had almost decided to give up his search, when he chanced to meet Bennie Barn-Swallow one day. Jasper happened to mention that he was on the lookout for Jolly Robin's strange bird; and Bennie Barn-Swallow said quickly: "Do you mean the bird of gold?"

"The bird of brass, I should say!" Jasper replied, with his nose in the air. "You haven't seen him, have you?"

"Why, yes!" said Bennie. "He stays right near my house."

Of course, Jasper Jay knew that Bennie lived in a mud house, under the eaves of Farmer Green's barn. So he cried at once: "Then my search is ended! I'll come over to the barn this afternoon and fight the upstart."

The news spread quickly--the news of the fight that was going to take place at Farmer Green's barn.

And as soon as he heard it, Jolly Robin went straight to the barn and asked the golden bird if he wouldn't leave Pleasant Valley at once.

But the great, gorgeous creature paid no attention to Jolly Robin's request. Indeed, he seemed not to hear his words at all--though Jolly Robin thought the stranger was just pretending.

Jolly had to sing a good many songs that day to keep up his spirits. Somehow, he felt that it was all his fault that there was going to be a fight.

"I wish I hadn't told anyone about the golden bird," he said. "Maybe he would have flown away before Jasper Jay heard of his being here."

Well, Jasper invited everybody to come to the barn late in the afternoon to see him whip the golden bird and pull out his tail-feathers.

"There's going to be some fun," said Jasper Jay. "Nobody ought to miss it."

So, as the afternoon waned, the feathered folk began to gather in the orchard. Jolly Robin was there, and his wife, and old Mr. Crow, Rusty Wren, Bobbie Bobolink, Miss Kitty Catbird, and a good many others as well.

There was a good deal of noise, for everyone was chattering. And Jasper Jay made almost as great a din as all his friends together. He boasted in a loud voice that he was going to give the golden bird a terrible beating. And he was so pleased with himself that some of his companions whispered to one another that it might be a good thing if the golden bird gave Jasper a sound whipping.

At last Jasper Jay called out that he was ready. And then he started for Farmer Green's barn, while the eager crew followed close behind him. They all alighted on the ridge of the barn. And like Jasper Jay, they sat there for a short time and stared at the golden bird, who shimmered like fire in the slanting rays of the setting sun.

Jolly Robin and Bennie Barn-Swallow had seen him before; so they weren't surprised. But all the others gazed at him in amazement.

Now, to Jasper Jay the golden bird looked enormous. He was perched high up on a rod which rose above the roof. And he seemed very proud and disdainful. In fact, he paid no attention at all to the curious flock that watched him.

For a little while nobody said a word. And Jasper Jay was the first to speak.

"Fiddlesticks!" he cried. "This is nothing but a barnyard fowl. He's a rooster--that's what he is!"

Day 18

1. Read *The Tale of Jolly Robin*, chapter 18.
2. What does the Roman numeral for number 18 look like?
3. Tell what happened in the chapter to a parent or older sibling.

Chapter XVIII ON TOP OF THE BARN

All the feathered folk on the roof of Farmer Green's barn saw at once that Jasper Jay had told the truth. The golden bird was a rooster, just as Jasper had said. But it seemed strange to them that a rooster should sit on so high a perch. "It looks to me," said old Mr. Crow, "it looks to me as if he had flown up here and lighted on that rod and then was afraid to fly down again."

"I'll knock him off!" cried Jasper Jay. And he made ready to swoop at the stranger.

"I wouldn't do that!" said Jolly Robin.

"No!" Jasper Jay replied. "I know you wouldn't. You'd be afraid to do such a thing."

"It's not that," Jolly Robin told him, "though he is ten times my size. This is what I mean: He's a peaceable fellow. And though I will admit that he seems a little too proud, he hasn't harmed anybody. So why should anybody harm him?"

"He's a barnyard fowl and he belongs on the ground," Jasper Jay declared. "If we let him stay up here in the air there's no knowing what Farmer Green's fowls will do. All his hens and roosters--and he has a hundred of 'em--may take to flying about where they don't belong. This golden gentleman is setting them a bad example. And it is my duty to teach him a lesson."

Now, the real reason why Jasper wanted to knock the golden rooster off his high perch was because he was so handsome. Jasper's fine blue suit looked quite dull beside the golden dress of the stranger. And that was more than Jasper could stand. "Here I go!" Jasper cried. And he left his friends and flew straight at the golden fowl.

Jasper struck the rooster such a hard blow that he spun around on his perch twice. But he didn't lose his balance. And he never said a single word.

"I'll pull out his tail-feathers this time!" Jasper squawked, as he darted at the stranger again. But Jasper had no luck at all. Though he pecked viciously at the tail of the golden rooster, he succeeded only in hurting his own bill.

Several times Jasper tried. But not one tail-feather came away. And some of the onlookers began to smile. Old Mr. Crow even guffawed aloud. But Jasper Jay pretended not to hear him.

"Don't you think we'd better go away?" Jolly Robin asked Jasper at last.

"I think you had better leave," Jasper screamed. He was very angry, because he knew that his friends were laughing at him. And instead of flying at the golden rooster again he made a swift attack on Jolly Robin.

Being angry, Jasper had forgotten that Jolly Robin's wife was present. And to the blue-coated rascal there seemed suddenly to be as many as six Jolly Robins, each one with a furious wife, too.

Jasper fought his hardest. But he was no match for them. Very soon he made for the woods; and as he flew away a blue tail-feather with a white tip floated down into the barnyard, where Johnnie Green had stood for some minutes, watching the strange sight on the roof of his father's barn.

Johnnie picked up the feather and stuck it in his hat. And when he told his father, later, how a big blue jay had tried to whip the new weather-vane and a pair of robins as well, Farmer Green threw back his head and laughed loudly.

"Don't you believe me?" Johnnie asked him. "Here's the blue jay's tail-feather, anyhow. And that ought to prove that I am telling the truth."

But Farmer Green only laughed all the more. You see, he could hardly believe all the strange things that happened in the neighborhood.

Day 19

1. Read *The Tale of Jolly Robin*, chapter 19.
2. What does the Roman numeral for number 19 look like?
3. Tell what happened in the chapter to a parent or older sibling.

Chapter XIX CURIOUS MR. CROW

Living in the orchard as they did, near the farmhouse, Jolly Robin and his wife knew more about Farmer Green's family than any of the other birds in Pleasant Valley, except maybe Rusty Wren. Being a house wren, Rusty was naturally on the best of terms with all the people in the farmhouse.

But all summer long Rusty Wren never strayed far from home. So it was Jolly Robin who told his friends in the woods many strange stories about what happened near the orchard. His account of the golden bird was only one of many curious tales that he related to the wondering wood-creatures.

Being so cheerful and having so much interesting news to tell, Jolly Robin was welcome wherever he went. And when his friends met him in the woods or the fields they were sure to stop and ask him if he hadn't some new story to tell. One day old Mr. Crow even took the trouble to fly all the way across the cornfield to the edge of the woods, where his sharp eyes had seen Jolly Robin eating wild cherries.

"I say, what do you know that's new?" Mr. Crow asked him. The old gentleman was a very curious person. Being a great gossip, he was always on the lookout for something to talk about.

"I don't believe I've seen anything lately that would interest you," Jolly replied, "unless it's the four-armed man."

Mr. Crow looked up quickly. "What's that you say?" he exclaimed.

"The four-armed man!" Jolly Robin repeated.

"Is that a joke?" Mr. Crow asked. He was inclined to be suspicious, because he always disliked having tricks played upon him. "I've heard of--and seen--a two-headed calf," he remarked. "But a four-armed man is a little too much for me to believe in, unless I behold him with my own eyes."

Jolly Robin laughed.

"It's no joke at all!" he declared.

"Then what are you laughing at?" Mr. Crow inquired severely.

"Nothing!" Jolly Robin answered. "It's just a habit of mine to laugh."

"Very well!" said Mr. Crow. "I accept your apology. But please don't do it again.... And now," he added, "where, pray, is this wonderful four-armed man?"

"In the barnyard!" Jolly Robin informed him. "I've often seen him lately, walking between the house and the barn. He looks a good deal like the hired-man. But of course it can't be he, for the hired-man--as you yourself know--has but two arms."

"I must have a look at this monster," Mr. Crow remarked. "When would be a good time for me to see him?"

"At milking-time," Jolly Robin told him. "If you'll meet me on the bridge down the road when you see Johnnie Green and old dog Spot driving the cows home from the pasture this afternoon, I'll be glad to show you the four-armed man. And then you'll admit that I'm not joking."

"I'll certainly be there--" Mr. Crow promised--"but on one condition. You must tell me now whether you have ever known this queer being to fire a gun. If a two-armed man can shoot one gun, I see no reason why a four-armed man could not fire at least two guns at the same time. And if there's any chance of such a thing happening, I would not care to be present."

Jolly Robin had hard work to keep from laughing again. The very idea of the four-armed man aiming two guns at old Mr. Crow struck him as being very funny. He couldn't speak at all for a few moments. But he shook his head violently.
"You think there's no danger, then?" said Mr. Crow, anxiously.

"None at all!" Jolly Robin answered him. "He carries nothing more dangerous than milk-pails."

"Then I'll meet you on the bridge," Mr. Crow promised.

Day 20

1. Read *The Tale of Jolly Robin*, chapter 20.
2. What does the Roman numeral for number 20 look like?
3. Tell what happened in the chapter to a parent or older sibling.

Chapter XX THE FOUR-ARMED MAN

Old dog Spot was driving the last cow down the lane when Jolly Robin and Mr. Crow met on the bridge near the farmhouse, as they had agreed.

"Now, then--" said Mr. Crow, even before his broad wings had settled smoothly along his back--"now, then, where's the four-armed man?"

Jolly looked towards the barnyard.

"I don't see him yet," he said. "But he ought to appear any moment now. Let's move over to the big oak, for we can get a better view of the barnyard from the top of it."

Mr. Crow was more than willing. So they flew to the oak and waited for a time. They saw the cows file into the barn, each finding her own place in one of the two long rows of stanchions that faced each other across the wide aisle running the length of the barn. It was through that aisle that the men walked with great forkfuls of hay in the winter time, which they flung down before the cows, who munched it contentedly.

But it was summer now. And the cows found their own food in the pasture on the hillside. They came to the barn only to be milked.

"It's milking-time right now," Jolly Robin remarked. "And pretty soon you'll see the four-armed man come out of the barn with some pails full of milk. He'll carry them into the house, to set them in the buttery. We'll have a good look at him without his knowing anything about it."

And that was exactly what happened.

"Here he comes!" Jolly Robin exclaimed, as a figure stepped out of the barn and began walking toward the house. "Now, you'll have to admit that I wasn't joking when I told you the news of this strange being. You ought to be pretty glad I let you know about the four-armed man, Mr. Crow. I guess you never saw anything quite so queer as he is, even if you have seen a two-headed calf." Jolly Robin said a great deal more to Mr. Crow. And he was so pleased that he started to sing a song.

But Mr. Crow quickly silenced him.

"Do keep still!" he whispered. "Do you want to get me into trouble? It's bad enough to have a trick like this played on me, without your making such a noise. Farmer Green might shoot me if he saw me so near his house. I thought--" Mr. Crow added--"I thought you laughed a little too much when you told me about your four-armed man. It's a hoax--a joke--a trick--and a very poor one, too."

Jolly Robin was puzzled enough by Mr. Crow's disagreeable remarks.

"I don't understand how you can say those things," he said.

Mr. Crow looked narrowly at his small companion before answering. And then he asked: "Do you mean to say you never heard of a neck-yoke?"

"Never!" cried Jolly Robin.

"Well, well!" said Mr. Crow. "The ignorance of some people is more than I can understand.... That was no four-armed man. You said he looked like Farmer Green's hired-man; and it is not surprising that he does, for he is the hired-man. He has found an old neck-yoke somewhere. It is just a piece of wood that fits about his shoulders and around his neck and sticks out on each side of him like an arm. And he hooks a pail of milk to each end of the yoke, carrying his load in that way. I supposed," said Mr. Crow, "that people had stopped using neck-yokes fifty years ago. It's certainly that long since I've seen one."

"Then it's no wonder that I made a mistake!" Jolly Robin cried. "For I'm too young ever to have heard of a neck-yoke, even." And he laughed and chuckled merrily. "It's a good joke on me!" he said.

But old Mr. Crow did not laugh. "There you go, making a noise again!" he said crossly. "A person's not safe in your company." And he hurried off across the meadow. Mr. Crow was always very nervous when he was near the farmhouse.

But Jolly Robin stayed right there until the hired-man walked back to the barn. He saw then that what Mr. Crow had told him was really so. And he never stopped laughing until long after sunset.

This is a picture to show you what a neck yoke looks like.

Do you think she looks like she has four arms?

Picture info:
"Glaspalast München 1891 076b" by Gari Melchers - Illustrierter Katalog der Münchener Jahresausstellung von Kunstwerken Aller Nationen im kgl. Glaspalaste 1891, 3. Auflage, ausgegeben am 24. Juli, München 1891 (Digitalisat der BSB). Licensed under Public domain via Wikimedia Commons - http://commons.wikimedia.org/wiki/File:Glaspalast_M%C3%BCnchen_1891_076b.jpg#mediaviewer/File:Glaspalast_M%C3%BCnchen_1891_076b.jpg

Day 21

1. Read *The Tale of Jolly Robin*, chapter 21.
2. What does the Roman numeral for number 21 look like?
3. Tell what happened in the chapter to a parent or older sibling.

Chapter XXI A DOLEFUL DITTY

Jolly Robin often complained about the wailing of Willie Whip-poor-will. Willie lived in the woods, which were not far from the orchard. And it was annoying to Jolly to hear his call, "Whip-poor-will, whip-poor-will," repeated over and over again for some two hours after Jolly's bed-time. Neither did Jolly Robin enjoy being awakened by that same sound an hour or two before he wanted to get up in the morning. And what was still worse, on moonlight nights Willie sometimes sang his favorite song from sunset to sunrise.

"What a doleful ditty!" said Jolly Robin. "I must see this fellow and tell him that he ought to change his tune." But the trouble was that Jolly Robin did not like to roam about at night. He was always too sleepy to do that. And in the daytime Willie Whip-poor-will was silent, resting or sleeping upon the ground in the woods.

But a day came at last when Jolly Robin stumbled upon Willie Whip-poor-will, sound asleep where he lived. And Jolly lost no time in waking him up. "I've been wanting to speak to you for some time," he told the drowsy fellow.

"What's the matter?" Willie Whip-poor-will asked, with a startled stare. "Are the woods on fire?"

"No!" said Jolly Robin. "I want to talk with you--that's all." And he was as cheerful as anyone could have wished. But Willie Whip-poor-will looked very cross.

"This is a queer time to make a call!" he grumbled. "I don't like to be disturbed in broad daylight. I supposed everybody knew that midnight is the proper time for a visit."

"But I'm always asleep then," Jolly Robin objected, "unless it's a moonlight night and you happen to be singing on my side of the woods."

Willie Whip-poor-will looked almost pleasant when Jolly said that. "So you stay awake to hear me!" he exclaimed. "I see you like my singing."

Jolly Robin laughed, because Willie had made such a funny mistake.

"You're wrong!" he said. "In fact, I've been wanting to talk with you about that very thing. I want you to change your song, which is a very annoying one. It's altogether too disagreeable. I'll teach you my 'Cheerily-cheerup' song. You'll like it much better, I think. And I'm sure all your neighbors will.... Why not learn the new song right now?" Jolly asked.

But Willie Whip-poor-will made no answer. Looking at him more closely, Jolly Robin was amazed to see that he was sound asleep.

"Here, wake up!" Jolly cried, as he nudged Willie under a wing.

Again Willie Whip-poor-will sprang up with a bewildered expression.

"Hullo!" he said. "What's the trouble? Did a tree fall?"

"You went to sleep while I was talking to you," Jolly Robin explained.

"Oh!" said Willie Whip-poor-will. "That doesn't matter. You must be used to that."

And the words were scarcely out of his mouth before he had fallen asleep again.

Jolly Robin looked at him in a puzzled way. He didn't see how he could teach Willie his "Cheerily-cheerup" song unless he could keep him awake. But he thought he ought to try; so he gave Willie a sharp tweak with his bill.

"Did you hear what I said about your singing?" he shouted right in Willie's ear.

Willie Whip-poor-will only murmured sleepily: "It's rheumatism. I just felt a twinge of it." He had no idea what Jolly Robin was talking about.

Day 22

1. Read *The Tale of Jolly Robin*, chapter 22.
2. Tell someone about the chapter.
3. Congratulations! You read a whole, big book!

Chapter 22 XXII SHOCKING MANNERS

Jolly Robin tried his best to rouse Willie Whip-poor-will out of his daytime nap. But he had to admit to himself at last that his efforts were in vain. It was plain that Willie was too sleepy to understand what was said to him. And as for his learning a new song when he was in that condition, that was entirely out of the question.

"I'll have to wait till sunset," Jolly Robin sighed at last. "That's the time that Willie always wakes up and begins to sing.... I'll come back here late this afternoon."

So he left the woods; and he was busy every moment all the rest of the day.

Shortly before sunset Jolly Robin went back to the place in the woods where he had left Willie Whip-poor-will sleeping. But Willie was no longer there. He had left only a few minutes before Jolly's arrival. And as Jolly sat on a low branch of a tree and looked all around, just as the sun dropped behind the mountain, a voice began singing from some point deeper in the woods. "Whip-poor-will! Whip-poor-will!" That was the way the song went.

"There's Willie now!" Jolly Robin exclaimed.

And he flew off at once to find his night-prowling friend. He knew that Willie Whip-poor-will was some distance away, because he couldn't hear the low "chuck!" with which Willie always began his song, as a sort of warning that he was going to sing, and that nobody could stop him.

Jolly had a good deal of trouble finding the singer, because Willie Whip-poor-will didn't stay in one place. Between his bursts of song he coursed about hunting for insects, which he caught as he flew. So it was not surprising that Jolly did not come upon him until it had grown almost dark in the woods.

"Hullo!" said Willie as soon as he saw Jolly Robin. "I haven't seen you for a long time."

Jolly Robin laughed merrily.

"Don't you remember my calling on you about noon to-day?" he asked.

"You must be mistaken," Willie Whip-poor-will replied. "I've been asleep since sunrise-- until a little while ago. And nobody came to see me."

"You've forgotten," said Jolly. "But it's no matter. I can talk to you now just as well. I want to speak to you about your singing."

Jolly paused then; and he yawned widely, for it was his bed-time that very moment.

"Talk fast, please!" said Willie Whip-poor-will. "I haven't finished my breakfast yet. And I'm pretty hungry."

It seemed queer, to Jolly Robin, that anyone should be eating his breakfast right after sunset. And he was about to say something about the matter. But just as he opened his mouth to speak he yawned again. And then, without realizing what he was doing, he tucked his head under his wing and fell asleep on the limb of the cedar tree where he was sitting.

Willie Whip-poor-will looked at him in astonishment. "What shocking manners!" he exclaimed. "He went to sleep while we were talking. But I suppose he knows no better."

Willie would have liked to know what Jolly Robin was going to say about his singing. But he was so hungry that he left Jolly asleep upon his perch and hurried off to look for more insects.

Since it was a moonlight night, Willie Whip-poor-will spent all the time until sunrise in hunting for food. Now and then he stopped to rest and sing his queer song, which Jolly Robin did not like. But Jolly Robin slept so soundly that for once Willie's singing never disturbed him at all.

THE END

Day 23

1. Read the first part of *The Tale of Peter Rabbit*.
2. Why was Peter the only rabbit to go to the garden? (Answers)

THE TALE OF PETER RABBIT
By Beatrix Potter

Once upon a time there were four little Rabbits, and their names were--Flopsy, Mopsy, Cotton-tail, and Peter.

They lived with their Mother in a sand-bank, underneath the root of a very big fir-tree.

'Now my dears,' said old Mrs. Rabbit one morning, 'you may go into the fields or down the lane, but don't go into Mr. McGregor's garden: your Father had an accident there; he was put in a pie by Mrs. McGregor.'

'Now run along, and don't get into mischief. I am going out.'

Then old Mrs. Rabbit took a basket and her umbrella, and went through the wood to the baker's. She bought a loaf of brown bread and five currant buns.

Flopsy, Mopsy, and Cottontail, who were good little bunnies, went down the lane to gather blackberries: But Peter, who was very naughty, ran straight away to Mr. McGregor's garden, and squeezed under the gate!

First he ate some lettuces and some French beans; and then he ate some radishes; And then, feeling rather sick, he went to look for some parsley.

But round the end of a cucumber frame, whom should he meet but Mr. McGregor!

Mr. McGregor was on his hands and knees planting out young cabbages, but he jumped up and ran after Peter, waving a rake and calling out, 'Stop thief!'

Peter was most dreadfully frightened; he rushed all over the garden, for he had forgotten the way back to the gate.

He lost one of his shoes among the cabbages, and the other shoe amongst the potatoes.

After losing them, he ran on four legs and went faster, so that I think he might have got away altogether if he had not unfortunately run into a gooseberry net, and got caught by the large buttons on his jacket. It was a blue jacket with brass buttons, quite new.

Peter gave himself up for lost, and shed big tears; but his sobs were overheard by some friendly sparrows, who flew to him in great excitement, and implored him to exert himself.

Mr. McGregor came up with a sieve, which he intended to pop upon the top of Peter; but Peter wriggled out just in time, leaving his jacket behind him.

And rushed into the tool-shed, and jumped into a can. It would have been a beautiful thing to hide in, if it had not had so much water in it.

Mr. McGregor was quite sure that Peter was somewhere in the tool-shed, perhaps hidden underneath a flower-pot. He began to turn them over carefully, looking under each.

Presently Peter sneezed--'Kertyschoo!' Mr. McGregor was after him in no time and tried to put his foot upon Peter, who jumped out of a window, upsetting three plants. The window was too small for Mr. McGregor, and he was tired of running after Peter. He went back to his work.

Day 24

1. Finish reading *The Tale of Peter Rabbit*.
2. What happened to Peter's new clothes? (Answers)

The Tale of Peter Rabbit, cont.

Peter sat down to rest; he was out of breath and trembling with fright, and he had not the least idea which way to go. Also he was very damp with sitting in that can.

After a time he began to wander about, going lippity--lippity—not very fast, and looking all round.

He found a door in a wall; but it was locked, and there was no room for a fat little rabbit to squeeze underneath.

An old mouse was running in and out over the stone doorstep, carrying peas and beans to her family in the wood. Peter asked her the way to the gate, but she had such a large pea in her mouth that she could not answer. She only shook her head at him. Peter began to cry.

Then he tried to find his way straight across the garden, but he became more and more puzzled. Presently, he came to a pond where Mr. McGregor filled his water-cans. A white cat was staring at some gold-fish, she sat very, very still, but now and then the tip of her tail twitched as if it were alive. Peter thought it best to go away without speaking to her; he had heard about cats from his cousin, little Benjamin Bunny.

He went back towards the tool-shed, but suddenly, quite close to him, he heard the noise of a hoe--scr-r-ritch, scratch, scratch, scritch. Peter scuttered underneath the bushes. But presently, as nothing happened, he came out, and climbed upon a wheelbarrow and peeped over. The first thing he saw was Mr. McGregor hoeing onions. His back was turned towards Peter, and beyond him was the gate!

Peter got down very quietly off the wheelbarrow; and started running as fast as he could go, along a straight walk behind some black-currant bushes.

Mr. McGregor caught sight of him at the corner, but Peter did not care. He slipped underneath the gate, and was safe at last in the wood outside the garden.

Mr. McGregor hung up the little jacket and the shoes for a scare-crow to frighten the blackbirds.

Peter never stopped running or looked behind him till he got home to the big fir-tree.

He was so tired that he flopped down upon the nice soft sand on the floor of the rabbit-hole and shut his eyes. His mother was busy cooking; she wondered what he had done with his clothes. It was the second little jacket and pair of shoes that Peter had lost in a fortnight!

I am sorry to say that Peter was not very well during the evening.

His mother put him to bed, and made some chamomile tea; and she gave a dose of it to Peter!

'One table-spoonful to be taken at bed-time.'

But Flopsy, Mopsy, and Cotton-tail had bread and milk and blackberries for supper.

THE END

Day 25

1.   Read the first part of *The Tale of Jemima Puddle-Duck*.
2.   What is Jemima looking for? (Answers)

THE TALE OF JEMIMA PUDDLE-DUCK
By Beatrix Potter

What a funny sight it is to see a brood of ducklings with a hen! Listen to the story of Jemima Puddle-duck, who was annoyed because the farmer's wife would not let her hatch her own eggs.

Her sister-in-law, Mrs. Rebeccah Puddle-duck, was perfectly willing to leave the hatching to someone else--"I have not the patience to sit on a nest for twenty-eight days; and no more have you, Jemima. You would let them go cold; you know you would!"

"I wish to hatch my own eggs; I will hatch them all by myself," quacked Jemima Puddle-duck. She tried to hide her eggs; but they were always found and carried off.

Jemima Puddle-duck became quite desperate. She determined to make a nest right away from the farm. She set off on a fine spring afternoon along the cart-road that leads over the hill. She was wearing a shawl and a poke bonnet.

When she reached the top of the hill, she saw a wood in the distance. She thought that it looked a safe quiet spot.

Jemima Puddle-duck was not much in the habit of flying. She ran downhill a few yards flapping her shawl, and then she jumped off into the air. She flew beautifully when she had got a good start.

She skimmed along over the tree-tops until she saw an open place in the middle of the wood, where the trees and brushwood had been cleared.

Jemima alighted rather heavily, and began to waddle about in search of a convenient dry nesting-place. She rather fancied a tree-stump amongst some tall fox-gloves.

But--seated upon the stump, she was startled to find an elegantly dressed gentleman reading a newspaper. He had black prick ears and sandy coloured whiskers.

"Quack?" said Jemima Puddle-duck, with her head and her bonnet on one side--"Quack?"

The gentleman raised his eyes above his newspaper and looked curiously at Jemima-- "Madam, have you lost your way?" said he. He had a long bushy tail which he was sitting upon, as the stump was somewhat damp.

Jemima thought him mighty civil and handsome. She explained that she had not lost her way, but that she was trying to find a convenient dry nesting-place.

"Ah! is that so? indeed!" said the gentleman with sandy whiskers, looking curiously at Jemima. He folded up the newspaper, and put it in his coat-tail pocket.

Jemima complained of the superfluous hen.

"Indeed! how interesting! I wish I could meet with that fowl. I would teach it to mind its own business!"

"But as to a nest--there is no difficulty: I have a sackful of feathers in my wood-shed. No, my dear madam, you will be in nobody's way. You may sit there as long as you like," said the bushy long-tailed gentleman.

He led the way to a very retired, dismal-looking house amongst the fox-gloves.
It was built of twigs and turf, and there were two broken pails, one on top of another, by way of a chimney.

"This is my summer residence; you would not find my earth--my winter house--so convenient," said the hospitable gentleman.

There was a tumble-down shed at the back of the house, made of old soap-boxes. The gentleman opened the door, and showed Jemima in.

The shed was almost quite full of feathers--it was almost suffocating; but it was comfortable and very soft.

Jemima Puddle-duck was rather surprised to find such a vast quantity of feathers. But it was very comfortable; and she made a nest without any trouble at all.

Day 26

1. Read the last part of *The Tale of Jemima Puddle-Duck*.
2. Who "helped" Jemima find a good spot for her nest? (Answers)
3. What did he really want? (Answers)

The Tale of Jemima Duck, continued

When she came out, the sandy whiskered gentleman was sitting on a log reading the newspaper--at least he had it spread out, but he was looking over the top of it.

He was so polite, that he seemed almost sorry to let Jemima go home for the night. He promised to take great care of her nest until she came back again next day.

He said he loved eggs and ducklings; he should be proud to see a fine nestful in his wood-shed.

Jemima Puddle-duck came every afternoon; she laid nine eggs in the nest. They were greeny white and very large. The foxy gentleman admired them immensely. He used to turn them over and count them when Jemima was not there.

At last Jemima told him that she intended to begin to sit next day--"and I will bring a bag of corn with me, so that I need never leave my nest until the eggs are hatched. They might catch cold," said the conscientious Jemima.

"Madam, I beg you not to trouble yourself with a bag; I will provide oats. But before you commence your tedious sitting, I intend to give you a treat. Let us have a dinner-party all to ourselves!

"May I ask you to bring up some herbs from the farm-garden to make a savoury omelette? Sage and thyme, and mint and two onions, and some parsley. I will provide lard for the stuff--lard for the omelette," said the hospitable gentleman with sandy whiskers.

Jemima Puddle-duck was a simpleton: not even the mention of sage and onions made her suspicious.

She went round the farm-garden, nibbling off snippets of all the different sorts of herbs that are used for stuffing roast duck. And she waddled into the kitchen, and got two onions out of a basket.

The collie-dog Kep met her coming out, "What are you doing with those onions? Where do you go every afternoon by yourself, Jemima Puddle-duck?"

Jemima was rather in awe of the collie; she told him the whole story. The collie listened, with his wise head on one side; he grinned when she described the polite gentleman with sandy whiskers.

He asked several questions about the wood, and about the exact position of the house and shed. Then he went out, and trotted down the village. He went to look for two fox-hound puppies who were out at walk with the butcher.

Jemima Puddle-duck went up the cart-road for the last time, on a sunny afternoon. She was rather burdened with bunches of herbs and two onions in a bag.

She flew over the wood, and alighted opposite the house of the bushy long-tailed gentleman.

He was sitting on a log; he sniffed the air, and kept glancing uneasily round the wood. When Jemima alighted he quite jumped.

"Come into the house as soon as you have looked at your eggs. Give me the herbs for the omelette. Be sharp!"

He was rather abrupt. Jemima Puddle-duck had never heard him speak like that. She felt surprised, and uncomfortable.

While she was inside, she heard pattering feet round the back of the shed. Someone with a black nose sniffed at the bottom of the door, and then locked it. Jemima became much alarmed.

A moment afterwards there were most awful noises--barking, baying, growls and howls, squealing and groans. And nothing more was ever seen of that foxy-whiskered gentleman.

Presently Kep opened the door of the shed, and let out Jemima Puddle-duck.

Unfortunately, the puppies rushed in and gobbled up all the eggs before he could stop them. He had a bite on his ear and both the puppies were limping. Jemima Puddle-duck was escorted home in tears on account of those eggs.

She laid some more in June, and she was permitted to keep them herself: but only four of them hatched. Jemima Puddle-duck said that it was because of her nerves; but she had always been a bad sitter.

Day 27

1. Read the poem "Stopping by Woods on a Snowy Evening."
2. Why does he think the horse would be confused about him stopping? (Answers)
3. Can he stay long and enjoy the peaceful, beautiful snowfall? (Answers)
4. I underlined the parts of the poem that will help you answer the questions.

"Stopping by Woods on a Snowy Evening" by Robert Frost

Stopping by Woods on a Snowy Evening
Whose woods these are I think I know.
His house is in the village though;
He will not see me stopping here
To watch his woods fill up with snow.
My little horse must think it queer
To stop without a farmhouse near
Between the woods and frozen lake
The darkest evening of the year.
He gives his harness bells a shake
To ask if there is some mistake.
The only other sound's the sweep
Of easy wind and downy flake.
The woods are lovely, dark and deep,
But I have promises to keep,
And miles to go before I sleep,
And miles to go before I sleep.

Day 28

1. Today you are going to read the beginning of *The Tale of Squirrel Nutkin*.
2. Squirrel Nutkin is impertinent. By the way he acts towards the owl, to whom everyone else shows respect, what do you think that word means?

THE TALE OF SQUIRREL NUTKIN
By Beatrix Potter

This is a Tale about a tail--a tail that belonged to a little red squirrel, and his name was Nutkin.

He had a brother called Twinkleberry, and a great many cousins: they lived in a wood at the edge of a lake.

In the middle of the lake there is an island covered with trees and nut bushes; and amongst those trees stands a hollow oak-tree, which is the house of an owl who is called Old Brown.

One autumn when the nuts were ripe, and the leaves on the hazel bushes were golden and green--Nutkin and Twinkleberry and all the other little squirrels came out of the wood, and down to the edge of the lake.

They made little rafts out of twigs, and they paddled away over the water to Owl Island to gather nuts. Each squirrel had a little sack and a large oar, and spread out his tail for a sail.

They also took with them an offering of three fat mice as a present for Old Brown, and put them down upon his door-step. Then Twinkleberry and the other little squirrels each made a low bow, and said politely--"Old Mr. Brown, will you favour us with permission to gather nuts upon your island?"

But Nutkin was excessively impertinent in his manners. He bobbed up and down like a little red cherry, singing--
  "Riddle me, riddle me, rot-tot-tote!
  A little wee man, in a red red coat!
  A staff in his hand, and a stone in his throat;
  If you'll tell me this riddle, I'll give you a groat."

Now this riddle is as old as the hills; Mr. Brown paid no attention whatever to Nutkin. He shut his eyes obstinately and went to sleep. The squirrels filled their little sacks with nuts, and sailed away home in the evening.

But next morning they all came back again to Owl Island; and Twinkleberry and the others brought a fine fat mole, and laid it on the stone in front of Old Brown's doorway, and said, "Mr. Brown, will you favour us with your gracious permission to gather some more nuts?"

Day 29

1. Read the next part of *The Tale of Squirrel Nutkin*.
2. Impertinent is the opposite of respectful. Do you think anything is going to happen to Nutkin because of his impertinence?

The Tale of Squirrel Nutkin, continued

But Nutkin, who had no respect, began to dance up and down, tickling old Mr. Brown with a nettle and singing--
  "Old Mr. B! Riddle-me-ree!
  Hitty Pitty within the wall,
  Hitty Pitty without the wall;
  If you touch Hitty Pitty,
  Hitty Pitty will bite you!"

Mr. Brown woke up suddenly and carried the mole into his house. He shut the door in Nutkin's face. Presently a little thread of blue smoke from a wood fire came up from the top of the tree, and Nutkin peeped through the key-hole and sang--
"A house full, a hole full!
And you cannot gather a bowl-full!"

The squirrels searched for nuts all over the island and filled their little sacks.

But Nutkin gathered oak-apples--yellow and scarlet--and sat upon a beech-stump playing marbles, and watching the door of old Mr. Brown.

On the third day the squirrels got up very early and went fishing; they caught seven fat minnows as a present for Old Brown.

They paddled over the lake and landed under a crooked chestnut tree on Owl Island.

Twinkleberry and six other little squirrels each carried a fat minnow; but Nutkin, who had no nice manners, brought no present at all. He ran in front, singing--
"The man in the wilderness said to me,
'How many strawberries grow in the sea?'
I answered him as I thought good--
'As many red herrings as grow in the wood.'"

But old Mr. Brown took no interest in riddles--not even when the answer was provided for him.

On the fourth day the squirrels brought a present of six fat beetles, which were as good as plums in plum-pudding for Old Brown. Each beetle was wrapped up carefully in a dock-leaf, fastened with a pine-needle pin. But Nutkin sang as rudely as ever--
"Old Mr. B! riddle-me-ree
Flour of England, fruit of Spain,
Met together in a shower of rain;
Put in a bag tied round with a string,
If you'll tell me this riddle, I'll give you a ring!"

Which was ridiculous of Nutkin, because he had not got any ring to give to Old Brown.

The other squirrels hunted up and down the nut bushes; but Nutkin gathered robin's pincushions off a briar bush, and stuck them full of pine-needle pins.

On the fifth day the squirrels brought a present of wild honey; it was so sweet and sticky that they licked their fingers as they put it down upon the stone. They had stolen it out of a bumble bees' nest on the tippitty top of the hill.

But Nutkin skipped up and down, singing--
   "Hum-a-bum! buzz! buzz! Hum-a-bum buzz!
   As I went over Tipple-tine
   I met a flock of bonny swine;
  Some yellow-nacked, some yellow backed!
   They were the very bonniest swine
   That e'er went over Tipple-tine."

Day 30

1. Today you are going to finish reading *The Tale of Squirrel Nutkin*.
2. What happened to Nutkin because he was impertinent? (Answers)

The Tale of Squirrel Nutkin, continued

Old Mr. Brown turned up his eyes in disgust at the impertinence of Nutkin. But he ate up the honey!

The squirrels filled their little sacks with nuts.

But Nutkin sat upon a big flat rock, and played ninepins with a crab apple and green fir-cones.

On the sixth day, which was Saturday, the squirrels came again for the last time; they brought a new-laid egg in a little rush basket as a last parting present for Old Brown.

But Nutkin ran in front laughing, and shouting--
   "Humpty Dumpty lies in the beck,

With a white counterpane round his neck,
Forty doctors and forty wrights,
Cannot put Humpty Dumpty to rights!"

Now old Mr. Brown took an interest in eggs; he opened one eye and shut it again. But still he did not speak.

Nutkin became more and more impertinent--
"Old Mr. B! Old Mr. B!
Hickamore, Hackamore, on the King's kitchen door;
All the King's horses, and all the King's men,
Couldn't drive Hickamore, Hackamore,
Off the King's kitchen door."

Nutkin danced up and down like a sunbeam; but still Old Brown said nothing at all.

Nutkin began again--
"Arthur O'Bower has broken his band,
He comes roaring up the land!
The King of Scots with all his power,
Cannot turn Arthur of the Bower!"

Nutkin made a whirring noise to sound like the wind, and he took a running jump right onto the head of Old Brown!...

Then all at once there was a flutterment and a scufflement and a loud "Squeak!" The other squirrels scuttered away into the bushes. When they came back very cautiously, peeping round the tree--there was Old Brown sitting on his door-step, quite still, with his eyes closed, as if nothing had happened.

But Nutkin was in his waistcoat pocket! This looks like the end of the story; but it isn't.

Old Brown carried Nutkin into his house, and held him up by the tail, intending to skin him; but Nutkin pulled so very hard that his tail broke in two, and he dashed up the staircase and escaped out of the attic window.

And to this day, if you meet Nutkin up a tree and ask him a riddle, he will throw sticks at you, and stamp his feet and scold, and shout--"Cuck-cuck-cuck-cur-r-r-cuck-k-k!"

THE END

Day 31

1. Read chapter 1 of *The Tale of Solomon Owl*.
2. Tell someone about the story. Who is the story about? (Answers)

<u>The Tale of Solomon Owl</u> By Arthur Scott Bailey

Chapter I   SCARING JOHNNY GREEN

When Johnnie Green was younger, it always scared him to hear Solomon Owl's deep-toned voice calling in the woods after dark.

"Whoo-whoo-whoo, whoo-whoo, to-whoo-ah!" That weird cry was enough to send Johnnie Green hurrying into the farmhouse, though sometimes he paused in the doorway to listen--especially if Solomon Owl happened to be laughing. His "haw-haw-hoo-hoo," booming across the meadow on a crisp fall evening, when the big yellow moon hung over the fields of corn-shocks and pumpkins, sounded almost as if Solomon were laughing at the little boy he had frightened. There was certainly a mocking, jeering note in his laughter.

Of course, as he grew older, Johnnie Green no longer shivered on hearing Solomon's rolling call. When Solomon laughed, Johnnie Green would laugh, too. But Solomon Owl never knew that, for often he was half a mile from the farm buildings.

A "hoot owl," Johnnie Green termed him. And anyone who heard Solomon hooting of an evening, or just before sunrise, would have agreed that it was a good name for him. But he was really a barred owl, for he had bars of white across his feathers.

If you had happened to catch Solomon Owl resting among the thick hemlocks near the foot of Blue Mountain, where he lived, you would have thought that he looked strangely like a human being. He had no "horns," or ear-tufts, such as some of the other owls wore; and his great pale face, with its black eyes, made him seem very wise and solemn.

In spite of the mild, questioning look upon his face whenever anyone surprised him in the daytime, Solomon Owl was the noisiest of all the different families of owls in Pleasant Valley. There were the barn owls, the long-eared owls, the short-eared owls, the saw-whet owls, the screech owls--but there! there's no use of naming them all. There wasn't one of them that could equal Solomon Owl's laughing and hooting and shrieking and wailing--at night.

During the day, however, Solomon Owl he was quiet about it. One reason for his silence then was that he generally slept when the sun was shining. And when most people were sleeping, Solomon Owl was as wide awake as he could be.

He was a night-prowler--if ever there was one. And he could see a mouse on the darkest night, even if it stirred ever so slightly.

That was unfortunate for the mice. But luckily for them, Solomon Owl couldn't be in more than one place at a time. Otherwise, there wouldn't have been a mouse left in Pleasant Valley--if he could have had his way.

And though he didn't help the mice, he helped Farmer Green by catching them. If he did take a fat pullet once in a while, it is certain that he more than paid for it.

So, on the whole, Farmer Green did not object to Solomon Owl's living in the wood-lot. And for a long time Solomon raised no objection to Farmer Green's living near Swift River.

But later Solomon Owl claimed that it would be a good thing for the forest folk if they could get rid of the whole Green family--and the hired man, too.

Day 32

1. Read chapter 2 of *The Tale of Solomon Owl.*
2. Tell someone about what happened.

Chapter 2 II A NEWCOMER

Upon his arrival, as a stranger, in Pleasant Valley, Solomon Owl looked about carefully for a place to live. What he wanted especially was a good, dark hole, for he thought that sunshine was very dismal.

Though he was willing to bestir himself enough to suit anybody, when it came to hunting, Solomon Owl did not like to work. He was no busy nest-builder, like Rusty Wren. In his search for a house he looked several times at the home of old Mr. Crow. If it had suited him better, Solomon would not have hesitated to take it for his own. But in the end he decided that it was altogether too light to please him.

That was lucky for old Mr. Crow. And the black rascal knew it, too. He had noticed that Solomon Owl was hanging about the neighborhood. And several times he caught Solomon examining his nest.

But Mr. Crow did not have to worry long. For as it happened, Solomon Owl at last found exactly what he wanted. In an old, hollow hemlock, he came across a cozy, dark cavity. As soon as he saw it he knew that it was the very thing! So he moved in at once. And except for the time that he spent in the meadow--which was considerably later--he lived there for a good many years.

Once Fatty Coon thought that he would drive Solomon out of his snug house and live in it himself. But he soon changed his mind—after one attempt to oust Solomon.

Solomon Owl--so Fatty discovered--had sharp, strong claws and a sharp, strong beak as well, which curled over his face in a cruel hook.

It was really a good thing for Solomon Owl--the fight he had with Fatty Coon. For afterward his neighbors seldom troubled him--except when Jasper Jay brought a crowd of his noisy friends to tease Solomon, or Reddy Woodpecker annoyed him by rapping on his door when he was asleep.

But those rowdies always took good care to skip out of Solomon's reach. And when Jasper Jay met Solomon alone in the woods at dawn or dusk he was most polite to the solemn old chap. Then it was "Howdy-do, Mr. Owl!" and "I hope you're well to-day!" And when Solomon Owl turned his great, round, black eyes on Jasper, that bold fellow always felt quite uneasy; and he was glad when Solomon Owl looked away.

If Solomon Owl chanced to hoot on those occasions, Jasper Jay would jump almost out of his bright blue coat. Then Solomon's deep laughter would echo mockingly through the woods.

You see, though not nearly so wise as he appeared, Solomon Owl knew well enough how to frighten some people.

Day 33

1. Read chapter 3 of *The Tale of Solomon Owl*.
2. Why is Mr. Frog uneasy and uncomfortable around Solomon? (Answers)

Chapter 3, III SOLOMON LIKES FROGS

It was a warm summer's evening--so warm that Mr. Frog, the tailor, had taken his sewing outside his tailor's shop and seated himself cross-legged upon the bank of the brook, where he sang and sewed without ceasing—except to take a swim now and then in the cool water, "to stretch his legs," as he claimed.

He was making a new suit of blue clothes for Jasper Jay. And since Jasper was a great dandy, and very particular Mr. Frog was taking special pains with his sewing.

Usually he did his work quickly. But now after every five stitches that he put into his work he stopped to take out ten. And naturally he was not getting on very fast. He had been working busily since early morning; and Jasper Jay's suit was further than ever from being finished.

Since he was a most cheerful person, Mr. Frog did not mind that. Indeed, he was more than pleased, because the oftener he took a swim the fewer stitches he lost. So he sang the merriest songs he knew.

The light was fast fading when a hollow laugh startled Mr. Frog. It seemed to come from the willow tree right over his head. And he knew without looking up that it was Solomon Owl's deep voice.

Mr. Frog tried to leap into the brook. But when he uncrossed his legs, in his haste he tangled them up in his sewing. And all he could do was to turn a somersault backward among some bulrushes, hoping that Solomon Owl had not seen him.

It is no secret that Mr. Frog was terribly afraid of Solomon Owl. Some of Mr. Frog's friends had mysteriously disappeared. And they had last been seen in Solomon's company.

As it happened, Mr. Frog had hoped in vain. For Solomon Owl only laughed more loudly than before. And then he said: "What are you afraid of, Mr. Frog?"

The tailor knew at once that he was caught. So he hopped nimbly to his feet and answered that there was nothing to be afraid of, so far as he could see.

It was a true statement, too; because Mr. Frog had not yet discovered Solomon Owl's exact whereabouts.

But he learned them soon; for Solomon immediately dropped down from the big willow and alighted on the bank near Mr. Frog--altogether too near him, in fact, for the tailor's comfort.

Solomon looked at Mr. Frog very solemnly. And he thought that he shivered.

"What's the matter? Are you ill?" Solomon Owl inquired. "You seem to be shaking."

"Just a touch of chills and fever, probably!" replied Mr. Frog with an uneasy smile. "You know it's very damp here."

"You don't look in the best of health--that's a fact!" Solomon Owl remarked. "You appear to me to be somewhat green in the face."

And he laughed once more--that same hollow, mirthless laugh.

Mr. Frog couldn't help jumping, because the sound alarmed him.

"Don't be disturbed!" said Solomon Owl. "I like all the Frog family."

At that remark, Mr. Frog started violently. That was exactly the trouble! Solomon Owl was altogether too fond of frogs, whether they were old or young, big or little.

It was no wonder that Mr. Frog swallowed rapidly sixteen times before he could say another word.

Day 34

1. Read chapter 4 of *The Tale of Solomon Owl*.
2. Tell someone about what happened.

Chapter 4, IV AN ODD BARGAIN

While Mr. Frog was swallowing nothing rapidly, he was thinking rapidly, too. There was something about Solomon Owl's big, staring eyes that made Mr. Frog feel uncomfortable. And if he had thought he had any chance of escaping he would have dived into the brook and swum under the bank.

But Solomon Owl was too near him for that. And Mr. Frog was afraid his caller would pounce upon him any moment. So he quickly thought of a plan to save himself. "No doubt---" he began. But Solomon Owl interrupted him.

"There!" cried Solomon. "You can speak, after all. I supposed you'd swallowed your tongue. And I was just waiting to see what you'd do next. I thought maybe you would swallow your head."

Mr. Frog managed to laugh at the joke, though, to tell the truth, he felt more nervous than ever. He saw what was in Solomon Owl's mind, for Solomon was thinking of swallowing Mr. Frog's head himself.

"No doubt--" Mr. Frog resumed--"no doubt you've come to ask me to make you a new suit of clothes."

Now, Solomon Owl had had no such idea at all. But when it was mentioned to him, he rather liked it. "Will you?" he inquired, with a highly interested air.

"Why, certainly!" the tailor replied. And for the first time since he had turned his backward somersault into the bulrushes, he smiled widely. "I'll tell you what I'll do!" he said. "First, I'll make you a coat free. And second, if you like it I will then make you a waistcoat and trousers, at double rates."

Solomon Owl liked the thought of getting a coat for nothing. But for all that, he looked at the tailor somewhat doubtfully.

"Will it take you long?" he asked.

"No, indeed!" Mr. Frog told him. "I'll make your coat while you wait."

"Oh, I wasn't going away," Solomon assured him with an odd look which made Mr. Frog shiver again. "Be quick, please! Because I have some important business to attend to."

Mr. Frog couldn't help wondering if it wasn't he himself that Solomon Owl was going to attend to. In spite of his fears, however, he caught up his shears and set to work to cut up some cloth that hung just outside his door.

"Stop!" Solomon Owl cried in a voice that seemed to shake the very ground. "You haven't measured me yet!"

"It's not necessary," Mr. Frog explained glibly. "I've become so skilful that one look at an elegant figure like yours is all that I need."

Naturally, Mr. Frog's remark pleased Solomon Owl. And he uttered ten rapid hoots, which served to make Mr. Frog's fingers fly all the faster. Soon he was sewing Solomon's coat with long stitches; and though his needle slipped now and then, he did not pause to take out a single stitch. For some reason, Mr. Frog was in a great hurry.

Solomon Owl did not appear to notice that the tailor was not taking much pains with his sewing. Perhaps Mr. Frog worked so fast that Solomon could not see what he was doing.

Anyhow, he was delighted when Mr. Frog suddenly cried:

"It's finished!" And then he tossed the coat to Solomon. "Try it on!" he said. "I want to see how well it fits you."

Solomon Owl held up the garment and looked at it very carefully. And as he examined it a puzzled look came over his great pale face.

There was something about his new coat that he did not understand.

Day 35

1. Read chapter 5 of *The Tale of Solomon Owl*.
2. Tell about the story of Solomon Owl so far to someone in your family.
3. Did Mr. Frog really make Solomon a coat? (Answers)
4. Why do you think Mr. Frog tricked him into putting a bag over his head?

Chapter 5, V THE COLD WEATHER COAT

Yes! As he held up his new coat and looked at it, Solomon Owl was puzzled. He turned his head toward Mr. Frog and stared at him for a moment. And then he turned his head away from the tailor and gazed upon the coat again.

Mr. Frog was most uncomfortable--especially when Solomon looked at him. "Everything's all right, isn't it?" he inquired.

Solomon Owl slowly shook his head.

"This is a queer coat!" he said. "What's this bag at the top of it?"

"Oh!" exclaimed Mr. Frog. "That's the hood! Knowing that you spend your winters here in Pleasant Valley, I made a hood to go over your head.... You'll find it very comfortable in cold weather--and it's the latest style, too. All the winter coats this year will have hoods, with holes to see through, you know."

Solomon Owl looked relieved at Mr. Frog's explanation. But there was still something more that appeared to trouble him.

"How shall I get into the coat?" he inquired. "It doesn't open in front, as it should."

"Another cold-weather style!" Mr. Frog assured him. "It's wind-proof! And instead of buttoning the coat, you pull it on over your head."

Solomon Owl said he didn't like that style very well.

"Then I can easily change it," the tailor told him. "But just try it on!" he urged. "It may please you, after all."

So Solomon Owl pulled the coat over his head. And it fell down about him, almost reaching his feet. But the coat did not seem to suit him at all, for he began to splutter and choke.

"What's the matter now?" Mr. Frog asked him.

"I can't see--that's what's the matter!" Solomon Owl cried in a voice that sounded hollower than ever, because it was muffled by the hood, which covered his head.

"I declare--I haven't cut the holes for your eyes!" the tailor exclaimed. "Just wait a moment and I'll make everything satisfactory." He clinked his shears together sharply as he spoke.

But Solomon Owl told him that he wouldn't think of letting anybody use shears so near his eyes.

"I'll take off the coat," he said. "And I know now that you're a very poor tailor, or you wouldn't have made such a mistake." He began to tug at the coat. But he soon found that taking it off was not so easy as putting it on. Solomon's sharp claws caught in the cloth; and his hooked beak, too, fastened itself in the hood the moment he tried to pull the coat over his head. "Here!" he cried to Mr. Frog. "Just lend me a hand! I can't see to help myself."

But Mr. Frog did not even answer him.

"Don't you hear me?" Solomon Owl shouted, as he struggled with his new coat, only to become tangled in it more than ever.

Still, the tailor said never a word, though something very like a giggle, followed by a splash, caught Solomon's ear.

"He's left me!" Solomon Owl groaned.

"Mr. Frog has left me to get out of this coat alone. And goodness knows how I'm ever going to do it."

He threshed about so vigorously that he tripped himself and fell upon the bank of the brook, rolling over and over toward the water.

He had a very narrow escape. If he hadn't happened to bring up against an old stump he would certainly have tumbled into the stream.

Though Solomon couldn't see, he knew that he was in danger. So he lay on his back on the ground and carefully tore his new coat into strings and ribbons.

At last he was free. And he rose to his feet feeling very sheepish, for he knew that Mr. Frog had played a sly trick on him.

"Never mind!" said Solomon Owl, as he flew way. "I'll come back to-morrow and ask Mr. Frog to make me a waistcoat and trousers. And then----" He did not finish what he was saying. But there is no doubt that whatever it was, it could not have been very pleasant for Mr. Frog.

Just as he had planned, Solomon Owl returned to the brook the next day. And he was both surprised and disappointed at what he found.

The door of Mr. Frog's tailor's shop was shut and locked. And on it there was a sign, which said: TO LET. (note: This means it's for rent.)

"He's moved away!" cried Solomon Owl. And he went off feeling that he had been cheated out of a good dinner--to say nothing of a new waistcoat—and new trousers, too.

He had not been gone long when the door opened. And Mr. Frog leaped nimbly outside. He took the sign off the door; and sitting down cross-legged upon the bank, he began to sew upon Jasper Jay's new blue suit, while his face wore a wider smile than ever.

He had suddenly decided not to let his shop, after all.

Day 36

1. Read chapter 6 of *The Tale of Solomon Owl*.
2. Tell someone about what happened.
3. Where does he go to find pullets to eat? Any guess what a pullet is? (Answers)

Chapter 6, VI SOLOMON NEEDS A CHANGE

For some time Solomon Owl had known that a queer feeling was coming over him. And he could not think what it meant. He noticed, too, that his appetite was leaving him. Nothing seemed to taste good any more.

So at last, one fine fall evening he went to see Aunt Polly Woodchuck, who was an herb doctor; for he had begun to worry about his health.

"It's lucky you came today," said Aunt Polly. "Because to-night I'm going to begin my winter's nap. And you couldn't have seen me again till spring--unless you happened to come here on ground-hog day, next February.... What appears to be your trouble?" she inquired.

"It's my appetite, partly," Solomon Owl said. "Nothing tastes as it did when I was a youngster. And I keep longing for something, though what it is I can't just tell."

Aunt Polly Woodchuck nodded her head wisely. "What have you been eating lately?" she asked.

Solomon Owl replied that he hadn't eaten anything but mice since the leaves began to turn.

"Hmm--the leaves are nearly all off the trees now," the old lady remarked. "How many mice have you eaten in that time?"

Solomon said that as nearly as he could remember he had eaten twenty-seven--or a hundred and twenty-seven. He couldn't say which--but one of those numbers was correct.

Aunt Polly Woodchuck threw up her hands.

"Sakes alive!" she cried. "It's no wonder you don't feel well! What you need is a change of food. And it's lucky you came to me now. If you'd gone on like that much longer I'd hate to say what might have happened to you. You'd have had dyspepsia, or some other sort of misery in your stomach."

"What shall I do?" asked Solomon Owl. "Insects are scarce at this season of the year. Of course, there are frogs--but I don't seem to care for them. And there are fish--but they're not easy to get, for they don't come out of the water and sit on the bank, as the frogs do."

"How about pullets?" Aunt Polly inquired.

At that Solomon Owl let out a long row of hoots because he was pleased.

"The very thing!" he cried. "That's what I've been wanting all this time. And I never guessed it.... I'll pay you for your advice the next time I see you," he told Aunt Polly. And Solomon Owl hurried away before she could stop him. Since he had no intention of visiting her on ground-hog day, he knew it would be spring before he saw Aunt Polly Woodchuck again.

The old lady scolded a bit. And it did not make her feel any pleasanter to hear Solomon's mocking laughter, which grew fainter and fainter as he left the pasture behind him. Then she went inside her house, for she was fast growing sleepy. And she wanted to set things to rights before she began her long winter's nap.

Meanwhile, Solomon Owl roamed restlessly through the woods. There was only one place in the neighborhood where he could get a pullet. That was at Farmer Green's chicken house. And for some reason he did not care to visit the farm buildings until it grew darker.

So he amused himself by making the woods echo with his strange cry, "Whoo-whoo-whoo, whoo-whoo, to-whoo-ah!" And now and then he threw in a few "wha-whas," just for extra measure.

Many of the forest folk who heard him remarked that Solomon Owl seemed to be in extra fine spirits.

"Probably it's the hunter's moon that pleases him!" Jimmy Rabbit remarked to a friend of his. "I've always noticed that old Solomon makes more noise on moonlight nights than at any other time."

The hunter's moon, big and yellow and round, was just rising over Blue Mountain. But for once it was not the moon that made Solomon Owl so talkative. He was in fine feather, so to speak, because he was hoping to have a fat pullet for his supper. And as for the moon, he would have been just as pleased had there been none at all that night. For Solomon Owl never cared to be seen when he visited Farmer Green's chicken house.

Day 37

1. Read chapter 7 of *The Tale of Solomon Owl*.
2. Tell someone what happened in the chapter.
3. A pullet is a kid hen, not a baby chick, not a grown hen.
4. Any idea what has "blazing eyes?"

Chapter 7, VII THE BLAZING EYES

It was some three hours after sunset when Solomon Owl at last reached Farmer Green's place. All was quiet in the chicken house because the hens and roosters and their families had long since gone to roost. And except for a light that shone through a window, the farmhouse showed not a sign of life.

Everything was as Solomon Owl wished it--or so he thought, at least, as he alighted in a tree in the yard to look about him. He wanted no one to interrupt him when he should go nosing around the chicken house, to find an opening.

To his annoyance, he had not sat long in the tree when the woodshed door opened. And Solomon stared in amazement at the strange sight he saw.

A great head appeared, with eyes and mouth--yes! and nose, too--all a glaring flame color. Solomon had never seen such a horrible face on man or bird or beast. But he was sure it was a man, for he heard a laugh that was not to be mistaken for either a beast's or

81

a bird's. And the worst of it was, those blazing eyes were turned squarely toward Farmer Green's chicken house!

Solomon Owl was too wary to go for his fat pullet just then. He decided that he would wait quietly in the tree for a time, hoping that the man would go away.

While Solomon watched him the stranger neither moved nor spoke. And, of course, Solomon Owl was growing hungrier every minute. So at last he felt that he simply must say something.

"Who-who-who-are-you?" he called out from his tree.

But the strange man did not answer. He did not even turn his head.

"He must be some city person," Solomon Owl said to himself. "He thinks he's too good to speak to a countryman like me."

Then Solomon sat up and listened. He heard a scratching sound. And soon he saw a plump figure crawl right up into his tree-top.

It was Fatty Coon!

"What are you doing here?" Solomon Owl asked in a low voice, which was not any too pleasant.

"I'm out for an airing," Fatty answered. "Beautiful night--isn't it?"

But Solomon Owl was not interested in the weather.

"I don't suppose you've come down here to get a chicken, have you?" he inquired.

Fatty Coon seemed greatly surprised at the question. "Why--no!" he exclaimed. "But now that you speak of it, it reminds me that Farmer Green's saving a pullet for me. He was heard to say not long ago that he would like to catch me taking one of his hens. So he must have one for me. And I don't want to disappoint him."

At first Solomon Owl didn't know what answer to make. But at last he turned his head toward Fatty.

"Why don't you go and get your pullet now?" he asked.

"There's that man down below, with the glaring eyes--" said Fatty Coon. "I've been waiting around here for quite a long time and he hasn't looked away from the chicken house even once.... Do you know him?"

"No! And I don't want to!" said Solomon Owl.

"S-sh!" Fatty Coon held up a warning hand. "Who's that?" he asked, peering down at a dark object at the foot of their tree.

Then both he and Solomon saw that it was Tommy Fox, sitting on his haunches and staring at the big head, with its blazing eyes and nose and mouth.

"Not looking for chickens, I suppose?" Solomon Owl called in a low tone, which was hardly more than a whisper.

But Tommy Fox's sharp ears heard him easily. And he looked up, licking his chops as if he were very hungry indeed. And all the while the stranger continued to stare straight at the chicken house, as if he did not intend to let anybody go prowling about that long, low building to steal any of Farmer Green's poultry.

It was no wonder that the three chicken-lovers (two in the tree and one beneath it) hesitated. If the queer man had only spoken they might not have been so timid.

But he said never a word.

Day 38

1. Read chapter 8 of *The Tale of Solomon Owl*.
2. Tell someone what happened in the chapter.

Chapter 8, VIII WATCHING THE CHICKENS

Solomon Owl and Fatty Coon couldn't help laughing at what Tommy Fox said to them, as they sat in their tree near the farmhouse, looking down at him in the moonlight.

"I'm here to watch Farmer Green's chickens for him--" said he--"to see that no rat--or anybody else--runs away with a pullet."

"Farmer Green has someone else watching for him to-night," said Solomon Owl, when he had stopped laughing. "There's that strange man! You can see how he keeps his glaring eyes fixed on the chicken house. And unless I'm mistaken, he's on the lookout for you."

"No such thing!" Tommy Fox snapped. And he looked up at Solomon as if he wished that he could climb the tree.

"Here comes somebody else!" Fatty Coon exclaimed suddenly. His keen eyes had caught sight of Jimmy Rabbit, hopping along on his way to the vegetable garden, to see if he couldn't find a stray cabbage or a turnip.

Solomon Owl called to him. Whereupon, Jimmy Rabbit promptly sat up and looked at the odd trio. If it hadn't been for Tommy Fox he would have drawn nearer.

"Do you know that stranger?" Solomon Owl asked him, pointing out the horrible head to Jimmy.

"I haven't the pleasure," said Jimmy Rabbit, after he had taken a good look.

"Well," said Solomon, "won't you kindly speak to him; and ask him to go away?"

"Certainly!" answered Jimmy Rabbit, who always tried to be obliging.

"I hope the stranger won't eat him," remarked Tommy Fox, "because I hope to do that some day, myself."

It was queer--but Jimmy Rabbit was the only one of the four that wasn't afraid of those glaring features. He hopped straight up to the big round head, which was just a bit higher than one of the fence posts, against which the stranger seemed to be leaning. And after a moment or two Jimmy Rabbit called to Solomon and Fatty and Tommy Fox: "He won't go away! He's going to stay right where he is!"

"Come here a minute!" said Tommy.

Jimmy Rabbit shook his head.

"You come over here!" he answered. And he did not stir from the side of the stranger. He knew very well that Tommy Fox was afraid of the man with the head with the glaring eyes.

As for Tommy Fox, he did not even reply--that is, to Jimmy Rabbit. But he spoke his mind freely enough to his two friends in the tree.

"It seems to me one of you ought to do something," said he. "We'll eat no pullets tonight if we can't get rid of this meddlesome stranger."

Fatty Coon quite agreed with him.

"The one who was here first is the one to act!" Fatty declared. "That's you!" he told Solomon Owl.

So Solomon Owl felt most uncomfortable.

"I don't know what I can do," he said. "I spoke to the stranger--asked him who he was. And he wouldn't answer me."

"Can't you frighten him away?" Tommy Fox inquired. "Fly right over his head and give him a blow with your wing as you pass!"

Solomon Owl coughed. He was embarrassed, to say the least.

"He's afraid!" Fatty Coon cried. And both he and Tommy Fox kept repeating, over and over again, "He's afraid! He's afraid! He's afraid!"

It was really more than Solomon Owl could stand.

"I'm not!" he retorted angrily. "Watch me and you'll see!" And without another word he darted out of the tree and swooped down upon the stranger, just brushing the top of his head. Solomon Owl knew at once that he had knocked something off the top of that dreadful head--something that fell to the ground and made Jimmy Rabbit jump nervously.

Then Solomon returned to his perch in the tree. "He hasn't moved," he said. "But I knocked off his hat."

"You took off the top of his head!" cried Fatty Coon in great excitement. "Look! The inside of his head is afire." And peering down from the tree-top, Solomon Owl saw that Fatty Coon had told the truth.

Day 39

1. Read chapter 9 of *The Tale of Solomon Owl*.
2. Tell someone what happened in the chapter.
3. This is a jack-o-lantern. It's a carved pumpkin with a candle inside.

Chapter 9, IX HALLOWEEN (There are no content issues with this chapter despite the title.)

Solomon Owl was afraid of fire. And when he looked down from his perch in the tree and saw, through the hole in the stranger's crown, that all was aglow inside his big, round head, Solomon couldn't help voicing his horror. He "whoo-whooed" so loudly that Tommy Fox, at the foot of the tree, asked him what on earth was the matter.

"His head's all afire!" Solomon Owl told him. "That's what makes his eyes glare so. And that's why the fire shines through his mouth and his nose, too. It's no wonder he didn't answer my question--for, of course, his tongue must certainly be burned to a cinder."

"Then it ought to be safe for anybody to enter the chicken house," Tommy Fox observed. "What could the stranger do, when he's in such a fix?"

"He could set the chicken house afire, if he followed you inside," replied Solomon Owl wisely. "And I, for one, am not going near the pullets to-night."

"Nor I!" Fatty Coon echoed. "I'm going straight to the cornfield. The corn is still standing there in shocks; and I ought to find enough ears to make a good meal."

But Solomon Owl and Tommy Fox were not interested in corn. They never ate it. And so it is not surprising that they should be greatly disappointed. After a person has his mouth all made up for chicken it is hard to think of anything that would taste even half as good.

"It's queer he doesn't go and hold his head under the pump," said Solomon Owl. "That's what I should do, if I were he."

"Jimmy Rabbit had better not go too near him, or he'll get singed," said Tommy Fox, anxiously. "I don't want anything to happen to him."

"Jimmy Rabbit is very careless," Solomon declared. "I don't see what he's thinking of--going so near a fire! It makes me altogether too nervous to stay here. And I'm going away at once."

Tommy Fox said that he felt the same way. And the moment Fatty Coon, with his sharp claws, started to crawl down the tree on his way to the cornfield, Tommy Fox hurried off without even stopping to say good-bye.

"Haw-haw-hoo!" laughed Solomon Owl. "Tommy Fox is afraid of you!" he told Fatty Coon. But Fatty didn't seem to hear him. He was thinking only of the supper of corn that he was going to have.

"Better come away!" Solomon Owl called to Jimmy Rabbit, turning his head toward the fence where Jimmy had been lingering near the hot-headed stranger.

But Jimmy Rabbit didn't answer him, either. He was no longer there. The moment he had seen Tommy Fox bounding off across the meadow Jimmy had started at once for Farmer Green's vegetable garden.

So Solomon Owl was the last to leave.

"There's really nothing else I can do," he remarked to himself. "I don't know what Aunt Polly Woodchuck would say if she knew that I didn't follow her advice to-night and eat a pullet for my supper.... But I've tried my best.... And that's all anybody can do."

Solomon Owl was upset all the rest of that night. And just before daybreak he visited the farmyard again, to see whether the strange man with the flaring head still watched the chicken house. And Solomon found that he had vanished.

So Solomon Owl alighted on the fence. There was nothing there except a hollowed-out pumpkin, with a few holes cut in it, which someone had left on one of the fence-posts.

"Good!" said he. "Maybe I can get my pullet after all!" He turned to fly to the chicken house. But just then the woodshed door opened again. And Farmer Green stepped outside, with a lantern in his hand. He was going to the barn to milk the cows. But Solomon Owl did not wait to learn anything more.

He hurried away to his house among the hemlocks. And having quickly settled himself for a good nap, he was soon fast asleep.

That was how Johnnie Green's jack-o'-lantern kept Tommy Fox and Fatty Coon and Solomon Owl from taking any chickens on Halloween.

Day 40

1. Read chapter 10 of *The Tale of Solomon Owl.*
2. Tell what happened in the chapter. What trouble is the wishbone causing? What is Solomon doing about it? (Answers)

Chapter 10, X A TROUBLESOME WISHBONE

Solomon Owl had pains--sharp pains--underneath his waistcoat. And not knowing what else to do, he set off at once for Aunt Polly Woodchuck's house under the hill, in the pasture, which he had not visited since the previous fall. Luckily, he found the old lady at home. And quickly he told her of his trouble.

"What have you been eating?" she inquired.

"I've followed your advice. I've been eating chickens," said he--"very small chickens, because they were all I could get."

Aunt Polly Woodchuck, who was an herb doctor--and a good one--regarded him through her spectacles.

"I'm afraid," said she, "you don't chew your food properly. Bolting one's food is very harmful. It's as bad as not eating anything at all, almost."

Solomon Owl showed plainly that her remark surprised him.

"Why," he exclaimed, "I always swallow my food whole--when it isn't too big!"

"Gracious me!" cried Aunt Polly, throwing up both her hands. "It's no wonder you're ill. It's no wonder you have pains; and now I know exactly what's the matter with you. You have a wishbone inside you. I can feel it!" she told him, as she prodded him in the waistcoat.

"I wish you could get it out for me!" said Solomon with a look of distress.

"All the wishing in the world won't help you," she answered, "unless we can find some way of removing the wishbone so you can wish on that. Then I'm sure you would feel better at once."

"This is strange," Solomon mused. "All my life I've been swallowing my food without chewing it. And it has never given me any trouble before....What shall I do?"

"Don't eat anything for a week," she directed. "And fly against tree-trunks as hard as you can. Then come back here after seven days."

Solomon Owl went off in a most doleful frame of mind. It seemed to him that he had never seen so many mice and frogs and chipmunks as he came across during the following week. But he didn't dare catch a single one, on account of what Aunt Polly Woodchuck had said.

His pains, however, grew less from day to day--at least, the pains that had first troubled him. But he had others to take their place. Hunger pangs, these were! And they were almost as bad as those that had sent him hurrying to see Aunt Polly Woodchuck.

On the whole, Solomon passed a very unhappy week. Flying head foremost into tree-trunks (as Aunt Polly had instructed him to do) gave him many bumps and bruises. So he was glad when the time came for him to return to her house in the pasture.

Solomon's neighbors had been so interested in watching him that they were all sorry when he ceased his strange actions. Indeed, there was a rumor that Solomon had become very angry with Farmer Green and that he was trying to knock down some of Farmer Green's trees. Before the end of that unpleasant week Solomon had often noticed as many as twenty-four of the forest folk following him about, hoping to see a tree fall.

But they were all disappointed. However, they enjoyed the sight of Solomon hurling himself against tree-trunks. And the louder he groaned, the more people gathered around him.

Vocabulary

1. Do you know what it means to "inquire?" Here's the sentence where it says that. *"What have you been eating?" she inquired.* Instead of the sentence being, *"What have you been*

eating?" she said, it uses the word inquire, not said, so we can figure out that it tells us about how she said it. If the sentence had used an exclamation point, then maybe the sentence would have been, *"What have you been eating!" she shouted.* What clues do we have about the word *inquire*? It tells us how she is saying those words, and we see a question mark. The question mark tells us that she is asking a question. So, inquire must mean something about asking a question. In fact it does. To inquire means to ask. Use your clues and your detective skills to figure out words you don't know.

Day 41

1. Read chapter 11 of *The Tale of Solomon Owl*.
2. Tell someone what happened in the chapter.

Chapter 11 XI CURED AT LAST

"How do you feel now?" Aunt Polly Woodchuck asked Solomon Owl, when he had come back to her house after a week's absence.

"No better!" he groaned. "I still have pains. But they seem to have moved and scattered all over me."

"Good!" she exclaimed with a smile. "You are much better, though you didn't know it. The wishbone is broken. You broke it by flying against the trees. And you ought not to have any more trouble. But let me examine you!" she said, prodding him in the waistcoat once more.

"This is odd!" she continued a bit later. "I can feel the wishbone more plainly than ever."

"That's my own wishbone!" Solomon cried indignantly. "I've grown so thin through not eating that it's a wonder you can't feel my backbone, too."

Aunt Polly Woodchuck looked surprised.

"Perhaps you're right!" said she. "Not having a wishbone of my own, I forgot that you had one."

A look of disgust came over Solomon Owl's face.

"You're a very poor doctor," he told her. "Here you've kept me from eating for a whole week--and I don't believe it was necessary at all!"

"Well, you're better, aren't you?" she asked him.

"I shall be as soon as I have a good meal," replied Solomon Owl, hopefully.

"You ought not to eat anything for another week," Aunt Polly told him solemnly.

"Nonsense!" he cried.

"I'm a doctor; and I ought to know best," she insisted.

But Solomon Owl hooted rudely.

"I'll never come to you for advice any more," he declared. "I firmly believe that my whole trouble was simply that I've been eating too sparingly. And I shall take good care to see that it doesn't happen again."

No one had ever spoken to Aunt Polly in quite that fashion--though old Mr. Crow had complained one time that she had cured him too quickly. But she did not lose her temper, in spite of Solomon's jeers.

"You'll be back here again the very next time you're ill," she remarked. "And if you continue to swallow your food whole----"

But Solomon Owl did not even wait to hear what she said. He was so impolite that he flew away while she was talking. And since it was then almost dark, and a good time to look for field mice, he began his night's hunting right there in Farmer Green's pasture.

By morning Solomon was so plump that Aunt Polly Woodchuck would have had a good deal of trouble finding his wishbone. But since he did not visit her again, she had no further chance to prod him in the waistcoat.

Afterward, Solomon heard a bit of gossip that annoyed him. A friend of his reported that Aunt Polly Woodchuck was going about and telling everybody how she had saved Solomon's life.

"Mice!" he exclaimed (he often said that when some would have said "Rats!"). "There's not a word of truth in her claim. And if people in this neighborhood keep on taking her advice and her catnip tea they're going to be sorry some day. For they'll be really ill the first thing they know. And then what will they do?"

Day 42

1. Read chapter 12 of *The Tale of Solomon Owl*
2. Tell someone what happened in the chapter.
3. Why do you think Benjamin Bat was nervous about staying at Solomon Owl's house?

Chapter 12, XII BENJAMIN BAT

Solomon Owl was by no means the only night-prowler in Pleasant Valley. He had neighbors that chose to sleep in the daytime, so they might roam through the woods and fields after dark. One of these was Benjamin Bat. And furthermore, he was the color of night itself.

Now, Benjamin Bat was an odd chap. When he was still he liked to hang by his feet, upside down. And when he was flying he sailed about in a zigzag, helter-skelter fashion. He went in so many different directions, turning this way and that, one could never tell where he was going. One might say that his life was just one continual dodge--when he wasn't resting with his heels where his head ought to be.

A good many of Benjamin Bat's friends said he certainly must be crazy, because he didn't do as they did. But that never made the slightest difference in Benjamin Bat's habits. He continued to zigzag through life--and hang by his heels--just the same. Perhaps he thought that all other people were crazy because they didn't do likewise.

Benjamin often dodged across Solomon Owl's path, when Solomon was hunting for field mice. And since Benjamin was the least bit like a mouse himself--except for his wings-- there was a time, once, when Solomon tried to catch him.

But Solomon Owl soon found that chasing Benjamin Bat made him dizzy. If Benjamin hadn't been used to hanging head downward, maybe he would have been dizzy, too.

Though the two often saw each other, Benjamin Bat never seemed to care to stop for a chat with Solomon Owl. One night, however, Benjamin actually called to Solomon and asked his advice. He was in trouble. And he knew that Solomon Owl was supposed by some to be the wisest old fellow for miles around.

It was almost morning. And Solomon Owl was hurrying home, because a terrible storm had arisen. The lightning was flashing, and peals of thunder crashed through the woods. Big drops of rain were already pattering down. But Solomon Owl did not care, for he had almost reached his house in the hollow hemlock near the foot of Blue Mountain.

It was different with Benjamin Bat. That night he had strayed a long distance from his home in Cedar Swamp. And he didn't know what to do. "I want to get under cover, somewhere," he told Solomon Owl. "You don't know of a good place near-by, do you, where I can get out of the storm and take a nap?"

"Why, yes!" answered Solomon Owl. "Come right along to my house and spend the day with me!"

But Benjamin Bat did not like the suggestion at all.

"I'm afraid I might crowd, you," he said. He was thinking of the time when Solomon Owl had chased him. And sleeping in Solomon Owl's house seemed far from a safe thing to do.

Solomon was wise enough to guess what was going on inside Benjamin's head.

"Come along!" he said. "We'll both be asleep before we know it. I'm sorry I can't offer you something to eat. But I haven't a morsel of food in my house. No doubt, though, you've just had a good meal. I ate seven mice tonight. And I certainly couldn't eat anything more."

When Solomon Owl told him that, Benjamin Bat thought perhaps there was no danger, after all. And since the rain was falling harder and harder every moment, he thanked Solomon and said he would be glad to accept his invitation.

"Follow me, then!" said Solomon Owl. And he led the way to his home in the hemlock.

For once, Benjamin Bat flew in a fairly straight line, though he did a little dodging, because he couldn't help it.

There was more room inside Solomon's house than Benjamin Bat had supposed. While Benjamin was looking about and telling Solomon that he had a fine home, his host quickly made a bed of leaves in one corner of the room--there was only one room, of course.

"That's for you!" said Solomon Owl. "I always sleep on the other side of the house." And without waiting even to make sure that his guest was comfortable, Solomon Owl lay down and began to snore--for he was very sleepy.

It was so cozy there that Benjamin Bat was glad, already, that he had accepted Solomon's invitation.

Day 43

1. Read chapter 13 of *The Tale of Solomon Owl.*
2. Tell someone what happened in the chapter.

Chapter 13, XIII THE LUCKY GUEST

In the middle of the day Solomon Owl happened to awake. He was sorry that he hadn't slept until sunset, because he was very hungry. Knowing that it was light outside his hollow tree, he didn't want to leave home to find something to eat.

Then, suddenly, he remembered that he had brought Benjamin Bat to his house early that morning, so Benjamin might escape the storm.... Why not eat Benjamin Bat?

As soon as the thought occurred to him, Solomon Owl liked it. And he moved stealthily over to the bed of leaves he had made for his guest just before daybreak.

But Benjamin Bat was not there. Though Solomon looked in every nook and cranny of his one-room house, he did not find him.

"He must have left as soon as it stopped raining," said Solomon Owl to himself. "He might at least have waited to thank me for giving him a day's lodging. It's the last time I'll ever bring any worthless vagabond into my house. And I ought to have known better than to have anything to do with a crazy person like Benjamin Bat."

Anybody can see that Solomon Owl was displeased. But it was not at all astonishing, if one stops to remember how hungry he was, and that he had expected to enjoy a good meal without the trouble of going away from home to get it.

Solomon Owl went to the door of his house and looked out. The sun was shining so brightly that after blinking in his doorway for a few minutes he decided that he would go to bed again and try to sleep until dusk. He never liked bright days. "They're so dismal!" he used to say. "Give me a good, dark night and I'm happy, for there's nothing more cheering than gloom."

In spite of the pangs of hunger that gnawed inside him, Solomon at last succeeded in falling asleep once more. And he dreamed that he chased Benjamin Bat three times around Blue Mountain, and then three times back again, in the opposite direction. But he never could catch him, because Benjamin Bat simply wouldn't fly straight. His zigzag course was so confusing that even in his dream Solomon Owl grew dizzy.

Now, Benjamin Bat was in Solomon's house all the time. And the reason why Solomon Owl hadn't found him was a very simple one. It was merely that Solomon hadn't looked in the right place.

Benjamin Bat was hidden--as you might say--where his hungry host never once thought of looking for him. And being asleep all the while, Benjamin didn't once move or make the slightest noise.

If he had snored, or sneezed, or rustled his wings, no doubt Solomon Owl would have found him.

When Benjamin awakened, late in the afternoon, Solomon was still sleeping. And Benjamin crept through the door and went out into the gathering twilight, without arousing Solomon.

"I'll thank him the next time I meet him," Benjamin Bat decided. And he staggered away through the air as if he did not quite know, himself, where he was going. But, of course, that was only his queer way of flying.

When he told his friends where he had spent the day they were astonished.

"How did you ever dare do anything so dangerous as sleeping in Solomon Owl's house?" they all asked him.

But Benjamin Bat only said, "Oh! There was nothing to be afraid of." And he began to feel quite important.

Day 44

1. Read chapter 14 of *The Tale of Solomon Owl*.
2. Tell someone what happened in the chapter.

Chapter 14, XIV HANGING BY THE HEELS

It was several nights before Solomon Owl and Benjamin Bat chanced to meet again in the forest.

"Hullo!" said Solomon.

"Hullo!" said Benjamin Bat. "I'm glad to see you, because I want to thank you for letting me spend the day in your house, so I wouldn't have to stay out in the storm."

"You must be a light sleeper," Solomon observed. (He did not tell Benjamin that he was welcome!)

"What makes you think that?" Benjamin Bat inquired.

"Why--you left my house before noon," Solomon told him.

"Oh, no!" said Benjamin. "I slept soundly until sunset. When I came away the crickets were chirping. And I was surprised that you hadn't waked up yourself."

"You were gone before midday," Solomon Owl insisted. And they had something very like a dispute, while Solomon Owl sat in one tree and Benjamin Bat hung head downward from another. "I ought to know," said Solomon. "I was awake about noon; and I looked everywhere for you."

"What for?" asked Benjamin.

Naturally, Solomon didn't like to tell him that he had intended to eat him. So he looked wise--and said nothing.

"You didn't look on the ceiling, did you?" Benjamin Bat inquired.

"No, indeed!" Solomon Owl exclaimed.

"Well, that's where I was, hanging by my feet," Benjamin Bat informed him.

Solomon Owl certainly was surprised to hear that.

"The idea!" he cried. "You're a queer one! I never once thought of looking on the ceiling for a luncheon!" He was so astonished that he spoke before he thought how oddly his remark would sound to another.

When he heard what Solomon Owl said, Benjamin Bat knew at once that Solomon had meant to eat him. And he was so frightened that he dropped from the limb to which he was clinging and flew off as fast as he could go. For once in his life he flew in a straight line, with no zigzags at all, he was in such a hurry to get away from Solomon Owl, who--for all he knew--might still be very hungry.

But Solomon Owl had caught so many mice that night that he didn't feel like chasing anybody. So he sat motionless in the tree, merely turning his head to watch Benjamin sailing away through the dusky woods. He noticed that Benjamin didn't dodge at all--except when there was a tree in his way. And he wondered what the reason was.

"Perhaps he's not so crazy as I supposed," said Solomon Owl to himself. And ever afterward, when he happened to awake and feel hungry, Solomon Owl used to look up at the ceiling above him and wish that Benjamin Bat was there.

But Benjamin Bat never cared to have anything more to do with Solomon Owl.

He said he had a good reason for avoiding him.

And ever afterward he passed for a very brave person among his friends. They often pointed him out to strangers, saying, "There's Benjamin Bat! He doesn't know what fear is. Why, once he even spent a whole day asleep in Solomon Owl's house! And if you don't think that was a bold thing to do, then I guess you don't know Solomon Owl."

Day 45

1. Read chapter 15 of *The Tale of Solomon Owl*.
2. Tell someone about the chapter.
3. What does it mean to settle a dispute? (Answers)

Chapter 15, XV DISPUTES SETTLED

Solomon Owl looked so wise that many of his neighbors fell into the habit of going to him for advice. If two of the forest folk chanced to have a dispute which they could not settle between them they frequently visited Solomon and asked him to decide which was in the right. And in the course of time Solomon became known far and wide for his ability to patch up a quarrel.

At last Jimmy Rabbit stopped Solomon Owl one night and suggested that he hang a sign outside his house, so that there shouldn't be anybody in the whole valley that wouldn't know what to do in case he found himself in an argument.

Solomon decided on the spot that Jimmy Rabbit's idea was a good one. So he hurried home and before morning he had his sign made, and put out where everyone could see it. It looked like this: DISPUTES SETTLED WITHIN.

There was only one objection to the sign. As soon as Jimmy Rabbit saw it he told Solomon that it should have said: DISPUTES SETTLED WITHOUT.

"Without what?" Solomon Owl inquired.

"Why, without going into your house!" said Jimmy Rabbit. "I can't climb a tree, you know. And neither can Tommy Fox. We might have a dispute to-night; and how could you ever settle it?"

"Oh, I shall be willing to step outside," Solomon told him. And he refused to change the sign, declaring that he liked it just as it was.

Now, there was only one trouble with Solomon Owl's settling of disputes. Many of the forest folk wanted to see him in the daytime. And night was the only time he was willing to see them. But he heard so many objections to that arrangement that in the end Solomon agreed to meet people at dusk and at dawn, when it was neither very dark nor very light. On the whole he found that way very satisfactory, because there was just enough light at dusk and at dawn to make him blink. And when Solomon blinked he looked even wiser than ever.

Well, the first disputing pair that came to Solomon's tree after he hung out his new sign were old Mr. Crow and Jasper Jay. They reached the hemlock grove soon after sunset and squalled loudly for Solomon. "Hurry!" Mr. Crow cried, as soon as Solomon Owl stepped outside his door. "It will be dark before we know it; and it's almost our bedtime."

"What's your difficulty?" Solomon asked them.

Mr. Crow looked at Jasper Jay. And then he looked at Solomon again.

"Maybe you won't like to hear it," he said. And he winked at Jasper. "But you've put out this sign--so we've come here."

"You've done just right!" exclaimed Solomon Owl. "And as for my not liking to hear the trouble, it's your dispute and not mine. So I don't see how it concerns me--except to settle it."

"Very Well," Mr. Crow answered. "The dispute, then, is this: Jasper says that in spite of your looking so wise, you're really the stupidest person in Pleasant Valley."

"He does, eh?" cried Solomon Owl, while Jasper Jay laughed loudly. "And you, of course, do not agree with him," Solomon continued.

"I do not!" Mr. Crow declared.

"Good!" said Solomon, nodding his head approvingly.

"No, I do not agree with Jasper Jay," Mr. Crow said. "I claim that there's one other person more stupid than you are--and that's Fatty Coon."

Well, Solomon Owl certainly was displeased. And it didn't make him feel any happier to hear Jasper Jay's boisterous shouts, or the hoarse "haw-haw" of old Mr. Crow.

"I hope you can decide which one of us is right," Mr. Crow ventured.

"I am, of course!" cried Jasper Jay.

"You're not!" Mr. Crow shouted. And to Solomon Owl he said, "We've been disputing like this all day long."

Solomon Owl didn't know what to say. If he announced that Jasper was right it would be the same as admitting that he was the stupidest person in the whole neighborhood. And if he said that old Mr. Crow's opinion was correct he would not be much better off. Naturally he didn't want to tell either of them that he was right.

"I'll have to think about this," Solomon observed at last.

"We don't want to wait," said Mr. Crow. "If we keep on disputing we're likely to have a fight."

Now, Solomon Owl hoped that they would have a fight. So he was determined to keep them waiting for his decision.

"Come back tomorrow at this time," he said.

Day 46

1.   Read this first paragraph of chapter 16 of *The Tale of Solomon Owl*.

The next evening, just at dusk, Jasper Jay and old Mr. Crow returned to Solomon Owl's house, looking much bedraggled. One of Mr. Crow's eyes was almost closed; and Jasper Jay's crest seemed to have been torn half off his head.

2.   What do you think happened to Jasper Jay?
3.   Now read the rest of the chapter and see if you were right.
4.   Tell someone about what happened in the chapter.

Chapter 16, XVI NINE FIGHTS

The next evening, just at dusk, Jasper Jay and old Mr. Crow returned to Solomon Owl's house, looking much bedraggled. One of Mr. Crow's eyes was almost closed; and Jasper Jay's crest seemed to have been torn half off his head.

"What's the matter?" asked Solomon, as soon as he saw them.

"We've had three fights," said Jasper Jay.

"Yes! And I've whipped him each time!" cried Mr. Crow. "So I must be in the right. And you'd better decide our dispute in my favor at once."

But Solomon Owl was still in no hurry.

"It's a difficult question to settle," said he. "I don't want to make any mistake. So I shall have to ask you to come back here to-morrow at this time."

Both Jasper and Mr. Crow seemed disappointed. Although Mr. Crow had won each fight, he was very weary, for he was older than Jasper Jay.

As they went off, Solomon Owl began to feel much pleased with himself.

The following evening, at sunset, old Mr. Crow and Jasper Jay visited Solomon Owl once more. And they looked more battered than ever.

"We've had three more fights," said Mr. Crow.

"Yes! And I won each time!" Jasper Jay piped up. "So I must be in the right. And you'd better decide in my favor without any further delay."

Solomon Owl thought deeply for some time.

"Maybe I ought to wait until to-morrow----" he began.

But his callers both shouted "No!"

"Well," said Solomon, "Mr. Crow has won three fights; and Jasper Jay has won three. So it is certain that each must be in the wrong."

But that announcement did not satisfy Jasper and Mr. Crow. And they left the hemlock grove, disputing more loudly than ever.

And the next day, at dusk, they came back again.

"We've had three more fights; and I won!" they both cried at the same time.

"That proves my claim," said Solomon Owl. "You're both wrong."

They whispered together for a few minutes.

"We don't like your way of settling disputes," Mr. Crow remarked shortly. "But we've decided to stop quarreling."

"Good!" said Solomon Owl. "That shows that you are sensible."

"Yes!" replied Jasper. "We've decided to stop quarreling and fight you!"

"Wait a moment!" said Solomon Owl hastily, as they drew nearer. "I don't want my new suit spoiled." And he ducked inside the hollow tree before they could reach him.

Jasper and Mr. Crow waited and waited. But Solomon Owl did not reappear. And since his two visitors did not dare follow him into the dark cavern where he lived, they decided at last that they would go home--and get into bed.

"Let's take away his sign, anyhow!" Jasper Jay suggested.

So they pulled down Solomon's sign, which said "Disputes Settled Within," and they carried it off with them and hid it in some bushes.

That same night Solomon Owl hunted for it for a long time. But he never found it.

He decided not to hang out another, for he saw that settling disputes was a dangerous business.

Day 47

1. Read the first paragraph of chapter 17 of *The Tale of Solomon Owl*.
2. What do you think Solomon and his cousin are going to do together? Why?

Solomon Owl had a small cousin named Simon Screecher. He was unlike Solomon in some respects, because he always wore ear-tufts, and his eyes were yellow instead of black. But in some other ways he was no different from Solomon Owl, for he was a noisy chap and dearly loved mice--to eat.

3. Read the rest of the chapter and see if you were right.

Chapter 17, XVII COUSIN SIMON SCREECHER

Solomon Owl had a small cousin named Simon Screecher. He was unlike Solomon in some respects, because he always wore ear-tufts, and his eyes were yellow instead of black. But in some other ways he was no different from Solomon Owl, for he was a noisy chap and dearly loved mice--to eat.

It happened that the two met in the woods one fine fall evening; and they agreed to go hunting mice together.

Now, being so much smaller than Solomon, Simon Screecher was all the spryer. In fact, he was so active that he could catch mice faster than Solomon Owl could capture them. And they had not hunted long before Solomon discovered that Simon had succeeded in disposing of six mice to his three.

That discovery did not please Solomon at all.

"Look here!" he said. "Since we are hunting together it's only fair to divide what we catch, half and half."

Simon Screecher hesitated. But after reflecting that his cousin was very big and very strong, he agreed to Solomon's suggestion.

So they resumed their hunting. And every time one of them caught two mice, he gave one mouse to his cousin.

Still Solomon Owl was not satisfied.

"Wait a moment!" Solomon called to Simon Screecher. "It has just occurred to me that I am more than twice as big as you are; so I ought to have twice as many mice as you."

This time Simon Screecher hesitated longer. He did not like the second suggestion even as well as the first. And in the end he said as much, too.

But Solomon Owl insisted that it was only fair.

"You surely ought to be glad to please your own cousin," he told Simon.

"It's not that," said Simon Screecher. "It seems to me that since I'm not half your size, I ought to have twice as many mice to eat, so I'll grow bigger."

Well, Solomon Owl hadn't thought of that. He was puzzled to know what to say. And he wanted time in which to ponder.

"I'll think over what you say," he told Simon Screecher. "And now, since it's almost dawn, we'd better not hunt any longer to-night. But I'll meet you again at dusk if you'll come to my house."

"Very well, Cousin Solomon!" Simon answered. "I'm sure that after you've had a good sleep you'll be ready to agree with me."

"If that's the case, I may not take any nap at all," Solomon replied.

"Oh! You ought to have your rest!" his cousin exclaimed. Simon knew that if Solomon went all day without sleep he would be frightfully peevish by nightfall.

"Well--I'll try to get forty winks," Solomon promised. "But I don't believe I can get more than that, because I have so much on my mind that I'm sure to be wakeful."

Simon Screecher was somewhat worried as they parted. His wailing, tremulous whistle, which floated through the shadowy woods, showed that he was far from happy.

Day 48

1. Read chapter 18 of *The Tale of Solomon Owl*.
2. When it talks about "39 winks," that is a joke. To "catch 40 winks" means to take a nap. So, if he only got 39 winks, he didn't get all his sleep. He's tired because he can't sleep since he's thinking and worrying.
3. Tell someone what happened in this chapter.

Chapter 18, XVIII A COUSINLY QUARREL

It proved to be just as Solomon Owl had told his cousin, Simon Screecher. Solomon had so much on his mind that he had no sooner fallen asleep than he awoke again, to study over the question that perplexed him. He certainly did not want Simon to have twice as many mice as he. But Simon's argument was a good one. He had said that since Solomon was more than twice his size, it was proper that he should have a chance to grow. And everybody knew--Solomon reflected--everybody knew that eating made one larger.

The longer Solomon pondered, the farther he seemed from any answer that he liked. And he had begun to fear that he would not succeed in getting more than thirty-nine winks all day--instead of forty--when all at once an idea came into his mind.

Solomon knew right away that he had nothing more to worry about. He dropped into a sound sleep with a pleasant smile upon his usually solemn face. And when he opened his eyes again it was time for Simon Screecher to arrive.

Yes! Solomon could hear his cousin's whistle even then. So he hurried to his door; and there was Simon, sitting on a limb of the big hemlock waiting for him!

"It's all right!" said Solomon to his cousin. "I agree to your suggestion. We'll hunt together again to-night; and if you will give me one-third of all the mice you catch, I promise to give you two-thirds of all the mice that I capture."

"Good!" said Simon Screecher. And he looked vastly relieved. "Just hoot when you have any mice for me!"

"Whistle when you have any for me!" Solomon Owl replied.

And at that they started out for their night's sport. It was not long before Simon Screecher's well known whistle brought Solomon hurrying to him. Simon already had three mice, one of which he gave to Solomon, according to their agreement.

That same thing happened several times; until at last Simon Screecher began to grumble.

"What's the matter?" he asked his cousin. "You are not hooting, as you promised you would."

"But I haven't caught any mice yet!" Solomon Owl replied.

Again and again and again Simon's call summoned Solomon. But not once did Solomon's summon Simon. And all the time Simon Screecher grew more discontented. Toward the end of the night he declared flatly that he wasn't going to hunt any more with his cousin. "I've done exactly as I agreed!" Solomon Owl protested.

"You're altogether too slow and clumsy," Simon Screecher told him bluntly. "If I'm going to hunt with anybody after this I'm going to choose someone that's as spry as I am. There's no sense in my working for you. Here I've toiled all night long and I'm still hungry, for I've given you a third of my food."

They parted then--and none too pleasantly.

In Simon's whistle, as he flew away toward his home, there was unmistakable anger. But Solomon Owl's answering hoots--while they were not exactly sweet--seemed to carry more than a hint of laughter.

One would naturally think that Solomon might have been even hungrier than his small cousin. But it was not so. He had had more to eat than usual; for he had been very busy catching locusts and katydids--and frogs, too. Solomon Owl had not tried to catch a single mouse that night.

You know now the idea that had come to him while he was lying awake in his house during the daytime. He had made up his mind that he would not hunt for mice. And since he had not promised Simon to give him anything else, there was no reason why he should not eat all the frogs and katydids and locusts that he could find.

Perhaps it was not surprising that Simon Screecher never guessed the truth. But he seemed to know that there was something queer about that night's hunting, for he never came to Solomon Owl's house again.

Day 49

1. Read the first paragraph of chapter 19 of *The Tale of Solomon Owl*.
2. Does Solomon want it to get warmer? How do you know?

It was winter. And for several days a strong south wind had swept up Pleasant Valley. That--as Solomon Owl knew very well--that meant a thaw was coming. He was not sorry, because the weather had been bitterly cold.

3. Read the rest of the chapter and see if you were right.

Chapter 19, XIX THE SLEET STORM

It was winter. And for several days a strong south wind had swept up Pleasant Valley. That--as Solomon Owl knew very well--that meant a thaw was coming. He was not sorry, because the weather had been bitterly cold.

Well, the thaw came. And the weather grew so warm that Solomon Owl could stay out all night without once feeling chilled. He found the change so agreeable that he strayed further from home than was his custom. Indeed, he was far away on the other side of Blue Mountain at midnight, when it began to rain.

Now, that was not quite so pleasant. But still Solomon did not mind greatly. It was not until later that he began to feel alarmed, when he noticed that flying did not seem so easy as usual.

Solomon had grown heavy all at once--and goodness knows it was not because he had overeaten, for food was scarce at that season of the year. Moreover, Solomon's wings were strangely stiff. When he moved them they crackled.

"It must be my joints," he said to himself. "I'm afraid this wetting has given me rheumatism." So he started home at once--though it was only midnight. But the further he went, the worse he felt--and the harder it was to fly.

"I'll have to rest a while," he said to himself at last. So he alighted on a limb; for he was more tired than he had ever been in all his life.

But he soon felt so much better that he was ready to start on again. And then, to his dismay, Solomon Owl found that he could hardly stir. The moment he left his perch he floundered down upon the ground. And though he tried his hardest, he couldn't reach the tree again.

The rain was still beating down steadily. And Solomon began to think it a bad night to be out. What was worse, the weather was fast turning cold.

"I'm afraid I'll have to stay in bed a week after this," he groaned. "If I sit here long, as wet as I am, while the thaw turns into a freeze, I shall certainly be ill."

Now, if it hadn't been for the rain, Solomon Owl would have had no trouble at all. Or if it hadn't been for the freezing cold he would have been in no difficulty. Though he didn't know it, his trouble was simply this: The rain froze upon him as fast as it fell, covering him with a coating of ice. It was no wonder that he felt strangely heavy--no wonder that he couldn't fly.

There he crouched on the ground, while the rain and sleet beat upon him. And the only comforting thought that entered his head was that on so stormy a night Tommy Fox and Fatty Coon would be snug and warm in their beds. They wouldn't go out in such weather.

And Solomon Owl wished that he, too, had stayed at home that night.

From midnight until almost dawn Solomon Owl sat there. Now and then he tried to fly. But it was no use. He could scarcely raise himself off the ground.

At last he decided he would have to walk home. Fortunately, a hard crust covered the soft snow. So Solomon started off on his long journey.

Flying, Solomon could have covered the distance in a few minutes. But he was a slow walker. By the time he reached his home among the hemlocks the sun was shining brightly--for the rain had stopped before daybreak.

Solomon wondered how he would ever succeed in reaching his doorway, high up in the hollow tree. He gazed helplessly upward. And as he sat there mournfully the bright sunshine melted the ice that bound his wings. After a time he discovered that he could move freely once more. And then he rose quickly in the air and in a twinkling he had disappeared into the darkness of his home--that darkness which to him was always so pleasant.

Day 50

1. Read chapter 20 of *The Tale of Solomon Owl*.
2. Tell someone about the chapter.

Chapter 20, XX A PAIR OF RED-HEADS

In the woods there was hardly one of Solomon Owl's neighbors that couldn't point out the big hemlock tree where he lived. And mischievous fellows like Reddy Woodpecker sometimes annoyed Solomon a good deal by rapping loudly on his door. When he thrust his head angrily out of his house and blinked in the sunlight, his tormentors would skip away and laugh. They laughed because they knew that they had awakened Solomon Owl. And they dodged out of his reach because he was always ill-tempered when anybody disturbed his rest in the daytime.

Solomon Owl did not mind so very much so long as that trick was not played on him too often. But after a time it became one of Reddy Woodpecker's favorite sports. Not only once, but several times a day did he go to the hemlock grove to hammer upon Solomon's hollow tree. And each time that he brought Solomon Owl to his door Reddy Woodpecker laughed more loudly than ever before.

Once Solomon forgot to take off his nightcap (though he wore it in the daytime, it really was a nightcap). And Reddy Woodpecker was so amused that he shouted at the top of his lungs.

"What's the joke?" asked Solomon Owl in his deep, rumbling voice. He tried to look very severe. But it is hard to look any way except funny with a nightcap on one's head.

As luck had it, Jasper Jay came hurrying up just then. He had heard Reddy Woodpecker's laughter. And if there was a joke he wanted to enjoy it, too.

Jasper Jay, alighting in a small hemlock near Reddy Woodpecker, asked the same question that Solomon Owl had just put to his rude caller.

"What's the joke?" inquired Jasper Jay.

Reddy could not speak. He was rocking back and forth upon a limb, choking and gasping for breath. But he managed to point to the big tree where Solomon Owl lived.

And when Jasper looked, and saw Solomon's great, round, pale, questioning face, all tied up in a red nightcap, he began to scream.

They were no ordinary screams--those shrieks of Jasper Jay's. That blue-coated rascal was the noisiest of all the feathered folk in Pleasant Valley. And now he fairly made the woods echo with his hoarse cries.

"This is the funniest sight I've ever seen!" Jasper Jay said at last, to nobody in particular. "I declare, there's a pair of them!"

At that, Reddy Woodpecker suddenly stopped laughing.

"A pair of what?" he asked.

"A pair of red-heads, of course!" Jasper Jay replied. "You've a red cap--and so has he!" Jasper pointed at Solomon Owl (a very rude thing to do!).

Then two things happened all at once. Solomon Owl snatched off his red night-cap--which he had quite forgotten. And Reddy Woodpecker dashed at Jasper Jay. He couldn't pull off his red cap, for it grew right on his head.

"So that's what you're laughing at, is it?" he cried angrily. And then nobody laughed any more--that is, nobody but Solomon Owl.

Solomon was so pleased by the fight that followed between Jasper Jay and Reddy Woodpecker that his deep, rumbling laughter could be heard for half an hour--even if it was midday. "Wha-wha! Whoo-ah!" The sound reached the ears of Farmer Green, who was just crossing a neighboring field, on his way home to dinner.

"Well, well!" he exclaimed. "I wonder what's happened to that old owl! Something must have tickled him--for I never heard an owl laugh in broad daylight before."

Day 51

1. Read chapter 21 of *The Tale of Solomon Owl*.
2. Draw a map of the book's setting as best as you can. The setting is where it takes place.
3. You might want to hold onto this for your portfolio.

Chapter 21, XXI AT HOME IN THE HAYSTACK

After what happened when he came to his door without remembering to take off his red nightcap, Solomon Owl hoped that Reddy Woodpecker would stop teasing him.

But it was not so. Having once viewed Solomon's red cap, Reddy Woodpecker wanted to see it some more. So he came again and again and knocked on Solomon's door.

Solomon Owl, however, remembered each time to remove his nightcap before sticking his head out. And it might be said that neither of them was exactly pleased. For Reddy Woodpecker was disappointed; and Solomon Owl was angry.

Not a day passed that Reddy Woodpecker didn't disturb Solomon's rest at least a dozen times. Perhaps if Solomon had just kept still inside his house Reddy would have grown tired of bothering him. But Solomon Owl—for all he looked so wise--never thought of that.

But he saw before a great while that he would have to make a change of some sort--if he wanted to enjoy a good, quiet sleep again.

For a long time Solomon Owl pondered. It was a great puzzle--to know just how to outwit Reddy Woodpecker. And Solomon almost despaired of finding a way out of the difficulty. But at last an idea came to him, all in a flash. He would take his daytime naps somewhere else!

Solomon spent several nights looking for a good place to pass his days. And in the end he decided on the meadow. It would be convenient, he thought, when he was hunting meadow mice at dawn, if he could stay right there, without bothering to go into the woods to sleep.

Since there were no trees in the meadow, but only a few scrubby bushes along the stone wall, one might naturally make the mistake of thinking that there could not possibly be a nook of any kind that would suit Solomon Owl, who could never sleep soundly unless his bedroom was quite dark.

But there was one hiding place that Solomon liked almost as well as his home in the hollow hemlock. And that was Farmer Green's haystack. He burrowed into one side of it and made himself a snug chamber, which was as dark as a pocket--and ever so much quieter. What pleased Solomon most, however, was this: Nobody knew about that new retreat except himself.

Even if Reddy Woodpecker should succeed in finding it, he never could disturb Solomon by drumming upon the haystack. If Reddy tried that trick, his bill would merely sink noiselessly into the hay.

So Solomon Owl at last had a good day's rest. And when he met Reddy Woodpecker just after sunset, Solomon was feeling so cheerful that he said "Good-evening!" quite pleasantly, before he remembered that it was Reddy who had teased him so often.

"Good-evening!" Reddy Woodpecker replied. He seemed much surprised that Solomon Owl should be so agreeable. "Can you hear me?" Reddy asked him.

"Perfectly!" said Solomon.

"That's strange!" Reddy Woodpecker exclaimed. "I was almost sure you had suddenly grown deaf." And he could not understand why Solomon Owl laughed loud and long.

"Wha-wha! Whoo-ah!" Solomon's deep-voiced laughter rolled and echoed through the woodland.

But Reddy Woodpecker did not laugh at all.

Day 52

1. Read chapter 22 of *The Tale of Solomon Owl*.
2. Congratulations on finishing the book!
3. Tell someone about what you read.

Read Chapter 22, XXII IT WAS SOLOMON'S FAULT

Reddy Woodpecker had a very good reason for not laughing when he met Solomon Owl. Of course, he knew nothing whatever of Solomon's new hiding place in the haystack. And that very morning Reddy had invited a party of friends to go with him to the hemlock grove where Solomon Owl had always lived, "to have some fun," as Reddy had explained.

For a long time he had knocked and hammered and pounded at Solomon Owl's door. But for once Solomon's great pale face did not appear.

"Where's the fun?" Reddy's friends had wanted to know, after they had waited until they were impatient.

And Reddy Woodpecker could only shake his head and say:

"I can't understand it! It's never happened like this before. I'm afraid Solomon Owl has lost his hearing."

Reddy Woodpecker's friends were no more polite than he. And they began to jeer at him.

"You didn't hammer loud enough," one of them told him.

So he set to work again and rapped and rapped until his head felt as if it would fly off, and his neck began to ache.

Still, Solomon Owl did not appear. And the party broke up in something very like a quarrel. For Reddy Woodpecker lost his temper when his friends teased him; and a good many unpleasant remarks passed back and forth.

Somehow, Reddy felt that it was all Solomon Owl's fault, because he hadn't come to the door.

Of course, Reddy had no means of knowing that all that time Solomon Owl was sleeping peacefully in Farmer Green's haystack in the meadow, a quarter of a mile away.

It was a good joke on Reddy Woodpecker. And though no one had told Solomon Owl about it, he was not so stupid that he couldn't guess at least a little that had happened.

Solomon Owl continued to have a very pleasant time living in the meadow. Since there were many mice right close at hand, little by little he visited the woods less and less. And there came a time at last when he hardly left the meadow at all.

Not flying any more than he could help, and eating too much, and sleeping very soundly each day, he grew stouter than ever, until his friends hardly knew him when they saw him.

"Solomon Owl is a sight--he's so fat!" people began to say.

But his size never worried Solomon Owl in the least. When he became too big for his doorway in the haystack, it was a simple matter to make the opening larger--much simpler than it would have been to make himself smaller. And that was another reason why he was delighted with his new home.

At last, however, something happened to put an end to his lazy way of living. One day the sound of men's voices awakened him, when he was having a good nap in the haystack. And he felt his bedroom quiver as if an earthquake had shaken it.

Scrambling to his doorway and peeping slyly out, Solomon saw a sight that made him very angry. A hayrack stood alongside the stack; and on it stood Farmer Green and his hired man. Each had a pitchfork in his hands, with which he tore great forkfuls of hay off the stack and piled it upon the wagon.

Solomon Owl knew then that his fine hiding place was going to be spoiled. As soon as the horses had pulled the load of hay away, with Farmer Green and the hired man riding on top of it, Solomon Owl crept out of his snug bedroom and hurried off to the woods.

He was so fat that it was several days before he could squeeze inside his old home in the hollow hemlock. And for the time being he had to sit on a limb and sleep in the daylight as best he could.

But to his surprise, Reddy Woodpecker troubled him no more. Reddy had drummed so hard on Solomon's door, in the effort to awake him when he wasn't there, that Aunt Polly Woodchuck told him he would ruin his bill, if he didn't look out. And since the warning thoroughly alarmed him, Reddy stopped visiting the hemlock grove.

In time Solomon Owl grew to look like himself again. And people never really knew just what had happened to him. But they noticed that he always hooted angrily whenever anybody mentioned Farmer Green's name. THE END

Day 53

1. Read the poems.
2. In the first poem, why can the author do nothing but sit? (Answers)
3. In the poem about autumn, what do you think it might mean that "the rose is out of town"? (Answers)
4. In the last poem, why won't she have to wash? (Answers)

August Heat by Anonymous (That means that the author is not known.)
In August, when the days are hot,
I like to find a shady spot,
And hardly move a single bit--
And sit--
And sit--
And sit--
And sit!

Nature XXVII, Autumn by Emily Dickinson (1830–1886)
The morns are meeker than they were,
The nuts are getting brown;
The berry's cheek is plumper,
The rose is out of town.

Beneath the Sea
Were I a fish beneath the sea,
 Shell-paved and pearl-brocaded,
Would you come down and live with me,
 In groves by coral shaded?
No washing would we have to do;
 Our cushions should be sponges--
And many a great ship's envious crew
 Should watch our merry plunges!

Day 54

1. Read the story of *Little Red Riding Hood.*
2. What happened first?
3. What happened last?

LITTLE RED RIDING HOOD

There was once a sweet little maid who lived with her father and mother in a pretty little cottage at the edge of the village. At the further end of the wood was another pretty cottage and in it lived her grandmother.

Everybody loved this little girl, her grandmother perhaps loved her most of all and gave her a great many pretty things. Once she gave her a red cloak with a hood which she always wore, so people called her Little Red Riding Hood.

One morning Little Red Riding Hood's mother said, "Put on your things and go to see your grandmother. She has been ill; take along this basket for her. I have put in it eggs, butter and cake, and other dainties."

It was a bright and sunny morning. Red Riding Hood was so happy that at first she wanted to dance through the wood. All around her grew pretty wild flowers which she loved so well and she stopped to pick a bunch for her grandmother.

Little Red Riding Hood wandered from her path and was stooping to pick a flower when from behind her a gruff voice said, "Good morning, Little Red Riding Hood." Little Red Riding Hood turned around and saw a great big wolf, but Little Red Riding Hood did not know what a wicked beast the wolf was, so she was not afraid.

"What have you in that basket, Little Red Riding Hood?"

"Eggs and butter and cake, Mr. Wolf."

"Where are you going with them, Little Red Riding Hood?"

"I am going to my grandmother, who is ill, Mr. Wolf."

"Where does your grandmother live, Little Red Riding Hood?"

"Along that path, past the wild rose bushes, then through the gate at the end of the wood, Mr. Wolf."

Then Mr. Wolf again said "Good morning" and set off, and Little Red Riding Hood again went in search of wild flowers.

At last he reached the porch covered with flowers and knocked at the door of the cottage.

"Who is there?" called the grandmother.

"Little Red Riding Hood," said the wicked wolf.

"Press the latch, open the door, and walk in," said the grandmother.

The wolf pressed the latch, and walked in where the grandmother lay in bed. He made one jump at her, but she jumped out of bed into a closet. Then the wolf put on the cap which she had dropped and crept under the bedclothes.

In a short while Little Red Riding Hood knocked at the door, and walked in, saying, "Good morning, Grandmother, I have brought you eggs, butter and cake, and here is a bunch of flowers I gathered in the wood." As she came nearer the bed she said, "What big ears you have, Grandmother."

"All the better to hear you with, my dear."

"What big eyes you have, Grandmother."

"All the better to see you with, my dear."

"But, Grandmother, what a big nose you have."

"All the better to smell with, my dear."

"But, Grandmother, what a big mouth you have."

"All the better to eat you up with, my dear," he said as he sprang at Little Red Riding Hood.

Just at that moment Little Red Riding Hood's father was passing the cottage and heard her scream. He rushed in and with his axe chopped off Mr. Wolf's head.
Everybody was happy that Little Red Riding Hood had escaped the wolf. Then Little Red Riding Hood's father carried her home and they lived happily ever after.

Day 55

1. Read the poems.
2. In the first poem there are homophones, words that sound the same but are spelled differently. What are they? (Answers)
3. Can you make mistakes like in "Eletelephony"? Take two words and mix up their beginning letters.

Weather from *Enchanted Tulips and Other Verses for Children*

Whether the weather be fine,
Or whether the weather be not,
Whether the weather be cold,
Or whether the weather be hot,
We'll weather the weather
Whatever the weather,
Whether we like it or not!

Eletelephony
by Laura E. Richards

Once there was an elephant,
Who tried to use the telephant--
No! no! I mean an elephone
Who tried to use the telephone--
(Dear me! I am not certain quite

That even now I've got it right.)
Howe'er it was, he got his trunk
Entangled in the telephunk;
The more he tried to get it free,
The louder buzzed the telephee--
I fear I'd better drop the song
Of elephop and telephong!)

Day 56

1. Read lessons 4 and 5 in the *McGuffey Second Reader*. (4 and 5 look like this IV and V, the V means 5 and the I means one, IV means one before five)
2. Say or write the pairs of rhyming words in the poem in lesson 4.

Lesson IV The Little Star

1. Twinkle, twinkle, little star;
   How I wonder what you are,
   Up above the world so high,
   Like a diamond in the sky!

2. When the blazing sun is set,
   And the grass with dew is wet,
   Then you show your little light;
   Twinkle, twinkle, all the night.

3. Then, if I wore in the dark,
   I would thank you for your spark.
   I could not see which way to go,
   If you did not twinkle so.

4. And when I am sound asleep,
   Oft you through my window peep;
   For you never shut your eye,
   Till the sun is in the sky.

LESSON V TWO DOGS

1. James White has two dogs. One is a Newfoundland dog, and the other is a Scotch terrier.

2. The Newfoundland is a large, noble fellow. He is black, with a white spot, and with long, shaggy hair. His name is Sport.

3. Sport is a good watchdog, and a kind playfellow. Every night he guards the house while James and his father are asleep.

4. In the daytime, James often uses Sport for his horse. He has a little wagon, and a set of small harness which just fits the dog.

5. He hitches Sport to this wagon, and drives over the country. In this way, he can go almost as fast as his father with the old family horse.

6. The name of James's Scotch terrier is Dodger. He is called Dodger because he jumps about so friskily. He is up on a chair, under the table, behind the door, down cellar, and out in the yard,--all in a minute.

7. Dodger has very bright eyes, and he does many funny things. He likes to put his paws up on the crib, and watch the baby.

8. The other day he took baby's red stocking, and had great fun with it; but he spoiled it in his play, and James had to scold him.

9. Everyone likes to see James White with his two dogs. They always seem very happy together.

Day 57

1. Read lessons 7 and 8 in the *McGuffey Second Reader*. (lessons VII and VIII)
2. Tell someone what the stories were about.

Lesson VII BABY BYE

1. Baby Bye,
   Here's a fly;
   We will watch him, you and I.
   How he crawls
   Up the walls,
   Yet he never falls!
   I believe with six such legs
   You and I could walk on eggs.
   There he goes
   On his toes,
   Tickling Baby's nose.

2. Spots of red
   Dot his head;
   Rainbows on his back are spread;
   That small speck
   Is his neck;
   See him nod and beck!
   I can show you, if you choose,
   Where to look to find his shoes,
   Three small pairs,
   Made of hairs;
   These he always wears.

3. Flies can see
   More than we;
   So how bright their eyes must be!
   Little fly,
   Open your eye;
   Spiders are near by.
   For a secret I can tell,
   Spiders never use flies well;
   Then away,
   Do not stay.
   Little fly, good day.

LESSON VIII PUSS AND HER KITTENS

1. Puss, with her three kittens, had lived in the coal cellar; but one day she thought she would carry them to the attic.

2. The servant thought that was not the proper place for them; so she carried them back to the cellar.

3. Puss was certain that she wanted them in the attic; so she carried them there again and again, five, six, seven, --yes, a dozen times; for each time the servant took them back to the cellar.

4. Poor puss was nearly tired out, and could carry them no longer.

5. Suddenly she went away. Where do you think she went?

6. She was gone a long time. When she returned, she had a strange cat with her that we had never seen before.

7. She seemed to tell him all about her great trouble, and he listened to her story.

8. Then the strange cat took the little kittens, one by one, and carried them to the attic. After this he went away, and we have never seen him since.

9. The servant then left the kittens in the attic, for she saw how anxious puss was to have them stay there.

10. Was not the strange cat kind to puss? This lesson should teach children to be ever ready to help one another.

Day 58

1. Read lessons 10 and 11 (X and XI) in the *McGuffey Second Reader*.
2. What is the lesson of lesson 10? (Answers)
3. What did the bird say in lesson 11? (Answers)

LESSON X AT WORK

1. A little play does not harm anyone, but does much good. After play, we should be glad to work.

2. I knew a boy who liked a good game very much. He could run, swim, jump, and play ball; and was always merry when out of school.

3. But he knew that time is not all for play; that our minutes, hours, and days are very precious.

4. At the end of his play, he would go home. After he had washed his face and hands, and brushed his hair, he would help his mother, or read in his book, or write upon his slate.

5. He used to say, "One thing at a time." When he had done with work, he would play; but he did not try to play and to work at the same time.

LESSON XI WHAT A BIRD TAUGHT

1. Why do you come to my apple tree,
   Little bird so gray?
   Twit-twit, twit-twit, twit-twit-twee!
   That was all he would say.

2. Why do you lock your rosy feet
   So closely round the spray?
   Twit-twit, twit-twit, twit-tweet!
   That was all he would say.

3. Why on the topmost bough do you get,
   Little bird so gray?
   Twit-twit-twee! twit-twit-twit!
   That was all he would say.

4. Where is your mate? come, answer me,
   Little bird so gray.
   Twit-twit-twit! twit-twit-twee!
   That was all he would say.

Day 59

1. Read lessons 12 and 13 (XII and XIII) in the *McGuffey Second Reader*.
2. What is the lesson of lesson 12? (Answers)
3. If you were a sunbeam, what would you do? Write or tell your answer.

LESSON XII SUSIE SUNBEAM

1. Susie Sunbeam was not her real name; that was Susan Brown. But every one called her Susie Sunbeam, because she had such a sweet, smiling face, and always brought brightness with her when she came.

2. Her grandfather first gave her this name, and it seemed to fit the little girl so nicely that soon it took the place of her own.

3. Even when a baby, Susie laughed and crowed from morning till night. No one ever heard her cry unless she was sick or hurt.

4. When she had learned to walk, she loved to go about the house and get things for her mother, and in this way save her as many steps as she could.

5. She would sit by her mother's side for an hour at a time, and ask her ever so many questions, or she would take her new book and read.

6. Susie was always pleasant in her play with other children. She never used an unkind word, but tried to do whatever would please her playmates best.

7. One day, a poor little girl with a very ragged dress was going by and Susie heard some children teasing her and making fun of her.

8. She at once ran out to the gate, and asked the poor little girl to come in. "What are you crying for?" Susie asked.

9. "Because they all laugh at me," she said.

10. Then Susie took the little girl into the house. She cheered her up with kind words, and gave her a nice dress and a pair of shoes.

11. This brought real joy and gladness to the poor child, and she, too, thought that Susie was rightly called Sunbeam.

LESSON XIII IF I WERE A SUNBEAM

1. "If I were a sunbeam,
   I know what I'd do;
  I would seek white lilies,
    Roaming woodlands through.
  I would steal among them,
    Softest light I'd shed,
  Until every lily
    Raised its drooping head.

2. "If I were a sunbeam,
   I know where I'd go;
  Into lowly hovels,
    Dark with want and woe:
  Till sad hearts looked upward,
    I would shine and shine;
  Then they'd think of heaven,
    Their sweet home and mine."

3. Are you not a sunbeam,
   Child, whose life is glad
  With an inner brightness
   Sunshine never had?
  Oh, as God has blessed you,
   Scatter light divine!
  For there is no sunbeam
   But must die or shine.

Day 60

1. Read lessons 17 and 18 (XVII and XVIII) in the *McGuffey Second Reader*.
2. What is the boy good for? (Answers)
3. What are some things you learned about the kingbird?

LESSON XVII MY GOOD-FOR-NOTHING

1.

"What are you good for, my brave little man?
Answer that question for me, if you can,--
You, with your fingers as white as a nun,--
You, with your ringlets as bright as the sun.
All the day long, with your busy contriving,
Into all mischief and fun you are driving;
See if your wise little noodle can tell
What you are good for. Now ponder it well."

2.

Over the carpet the dear little feet
Came with a patter to climb on my seat;
Two merry eyes, full of frolic and glee,
Under their lashes looked up unto me;
Two little hands pressing soft on my face,
Drew me down close in a loving embrace;
Two rosy lips gave the answer so true,
"Good to love you, mamma, good to love you."

Emily Huntington Miller.

LESSON XVIII THE KINGBIRD

1. The kingbird is not bigger than a robin.

2. He eats flies, and worms, and bugs, and berries.

3. He builds his nest in a tree, near some house.

4. When there are young ones in the nest, he sits on the top of a tree near them.

5. He watches to see that no bird comes to hurt them or their mother.

6. If a hawk, a crow, or even an eagle comes near, he makes a dash at it.

7. Though he is so small, he is brave, and he is also very active.

8. He never fails to drive off other birds from his nest.

9. He flies around and around the eagle, and suddenly strikes him with his sharp bill.

10. He strikes at his eye, and then darts away before the eagle can catch him.

11. Or he strikes from behind, and is off again before the eagle can turn round.

12. In a short time, the great eagle is tired of such hard blows, and flies away. He is very glad to get rid of his foe.

13. Is not the little fellow a brave bird?

14. Because he can drive off all other birds, he is called the KINGBIRD.

Day 61

1. Read lessons 23 and 24. (XXIII and XXIV)
2. What lesson did the little girl, Mary, need to learn? (Answers)
3. What steps are taken to shear sheep? (Answers)

LESSON XXIII THE TORN DOLL

1. Mary Armstrong was a pretty little girl, but she was heedless about some things.

2. Her way of leaving her books and playthings just where she had used them last, gave her mother much trouble in picking them up and putting them in their proper places.

3. She had often told Mary the evil effects of being so careless. Her books became spoiled, and her toys broken.

4. But worse than this was the growing habit of carelessness, which would be of great harm to her all her life. It would make her unhappy, and would annoy her friends.

5. One day Mary and her mother went out into their pleasant yard, to spend an hour in the open air. Mrs. Armstrong took her work with her.

6. Mary ran about and played with Dash, her pet dog, and was having a happy time.

7. But in a corner of the yard she found her nicest doll all torn and broken, and its dress covered with mud.

8. She knew, at once, that Dash had done this, and she scolded him harshly.

9. Carrying the broken doll to her mamma. she showed it to her, and could hardly keep from crying.

10. Mrs. Armstrong asked Mary if she had not left the doll on the porch where Dash could easily get it; and Mary had to answer, "Yes, ma'am."

11. "Then you must not blame the dog, Mary, for he does not know it is wrong for him to play with your doll. I hope this will be a lesson to you hereafter, to put your things away when you are through playing."

12. "I will try," said Mary. And her mother promised to mend the doll as well as she could.

LESSON XXIV SHEEP-SHEARING

1. Sheep are washed and sheared some time in the month of June. This should be done quite early in the month, before the hot days begin.

2. It is fine sport for those who look on, but not much fun for the sheep.

3. It is best for the sheep to have the wool taken off; otherwise they would suffer in the summer time.

4. When the time comes for washing the sheep, they are driven to a pond or a little river.

5. Then they are thrown into the water, one at a time. The men who are in the water catch them, and squeeze the wet wool with their hands to get the dirt all out of it.

6. Then the wool is thoroughly dried, the sheep are taken to the shearer; and he cuts off the wool with a large pair of shears.

7. It is then dyed, spun, and woven into cloth.

8. In a short time, before the cold winter comes, new wool grows out on the sheep. By the coming of spring there is so much, that it must be cut off again.

Day 62

1. Read lessons 26 and 27 (XXVI and XXVII).
2. How did Patty tame the squirrel? (Answers)
3. Does there seem to be a problem in the poem? In stanza #4? What is it? Maybe long ago they pronounced the words differently? Or is it just a mistake? What do you think? (Answers)

LESSON XXVI PATTY AND THE SQUIRREL

1. Little Patty lives in a log house near a great forest. She has no sisters, and her big brothers are away all day helping their father.

2. But Patty is never lonely; for, though the nearest house is miles away, she has many little friends. Here are two of them that live in the woods.

3. But how did Patty teach them to be so tame? Patty came to the woods often, and was always so quiet and gentle that the squirrels soon found they need not be afraid of her.

4. She brought her bread and milk to eat under the trees, and was sure to leave crumbs for the squirrels.

5. When they came near, she sat very still and watched them. So, little by little, she made them her friends, till, at last, they would sit on her shoulder, and eat from her hand.

6. Squirrels build for themselves summer houses. Those are made of leaves, and sticks, and moss. They are nice and cool for summer, but would never do for the winter cold and snow.

7. So these wise little people find a hollow in an old tree. They make it warm and snug with soft moss and leaves; and here the squirrels live all through the long winter.

LESSON XXVII THE SPARROW

1. Glad to see you, little bird;
   'Twas your little chirp I heard:
   What did you intend to say?
   "Give me something this cold day"?

2. That I will, and plenty, too;
   All the crumbs I saved for you.
   Don't be frightened--here's a treat:
   I will wait and see you eat.

3. Shocking tales I hear of you;
   Chirp, and tell me, are they true?
   Robbing all the summer long;
   Don't you think it very wrong?

4. Thomas says you steal his wheat;
   John complains, his plums you eat--
   Choose the ripest for your share,
   Never asking whose they are.

5. But I will not try to know
   What you did so long ago:
   There's your breakfast, eat away;
   Come to see me every day.

Day 63

1. Read lessons 32 and 33 (XXXII and XXXIII).
2. What are two things you learned about tigers?
3. What lesson did the girls learn? (Answers)

LESSON XXXII THE TIGER

1. The tiger is a giant cat. His body is nearly covered with black stripes.

2. Unlike the lion, he runs so fast that the swiftest horse can not overtake him. He goes over the ground by making bounds or springs, one after another.

3. By night, as well as by day, the tiger watches for his prey. With a frightful roar, he will seize a man, and carry him off.

4. Have you ever thought what use whiskers are to cats? Lions have great whiskers, and so have tigers and all other animals of the cat kind.

5. Whenever you find an animal with whiskers like the cat's, you may be sure that animal steals softly among branches and thick bushes.

6. By the slightest touch on the tiger's whiskers, he knows when there is anything in his road.

7. A few years ago, some English officers went out to hunt. When coming home from their day's sport, they found a little tiger kitten.

8. They took it with them and tied it, with a collar and chain, to the pole of their tent. It played about, to the delight of all who saw it.

9. One evening, just as it was growing dark, they heard a sound that frightened them greatly. It was the roar of a tiger.

10. The kitten pulled at the chain, and tried to break away. With a sharp cry, it answered the voice outside.

11. All at once, a large tigress bounded into the middle of the tent. She caught her kitten by the neck, and broke the chain which bound it.

12. Then turning to the door of the tent, she dashed away as suddenly as she had come.

LESSON XXXIII THE FIRESIDE

1. One winter night, Mrs. Lord and her two little girls sat by a bright fire in their pleasant home. The girls were sewing, and their mother was busy at her knitting.

2. At last, Katie finished her work, and, looking up, said, "Mother, I think the fire is brighter than usual. How I love to hear it crackle!"

3. "And I was about to say," cried Mary, "that this is a better light than we had last night."

4. "My dears," said their mother, "it must be that you feel happier than usual to-night. Perhaps that is the reason why you think the fire better, and the light brighter."

5. "But, mother," said Mary, "I do not see why we are happier now than we were then; for last night cousin Jane was here, and we played 'Puss in the corner' and 'Blind man' until we all were tired."

6. "I know! I know why!" said Katie. "It is because we have all been doing something useful to-night. We feel happy because we have been busy."

7. "You are right, my dear," said their mother. "I am glad you have both learned that there may be something more pleasant than play, and, at the same time, more instructive."

Day 64

1. Read lessons 35 and 36 (XXXV and XXXVI).
2. Retell the story to someone.

LESSON XXXV WILLIE AND BOUNCE

1. Two fast friends were Willie Brown and his little dog Bounce. Willie could never think of taking a walk without Bounce. Cake and play were equally shared between them.

2. Willie taught his dog many cunning tricks, and often said that Bounce could do almost anything in the world but talk.

3. There came a time, however, when Bounce really told Willie's father something, though he could not talk. Let me tell you how he did this.

4. It was on a bright summer afternoon. Willie had strolled with Bounce down to the river, which was not more than two blocks from his father's store.

5. Willie began to throw stones into the water, and to watch the ripples as they made one circle after another.

6. Bounce lay on the grass, watching the flies that buzzed around his nose, and catching any that came too near.

7. There were some logs floating in the river near the shore. Willie jumped upon one of them, to see if he could throw a stone across the river.

8. He drew back, and sent the stone with all his might. Just as it left his hand, the log turned, and he fell into the water.

9. He was very much frightened, for he did not know how to swim, and there was no one to hear, though he called as loud as he could for help.

LESSON XXXVI WILLIE AND BOUNCE (CONCLUDED)

1. Poor little Bounce gave a great yelp of distress. If he had been a big water dog, he could have jumped in and brought his master out.

2. He ran up and down the bank two or three times, barking, looking first at Willie and then around. Then he started, as fast as he could run, up the street to the store.

3. When he got there the door was shut, but he scratched against it and barked loudly, until some one came and opened it.

4. He caught hold of Mr. Brown's clothes, then ran to the door, then back again, catching at him, barking, and jumping.

5. A friend who was in the store said to Mr. Brown, "Something must be wrong; I would put on my hat, and go with the dog." Bounce, seeing Mr. Brown take his hat, started for the river.

6. Then Mr. Brown thought of Willie. As he came to the river, he saw Willie's hat floating on the water, and his small arm thrown up.

7. He sprang in and caught him just as he was going down for the last time, and quickly carried him to the bank. "Willie soon got over his fright, and no one seemed to be more delighted than Bounce.

Day 65

1. Read lessons 37 and 38 (XXXVII and XXXVIII).
2. How did the boy build the scale?

LESSON XXXVII THE KITCHEN CLOCK

1. Listen to the kitchen clock!
   To itself it ever talks,
   From its place it never walks;
  "Tick-tock-tick-tock: "
   Tell me what it says.

2. "I'm a very patient clock,
   Never moved by hope or fear,
   Though I've stood for many a year;
  Tick-tock-tick-tock: "
   That is what it says.

3. "I'm a very truthful clock:
   People say about the place,
   Truth is written on my face;
  Tick-tock-tick-tock: "
   That is what it says.

4. "I'm a most obliging clock;
   If you wish to hear me strike,
   You may do it when you like;
  Tick-tock-tick-tock: "
   That is what it says.

5. "I'm a very friendly clock;
   For this truth to all I tell,
   Life is short, improve it well;
  Tick-tock-tick-tock: "
   That is what it says.

6. What a talkative old clock!
   Let us see what it will do
   When the hour hand reaches two;
   "Ding-ding--tick-tock: "
   That is what it says.

LESSON XXXVIII THE NEW SCALES

1. "Herbert, will you please peel my orange?" said Lucy. Herbert was reading his new book, but he put it down at once, and took the orange from his little sister.

2. "Shall I make a pair of scales, Lucy, for you to use when you play store?"

3. "Oh yes! but how can you do that!"

4. "I'll show you. First, we must take the peel off in two little cups, one just as large as the other. While I do this, see if you can find me two nice sticks about ten inches long."

5. Lucy ran out to the woodhouse to find the sticks.--" Will these do?"

6. "No, they are too hard. Find some pine sticks if you can."

7. "Here are some."

8. "These will do nicely. Now I must make a scale beam and a post. Can you find me a little block for a post, Lucy!"

9. "Will a ribbon block do, Herbert?"

10. "Yes, if it is not too thick."

11. "Here is one an inch thick."

12. "That will be just right. Now get the little gimlet."

[Note: a gimlet is a hand tool with a spiraled shank, a screw tip, and a cross handle; used for boring/drilling holes]

13. Herbert worked away until he had made the beam and the post. Then he made a hole in the middle of the block, and put the post in. Next, he put the beam into a little groove at the top of the post, so that it would balance nicely.

14. "Now, Lucy, we must have a needle and some thread. We must put four threads to each cup; then we will tie the threads to the ends of the beam.

15. "There, Lucy, what do you think of that?"

16. "Why, Herbert, that is just as nice as the real scales in father's store; and you may have all my orange for making them."

Day 66

1. Read lessons 41 and 42. (XLI and XLII)
2. Tell someone something you learned about the fishhawk.

LESSON XLI THE FISHHAWK

1. The fishhawk, or osprey, is not so large as the eagle; but he has, like the eagle, a hooked bill and sharp claws.

2. His color is a dark brown, with black and white spots, and his length is from twenty to twenty-two inches. His breast is mostly white. His tail and wings are long.

3. The fishhawk is often found sitting upon a tree over a pond, or lake, or river. He is also found by the seaside.

4. He watches the fish as they swim in the water beneath him; then he darts down suddenly and catches one of them.

5. When he catches a fish in his sharp, rough claws, he carries it off to eat, and, as he flies away with it for his dinner, an eagle sometimes meets him.

6. The eagle flies at him fiercely with his sharp bill and claws, and compels the hawk to drop the fish.

7. Then the eagle catches the fish as it falls, before it reaches the ground, and carries it off.

8. The poor fish hawk, with a loud cry, timidly flies away. He must go again to the water and catch another fish for his dinner.

9. Thus you see, that the eagle is a robber. He robs fishhawks, whose only mode of getting a living is by catching fish.

LESSON XLI WHAT THE LEAF SAID

1. Once or twice a little leaf was heard to cry and sigh, as leaves often do, when a gentle wind is blowing. And the twig said, "What is the matter, little leaf?"

2. "The wind," said the leaf, "just told me that one day it would pull me off, and throw me on the ground to die."

3. The twig told it to the branch, and the branch told it to the tree. When the tree heard it, it rustled all over, and sent word back to the trembling leaf.

4. "Do not be afraid," it said; "hold on tight, and you shall not go off till you are ready."

5. So the leaf stopped sighing, and went on singing and rustling. It grew all the summer long till October. And when the bright days of autumn came, the leaf saw all the leaves around growing very beautiful.

6. Some were yellow, some were brown, and many were striped with different colors. Then the leaf asked the tree what this meant.

7. The tree said, "All these leaves are getting ready to fly away, and they have put on these colors because of their joy."

8. Then the little leaf began to want to go, and grew very beautiful in thinking of it. When it was gay in colors, it saw that the branches of the tree had no bright colors on them.

9. So the leaf said, "O branch! why are you lead- colored while we are all beautiful and golden?"

10. "We must keep on our working clothes," said the tree, "for our work is not yet done; but your clothes are for holidays, because your task is now over."

11. Just then a little puff of wind came, and the leaf let go without thinking, and the wind took it up and turned it over and over.

12. Then it fell gently down under the edge of the fence, among hundreds of leaves, and has never waked to tell us what it dreamed about.

Day 67

1. Read lessons 43 and 44. (XLIII and XLIV)
2. What was mother's Christmas present? (Answers)

LESSON XLIII THE WIND AND THE LEAVES
1.
"Come, little leaves," said the wind one day.
"Come o'er the meadows with me, and play;
Put on your dress of red and gold
Summer is gone, and the days grow cold."

2.
Soon as the leaves heard the wind's loud call,
Down they came fluttering, one and all;
Over the brown fields they danced and flew,
Singing the soft little songs they knew.

3.

"Cricket, good-by, we've been friends so long;
Little brook, sing us your farewell song,--
Say you are sorry to see us go;
Ah! you will miss us, right well we know.

4.

"Dear little lambs, in your fleecy fold,
Mother will keep you from harm and cold;
Fondly we've watched you in vale and glade;
Say, will you dream of our loving shade?"

5.

Dancing and whirling, the little leaves went;
Winter had called them, and they were content.
Soon fast asleep in their earthy beds,
The snow laid a coverlet over their heads.

George Cooper.

LESSON XLIV MAMMA'S PRESENT

1. Jessie played a good joke on her mamma. This is the way she did it.

2. Jessie had gone to the woods with Jamie and Joe to get green branches to trim up the house for Christmas. She wore her little cap, her white furs, and her red leggings.

3. She was a merry little girl, indeed; but she felt sad this morning because her mother had said, "The children will all have Christmas presents, but I don't expect any for myself. We are too poor this year."

4. When Jessie told her brothers this, they all talked about it a great deal. "Such a good, kind mamma, and no Christmas present! It's too bad."

5. "I don't like it," said little Jessie, with a tear in her eye.

6. "Oh, she has you," said Joe.

7. "But I am not something new," said Jessie.

8. "Well, you will be new, Jessie," said Joe, "when you get back. She has not seen you for an hour."

9. Jessie jumped and laughed. "Then put me in the basket, and carry me to mamma, and say, 'I am her Christmas present.' "

10. So they set her in the basket, and put green branches all around her. It was a jolly ride. They set her down on the doorstep, and went in and said, "There's a Christmas present out there for you, mamma."

11. Mamma went and looked, and there, in a basket of green branches, sat her own little laughing girl.

12. "Just the very thing I wanted most," said mamma.

13. "Then, dear mamma," said Jessie, bounding out of her leafy nest, "I should think it would be Christmas for mammas all the time, for they see their little girls every day."

Day 68

1. Read lessons 45 and 46. (XLV and XLVI)
2. What happened to Ralph when he threw a fit and grabbed what he wanted? (Answers)

LESSON XLV MARY'S STORY

1. Father, and Charles, and Lucy, and I went to the beach yesterday. We took our dinner, and stayed all day.

2. Father and Charles went out a little way from the shore in a boat, and fished, while Lucy and I gathered sea mosses.

3. We took off our shoes and stockings, and waded into the shallow water. We had a pail to put our seaweeds in.

4. We found such beautiful ones. Some wore purple, some pink, and some brown. When they were spread out in the water, the purple ones looked like plumes, and the brown ones like little trees.

5. Such a funny thing happened to Lucy. She slipped on a stone, and down she went into the water. How we both laughed! But the wind and sun soon dried Lucy's dress.

6. Then father came and took us in the boat for a row. After that we had a picnic dinner in the woods.

7. Then father spread his coat on the grass, and took a nap while we children played on the beach.

LESSON XLVI RALPH WICK

1. Ralph Wick was seven years old. In most things he was a fine boy, but he was too apt to cry.

2. When he could not have what he wanted, he would cry for it and say, "I will have it."

3. If he was told that it would hurt him, and he could not have it, he would begin to tease and cry.

4. One day, he went with his mother into the fields. The sun shone. The grass was cut. The flowers were in bloom.

5. Ralph thought he was, for once, a good boy. A smile was on his face. He wished to do as he was told.

6. He said, "Mother, I will be good now. I will do as you bid me. Please let me toss this hay."

7. "That I will," said his mother. So they threw the hay, as Ralph wished, and he was very happy.

8. "Now you must be tired," said his mother. "Sit down here, and I will get a nice red rose for you."

9. "I would like to have one," said Ralph. So his mother brought the red rose to him.

10. "Thank you, mother," he said. "But you have a white one, also. Please give me that."

11. "No, my dear," said his mother. "See how many thorns it has on its stem. You must not touch it. If you should try to pluck a rose like this, you would be sure to hurt your hand."

12. When Ralph found that he could not have the white rose, he began to scream, and snatched it. But he was soon very sorry. The thorns tore his hand. It was so sore he could not use it for some time.

13. Ralph did not soon forget this. When he wanted what he should not have, his mother would point to his sore hand. He at last learned to do as he was told.

Day 69

1. Read lesson 49. (XLIX)
2. What does it mean, pretty is as pretty does? (Answers)

LESSON XLIX PRETTY IS THAT PRETTY DOES

1. The spider wears a plain brown dress,
   And she is a steady spinner;
 To see her, quiet as a mouse,
 Going about her silver house,
 You would never, never, never guess
   The way she gets her dinner.
2. She looks as if no thought of ill

In all her life had stirred her;
But while she moves with careful tread,
And while she spins her silken thread,
She is planning, planning, planning still
The way to do some murder.

3. My child, who reads this simple lay,
With eyes down-dropt and tender,
Remember the old proverb says
That pretty is which pretty does,
And that worth does not go nor stay
For poverty nor splendor.

4. 'Tis not the house, and not the dress,
That makes the saint or sinner.
To see the spider sit and spin,
Shut with her walls of silver in,
You would never, never, never guess
The way she gets her dinner.

Alice Cary.

Day 70

1. Read some knock-knock jokes.
2. Which are your favorites?

Knock Knock
Who's there !
Adam !
Adam who ?
Adam up and tell me the total !

Knock Knock
Who's there !
Adder !
Adder who ?
Adder you get in here ?

Knock Knock
Who's there !
Abbey !
Abbey who ?
Abbey stung me on the nose !

Knock Knock
Who's there !
Abe !Abe who ?
Abe C D E F G H... !

Knock Knock
Who's there !
Adolf !
Adolf who ?
Adolf ball hit me in the mouth !

Knock Knock
Who's there !
Ahmed !
Ahmed who ?
Ahmed a big mistake coming here !

Knock Knock
Who's there !
Anka !
Anka who ?
Anka the ship !

Knock Knock
Who's there !
Barbie !
Barbie who ?
Barbie Q !

Knock Knock
Who's there !
Ben !
Ben who ?
Ben knocking on this door all morning !

Knock Knock
Who's there !
Avery !
Avery who ?
Avery time I come to your house we go through this !

Knock Knock
Who's there !
Beaver E !
Beaver E who ?
Beaver E quiet and nobody will find us !

Knock Knock
Who's there !
Bruce !
Bruce who ?
I Bruce easily, don't hit me !

Knock Knock
Who's there !
C-2 !
C-2 who ?
C-2 it that you don't forget my name
next time !

Knock Knock
Who's there !
Canoe !
Canoe who ?
Canoe come out and play with me ?

Knock Knock
Who's there ?
Chuck !
Chuck who ?
Chuck in a sandwich for lunch

Knock Knock
Who's there !
Costa !
Costa who ?
Costa lot !

Knock Knock
Who's there ?
Cotton !
Cotton who ?
Cotton a trap !

Knock Knock
Who's there !
Cumin !
Cumin who?
Cumin side, its freezing out there !
(from www.funmint.com/knock-knock-jokes/
Site says the jokes are public domain or free.)

Day 71

1. Read the poems.
2. Why was grandpa seeing everything purple? (Answers)
3. Who is causing all the problems in the house in the second poem? Do you have a guess what that means? That "nobody" is making the messes in the house?

Grandpa Dropped His Glasses
by Leroy F. Jackson

Grandpa dropped his glasses once
In a pot of dye,
And when he put them on again
He saw a purple sky.
Purple fires were rising up
From a purple hill,
Men were grinding purple cider
at a purple mill.
Purple Adeline was playing
With a purple doll;
Little purple dragon flies
Were crawling up the wall.
And at the supper-table
He got crazy as a loon
From eating purple apple dumplings
With a purple spoon.

Mr. Nobody
I know a funny little man,
As quiet as a mouse,
Who does the mischief that is done
In everybody's house!
There's no one ever sees his face,
And yet we all agree
That every plate we break was cracked
By Mr. Nobody.

'Tis he who always tears our books,
Who leaves the door ajar,
He pulls the buttons from our shirts,
And scatters pins afar;
That squeaking door will always squeak,
For, prithee, don't you see,
We leave the oiling to be done
By Mr. Nobody.
He puts damp wood upon the fire,
That kettles cannot boil;
His are the feet that bring in mud,
And all the carpets soiled.
The papers always are mislaid,
Who had them last but he?
There's no one tosses them about
But Mr. Nobody.
The finger marks upon the door
By none of us are made;
We never leave the blinds unclosed,
To let the curtains fade.
The ink we never spill; the boots
that lying round you see
Are not our boots -- they all belong
To Mr. Nobody.

Day 72

1. Read the poems.
2. Why couldn't Jonathan see the king? (Answers)
3. In the second poem, look at the words that rhyme with Antonio. What real words are they supposed to be? Can you figure it out?

Jonathan Bing
by Beatrice Curtis Brown

Poor old Jonathan Bing
Went out in his carriage to visit the King,
But everyone pointed and said, "Look at that!
Jonathan Bing has forgotten his hat!"
(He'd forgotten his hat!)
Poor old Jonathan Bing
Went home and put on a new hat for the King,
But by the palace the soldier said, "Hi!
You can't see the King; you've forgotten your tie!"
(He'd forgotten his tie!)
Poor old Jonathan Bing,
He put on a beautiful tie for the King,
But when he arrived, and Archbishop said, "Ho!
You can't come to court in pajamas, you know!"
Poor old Jonathan Bing
Went home and addressed a short note to the King:
"If you please will excuse me, I won't come to tea;
For home's the best place for all people like me!"

Antonio
by Laura E. Richards

Antonio, Antonio
Was tired of living alonio.
He thought he would woo
Miss Lissamy Lu,
Miss Lissamy Lucy Molonio.
Antonio, Antonio,
Rode off on his polo-ponio.
He found the fair maid
In a bowery shade,
A-sitting and knitting alonio.
Antonio, Antonio,

Said, "If you will be my ownio,
I'll love you true,
And I'll buy for you
An icery creamery conio!"
Oh, Nonio, Antonio!
You're far too bleak and bonio!
And all that I wish,
You singular fish,
Is that you will quickly begonio."
Antonio, Antonio,
He uttered a dismal moanio;
Then he ran off and hid
(Or I'm told that he did)
In the Antecatarctical Zonio.

Day 73

1. Read the poems.
2. The first one has words in another language. Say them the best you can.
3. In the second poem can you figure which word says more than one hippopotamus?

Iroquois Lullaby

Ho, Ho, Watanay,
Ho, Ho, Watanay,
Ho, Ho, Watanay,
Kiyokena, Kiyokena.
Do, do, mon petit,
Do, do, mon petit,
Do, do, mon petit,
et bonne nuit, et bonne nuit.
Slumber, my little one,
Slumber, my little one,
Slumber, my little one
and gently sleep, so gently sleep.
Land of the Silver Birch

Land of the silver birch
Home of the beaver
Where still the mighty moose
Wanders at will
Blue lake and rocky shore,
I will return once more,
Boom de boom, boom de boom
Boo-oo-oo-oo-oom.
http://www.earlyliterature.ecsd.net/cultures.htm

The Hippopotamus
by Ogden Nash

Behold the hippopotamus!
We laugh at how he looks to us,
And yet in moments dank and grim,
I wonder how we look to him.
Peace, peace, thou hippopotamus!
We really look all right to us,
As you no doubt delight the eye
Of other hippopotami.

Day 74

1. Read the poems.
2. Where can you find a yak? Can you find a place name in the poem? Maybe you'd like to find it on a map.

The Yak
By Hilaire Belloc

As a friend to the children commend me the Yak.
You will find it exactly the thing:
It will carry and fetch, you can ride on its back,
Or lead it about with a string.
The tartar who dwells on the plains of Tibet
(A desolate region of snow)

153

Has for centuries made it a nursery pet,
And surely the Tartar should know!
Then tell your papa where the yak can be got,
And if he is awfully rich
He will buy you the creature - or else he will not,
(I can not be positive which.)

Some One
by Walter De La Mare

Some one came knocking
At my wee, small door;
Some one came knocking,
I'm sure - sure - sure;
I listened, I opened,
I looked to left and right,
But naught there was a-stirring
In the still dark night;
Only the busy beetle
Tap-tapping in the wall,
Only from the forest
The screech-owl's call,
Only the cricket whistling
While the dewdrops fall,
So I know not who came knocking,
At all, at all, at all.

Day 75

1. Read the poems.
2. In the first poem a "yarn" is a story.
3. Who is the poet talking to in the second poem? (Answers)

Sea Fever
by John Mansfield

I must go down to the seas again, to the lonely sea and the sky,
And all I ask is a tall ship and a star to steer her by,
And the wheel's kick and the wind's song and the white sail's shaking,
And a grey mist on the sea's face and a grey dawn breaking.
I must go down to the seas again, for the call of the running tide
Is a wild call and a clear call that may not be denied;
And all I ask is a windy day with the white clouds flying,
And the flung spray and the blown spume, and the sea-gulls crying.
I must go down to the seas again, to the vagrant gypsy life,
To the gull's way and the whale's way where the wind's like a whetted knife;
And all I ask is a merry yarn from a laughing fellow-rover,
And quiet sleep and a sweet dream when the long trick's over.

There is Another Sky
by Emily Dickinson

There is another sky,
Ever serene and fair,
And there is another sunshine,
Though it be darkness there;
Never mind faded forests, Austin,
Never mind silent fields -
Here is a little forest,
Whose leaf is ever green;
Here is a brighter garden,
Where not a frost has been;
In its unfading flowers
I hear the bright bee hum:
Prithee, my brother,
Into my garden come!

Day 76

1. Read the poems.
2. In the first poem, how do you think a frog announces his name?
3. In the second poem, what does the poet think we should all do? (Answers)

<u>I'm Nobody! Who Are You?</u>
by Emily Dickinson

I'm Nobody! Who are you?
Are you -- Nobody -- Too?
Then there's a pair of us!
Don't tell! they'd advertise -- you know!
How dreary -- to be -- Somebody!
How public -- like a Frog --
To tell one's name -- the livelong June --
To an admiring Bog!

<u>To You</u>
by Walt Whitman

STRANGER! if you, passing, meet me,
and desire to speak to me,
why should you not speak to me?

And why should I not speak to you?

Day 77

1. Begin reading *The Tale of Reddy Woodpecker*. Read chapter 1.
2. Tell someone what happened in the chapter. (Remember, it's normal at this age to need to ask leading questions if they are having trouble getting started. Who was it about? What did he do? Then what happened?)

THE TALE OF REDDY WOODPECKER
BY ARTHUR SCOTT BAILEY

Chapter 1 MRS. ROBIN'S NEWS

IF you had been in Farmer Green's door-yard on a certain day in May you would have heard an unusual twittering and chirping and squawking.

Now, there was a reason for all this chatter. Jolly Robin's wife had seen a handsome stranger in the orchard. And she had hurried away to spread the news among her friends.

"He's a dashing person, very elegantly dressed," Mrs. Robin told everybody.

That remark did not seem to please the good lady's husband. For Jolly Robin turned up his nose or his bill slightly, and he said to his wife, "The question is: What are his manners like?"

Mrs. Robin admitted that the stranger's manners were not all that one might wish.

"He was somewhat noisy," she explained. "And I fear he may be quarrel-some. But his clothes certainly were beautiful."

Jasper Jay, who was something of a dandy, wanted to know exactly what the stranger wore. He said he doubted that the newcomer was as fashionable as Mrs. Robin supposed.

"I can't tell you much about his suit," Mrs. Robin went on, "except that it was new and stylish. What I noticed specially was his cap. It was a big one and it was a brilliant red."

Jasper Jay sniffed when he heard that.

"They're not wearing red caps this season," he declared. He flew off then, to find his cousin Mr. Crow and tell him the news. For he hoped that Mr. Crow would give the stranger a disagreeable greeting. Jasper Jay did not like other birds to be more gayly dressed than he.

While all the feathered folk in the neighborhood were wondering who the stranger could be, old Mr. Crow came winging over from the edge of the woods.

"Where is he?" he squalled. "Let me have one look at this new arrival! I think I know who he is."

A little later Mr. Crow had his look, over in the orchard. Then he came back and alighted in the tall grass behind the farmhouse.

"He's a Red-headed Woodpecker," Mr. Crow announced with a wise tilt of his own head. "There hasn't been one of his kind in Pleasant Valley for years and years.... It's a pity," he added, "that this one has stopped here."

The old gentleman's words threw little Mrs. Chippy into a flutter.

"Is he a dangerous person?" she quavered.

"I believe so," said Mr. Crow darkly.

"Does he eat eggs?" Mrs. Chippy faltered. "And nestlings?"

For a moment or two old Mr. Crow couldn't make up his mind whether he ought to get angry or not. Eating eggs and young birds was a subject he liked to avoid. He was aware that his neighbors knew he was a rascal. But he was a quick-witted old fellow. Suddenly he saw how the presence of this stranger might help him.

"Yes!" he told Mrs. Chippy. "This woodpecker family all eat eggs and nestlings. And if you people miss any of your treasures, later, you'll know who took them."

At that little Mr. Chippy nodded his chestnut-crowned head.

"If it isn't you," he remarked to Mr. Crow, "then it will be the stranger."

"Not at all! Not at all!" the old gentleman squawked. "You'll be safe in thinking the newcomer guilty." Then he turned his back on Mr. Chippy, as if that small, shrinking chap weren't worth noticing. And favoring Mrs. Chippy with what he thought was a pleasant smile, Mr. Crow said to her, "You mustn't let this Red-head know where your nest is. No doubt you have eggs in it already."

"Yes, I have!" she twittered proudly.

"I certainly hope Red-head won't steal them," said Mr. Crow. "It would be a shame if you lost your beautiful eggs. . . . Where is your nest, Mrs. Chippy?"

"Don't tell him!" peeped Mr. Chippy to his wife. "He wants to eat our eggs himself."

As for Mr. Crow, he gave a hoarse cry of rage, before he flapped himself away.

Day 78

1. Read chapter 2 of *The Tale of Reddy Woodpecker*.
2. Tell someone what happened in the chapter.

Chapter 2, II GETTING ACQUAINTED

"I DON'T believe," said Mrs. Jolly Robin after old Mr. Crow had flown off in a rage. "I don't believe this Mr. Woodpecker can be such a bad person as Mr. Crow thinks. He certainly wears very stylish clothes and a very handsome red cap."

"Clothes," said little Mr. Chippy severely, "clothes don't tell whether their wearer has a taste for eggs. Now, I wear a red cap. To be sure, it isn't as bright, perhaps, nor as big, as Mr. Woodpecker's. But it's a red cap, all the same. And everybody knows that I don't eat eggs. Everybody knows I'm no nest robber."

"You don't look like one!" cried a strange voice which made everybody jump. It was the newcomer, Mr. Woodpecker, himself! Unnoticed, he had flown up. And now he perched on a limb nearby. "You don't look any more like a nest robber than I do," he told Mr. Chippy.

The whole company stared at him; and then stared at little Mr. Chippy. There was a vast difference between them. Mr. Chippy was a tiny, meek person, while Mr. Woodpecker was as bold as brass. Mr. Chippy was modestly dressed; and his cap, though it was reddish, was of a dull hue. But the newcomer wore a flashy suit of dark steel blue and white; and his cap was both very big and very red. Mr. Chippy was a shy body who said little; and when he did speak it was usually only to utter a faint chip, chip, chip, chip. But Mr. Woodpecker was very talkative.

When he spoke you didn't have to strain your ears to hear what he said.

Mr. Woodpecker gave a quick glance all about and cried, "Howdy do!"

"Good morning, Mr. Woodpecker!" the birds greeted him.

"Don't call me 'Mister!'" he said. "My name is Reddy, Reddy Woodpecker." Then he turned to little, shrinking Mr. Chippy and his wife. "I can see that you're worried about your eggs," he remarked. "I suppose your nest is hidden not far away."

Mr. and Mrs. Chippy looked most uncomfortable. They didn't quite dare speak to such a grand person as Reddy.

"Where's your nest?" Reddy asked them bluntly.

"Chip, chip, chip, chip!" said Mr. Chippy. "Chip, chip, chip, chip!" said his wife.

"What sort of answer is that to a civil question?" Reddy Woodpecker blustered. "Here I've just made your acquaintance. And I've asked you to call me by my first name. And you won't even tell me where you live!"

Mr. and Mrs. Chippy didn't know what to say. It was lucky for them that Mr. Catbird came to their rescue.

"Don't bully these good people!" Mr. Catbird cried, as he settled himself right in front of Reddy Woodpecker. "If you had heard what old Mr. Crow said about you, just before you arrived, you'd understand why Mr. and Mrs. Chippy don't care to tell you where their nest is."

Reddy glared at Mr. Catbird.

"Old Mr. Crow? Who's he?" Reddy demanded. "I haven't made his acquaintance. I'm sure he can't know anything about me."

"Ah! Perhaps not!" Mr. Catbird answered. "But he knows what sort of family yours is. He has met others like you."

Reddy sniffed. "I never saw a Crow that wasn't a rascally blackguard," he snapped. "There never was a Crow that wasn't a nest robber."

"Chip, chip, chip, chip!" Mr. Chippy interrupted.

"What's he saying?" Reddy Woodpecker asked Mr. Catbird.

"He says he agrees with you."

"Then he has more sense than I thought," Reddy observed. "And if Mr. Crow spoke ill of me I hope Mr. Chippy has enough sense not to believe him."

"Chip, chip, chip, chip!"

"What's he saying now?" Reddy Woodpecker demanded of Mr. Catbird.

"He says he agrees with Mr. Crow," Mr. Catbird explained very pleasantly.

"Then he hasn't any sense at all!" cried Reddy.

The whole company couldn't help giggling when he said that. And Reddy Woodpecker promptly lost his temper.

"I've planned to spend the summer here," he said. "It's too late now to move on. But I can understand at last why none of my family has visited this neighborhood for many years. It's a pleasant enough place. But the neighbors aren't my sort at all."

"Chip, chip, chip, chip!" piped Mr. Chippy.

"He says he agrees with you," Mr. Catbird told Reddy Woodpecker. And then he added, "Meaow!" And he gave himself a jerk and spread his tail, all of which told Reddy Woodpecker plainly that Mr. Catbird had a very poor opinion of him.

Day 79

1.   Read chapter 3 of *The Tale of Reddy Woodpecker*.
2.   Tell someone what happened in the chapter.

Chapter 3, III MORNING TATTOOS

IN the spring Reddy Woodpecker liked to drum.

He never felt that a pleasant day was rightly begun unless he played a tattoo early in the morning. So upon his arrival in Pleasant Valley he began promptly to look about for a good drumming place.

It wasn't long before he discovered a strip of tin nailed upon the roof of Farmer Green's barn.

"Ah!" cried Reddy the moment he spied this treasure. "Just what I need!" And settling himself down upon it he hammered out a long, rolling tattoo with his strong bill.

It mattered not to him that Farmer Green's family was sound asleep. He didn't care whether he disturbed anybody. He liked to hear his own drumming; and he intended to drum.

"This is the finest drumming place I've ever had!" Reddy Woodpecker cried aloud. "I don't care if the neighbors are disagreeable to me. I'm glad I came here to spend the summer."

So he made good use of that bit of tin with which Farmer Green had mended the roof of the barn. Each morning (if it wasn't raining) he flew to the barn to beat his tattoo. And he began to speak of "My tin," and "My roof," and even of "My barn!"

Then, one morning, Reddy was a bit lazy. He was late about his morning drumming. And before he had left the orchard where he had decided to live he heard a sound that gave him a great start. From the direction of the barn came a rolling beat which filled him with dismay.

"Who's that drumming?" he exclaimed. "It can't be myself, because I'm here in the orchard." Then all at once he became terribly angry. "It's somebody else!" he muttered. "Somebody has stolen my drumming place, my piece of tin, my roof my barn!"

He flung himself off the old, dead apple tree where he had been looking for grubs for his breakfast and flew straight towards the rolling sound which still beat upon the air.

It was just as he had feared. A stranger sat upon the strip of tin pounding away with his bill as if it were his duty to waken everybody in Pleasant Valley. He wasn't as handsomely dressed as Reddy Woodpecker. He wore a brown and gray and black suit, with a patch of white low down upon his back and a splash of red on the back of his head. From each side of his bill reached a black mustache. This mustache gave the strange drummer a brigandish air which made Reddy Woodpecker think twice before he spoke to him. But Reddy was so angry that he just had to say something.

"Hop away from there!" he cried.

The stranger stopped drumming and looked up with a smile. He said only one word. It was "Why?"

"Because," said Reddy Woodpecker, "that bit of tin belongs to me."

"Does it?" asked the other. "I thought it belonged to Farmer Green."

Reddy Woodpecker noticed that the stranger was bigger than he was. And that fact, as well as the fierce mustache, made him hesitate again. He wanted to call the stranger a name. But he didn't quite dare.

Then the stranger spoke again. He spoke very agreeably, too.

"What use do you make of this tin?" he inquired.

"I drum on it," Reddy replied.

"Oh!" said the gentleman with the mustache. "Why didn't you say so before?" And he bowed and scraped in a most polite fashion. "I resign!" he cried. In another moment he was gone.

Reddy Woodpecker hastened to beat his morning tattoo upon the tin. And while he was drumming he noticed a Barn Swallow watching him.

"Who was that chap that just left?" he asked.
"Don't you know him?" Mr. Barn Swallow exclaimed. "That's Mr. Flicker."

"Huh!" Reddy Woodpecker grunted. "I don't think much of his drumming."

"You ought to," remarked Mr. Barn Swallow.

"Why?" Reddy inquired.

"Because he's a distant cousin of yours," Mr. Barn Swallow explained. "He belongs to the Woodpecker family."

Day 80

1. Read chapter 4 of *The Tale of Reddy Woodpecker*.
2. Tell someone what happened in the chapter.

Chapter 4, IV THE HIGH-HOLE

REDDY WOODPECKER lost no time in making friends with his cousin Mr. Flicker. Reddy knew well enough that most of the birds in the neighborhood wished he hadn't come there to live. So he thought it wise to be pleasant and polite to Mr. Flicker. There was no knowing when he might need one friend among so many enemies. He even let Mr. Flicker drum upon the strip of tin upon the roof of the barn. But secretly Reddy thought him a queer chap.

"There's one thing that's very odd about you," Reddy said to Mr. Flicker one day. "If you're a Woodpecker, why don't you peck wood? I've noticed that you spend most of your time on the ground when you're not drumming upon my tin."

Mr. Flicker laughed. "Oh!" he said lightly, "we Flickers have found an easier way to get a living than by drilling wood with our bills to find grubs. We eat ants," he explained. "And that's why you see me on the ground so much, because that's where the ants live." At the moment Mr. Flicker was on the ground, while Reddy clung to the trunk of a tree near him. And just to prove the truth of his statement Mr. Flicker made a quick jab into the turf with his bill. He pulled his bill out at once, giving Reddy Woodpecker a glimpse of an ant before he swallowed it.

Reddy Woodpecker stared at him in amazement. "Where's your home?" he asked Mr. Flicker. "Is your home on the ground?"

"Bless you, no!" cried Mr. Flicker. "I'm no ground bird. My wife and I have a fine hole in an old apple tree in the orchard."

Reddy Woodpecker had to approve of that, anyhow. So he nodded his red-capped head.

"You're sensible in one way, at least," he remarked. "That's the way to live, if only you build high enough, out of harm's way."

Mr. Flicker grinned at him.

"It's plain that you don't know we Flickers are sometimes called High-holes," he said, "because of the way we nest."

"Ah! So you have two names, eh?" Reddy Woodpecker exclaimed, as he speared a grub with his tongue and drew it out from under a bit of bark. "I should think you'd find that confusing. I should think you'd forget who you were, sometimes."

"Oh! It's easy when you get used to it," Mr. Flicker replied. He paused to capture another ant. And then he added, "I have more than just two names. I have one hundred and twenty-four in all."

"My goodness!" cried Reddy. He was so astonished that he missed a stab at a fine grub that was right under his nose. "My goodness! Has your wife as many names as that?"

"Yes!" said Mr. Flicker.

"And your children?" Mr. Flicker nodded. "Sakes alive!" Reddy exclaimed. "How do you ever feed them all?"

Mr. Flicker gave a long, rolling, curious laugh. "We feed the children under only one name," he explained, "although I must confess it sometimes seems to me that each of them eats enough for one hundred and twenty-four youngsters."

"I know how that is," said Reddy Woodpecker. "My home is in a tree in the orchard, too. And I'm raising a family of four myself."

Day 81

1. Read chapter 5 of *The Tale of Reddy Woodpecker*.
2. Tell someone what happened in the chapter.

Chapter 5, V TOO MUCH COUSIN

REDDY WOODPECKER wished that he hadn't been so pleasant to his cousin Mr. Flicker. It was all well enough for Mr. Flicker to drum upon Reddy's bit of tin on the roof of the barn so long as he drummed late in the morning. But when he drummed early, as he sometimes did, it usually happened that Reddy had to wait before he could begin his own morning tattoo.

And Reddy Woodpecker didn't like that at all. In fact it seemed to him that Mr. Flicker had quite forgotten his manners. For if he happened to reach the barn first, he never stopped drumming until he had all but drummed his head off. At least, that was the way it seemed to Reddy Woodpecker.

At such times Reddy did everything he could think of short of actually fighting to make Mr. Flicker stop. He made a sound like a tree toad, Utr-rr, Utr-r-r. He tapped on the shingles with his bill. He flew right over Mr. Flicker's head. But it seemed as if Mr. Flicker simply couldn't take a hint.

"I don't like to order him to hop away," thought Reddy. "He's my cousin. Besides, he's bigger than I am; and he does look terribly fierce with that black mustache."
Though he may have looked fierce, Mr. Flicker always acted in the most pleasant manner possible. And when he finished his drumming he never failed to ask Reddy Woodpecker how he liked it.

It was a hard question for Reddy to answer, because he didn't care in the least for Mr. Flicker's tattoos. He thought his own were far better. Sometimes Reddy pretended not to hear his cousin's question, but started drumming at once. Sometimes he said, "I believe that's an improvement over yesterday's tattoo." And at last he exclaimed one morning, "You ought to join the Woodchuck brothers!"

Mr. Flicker was a great person to ask, "Why?" He asked it now.

"Because," Reddy told him, "the Woodchuck brothers are famous whistlers. And they need somebody to drum for them while they whistle. I've often heard them chirping away by themselves over in the pasture. And as you must know, there's no music that sounds better than drumming, with a little shrill whistling to go with it unless it's a little whistling, with a plenty of loud drumming."

Mr. Flicker's favorite word "Why" sprang to his bill again. "Why," he inquired, "do you not drum for the Woodchuck brothers yourself?"

Reddy Woodpecker shook his head.

"I want to practice more, before I join a troupe," he said.

"There!" Mr. Flicker exclaimed. "I like to hear people talk that way. That shows that you don't think you're the best drummer in Pleasant Valley."

"I don't, eh?" said Reddy.

"No, you don't!" said Mr. Flicker. And it was plain that he didn't think so, either. But before Reddy could make up his mind to quarrel with his cousin Mr. Flicker asked him another question not "Why?" but "Where!" "Where" said Mr. Flicker earnestly "where can one find these Woodchuck brothers?"

"One can find them in the pasture, unless they're in the clover patch. Just now they are probably in the pasture, for it's a bit early in the season for clover."

"The pasture!" repeated Mr. Flicker. "Ah! There must be ant hills in the pasture."

"Hundreds of them!" said Reddy.

"Then I'll go to see the Woodchuck brothers at once," Mr. Flicker decided. So he flew off.

Day 82

1. Read chapter 6 of *The Tale of Reddy Woodpecker*.
2. Tell someone what happened in the chapter.

Chapter 6, VI MR. FLICKER'S PLANS

IN a little while Mr. Flicker returned from his trip to the pasture to see the Woodchuck brothers. Hurrying into the orchard he called to Reddy Woodpecker, "They're thinking it over."

"They'll want you to drum for them," Reddy assured him. "There's no doubt that the Woodchuck brothers will accept your offer....Why don't you move up to the pasture at once? You'd find it handy, living in the Woodchucks' dooryard."

"I can't do that," said Mr. Flicker. "You forget my family."

"Move them too!' Reddy urged him.

But Mr. Flicker shook his head. "I don't believe my wife would be willing," he replied. "Besides, there's that piece of tin on the roof of the barn. Would you advise me to move that?"'

"No!" Reddy cried hastily. "Don't move the tin! In fact, Mr. Flicker, I shouldn't move at all, if I were you."

But Mr. Flicker had liked the plan of moving to the pasture to live. He had found great quantities of ants there. And to Reddy's dismay he insisted that he should move and take the strip of tin with him. That is to say, he intended to move as soon as his wife gave him permission.

It was no wonder Reddy wished he had never put such an idea into his cousin Mr. Flicker's head. He had hoped to get rid only of Mr. Flicker and his drumming. He had never dreamed that Mr. Flicker would want to take the precious bit of tin with him when he went.

Shortly afterward Mr. Flicker reported that it was just as he had thought. Mrs. Flicker wouldn't listen to moving just then. But later, after the children learned to fly, and could feed themselves, she would have no objection to the change of residence.

Reddy Woodpecker cocked an eye toward the roof of the barn.

"That tin," he said, "you can't take it with you when you move. It belongs to Farmer Green."

"Oh!" Mr. Flicker exclaimed. "I thought it belonged to you. And I knew you wouldn't object to your cousin's borrowing it for the rest of the season now would you?"

But Reddy Woodpecker wasn't going to answer any dangerous questions. "The tin is Farmer Green's," he declared.

It seemed as if Mr. Flicker were full of alarming thoughts. "I wish," he said, "we'd have a cyclone that would rip that tin off the barn and carry it up to the pasture."

"Oh, my goodness!" cried Reddy Woodpecker. And he worried dreadfully all the rest of that day. There's no knowing when he would have stopped fretting had Mr. Flicker not made a certain report to him the following morning.

"The Woodchuck brothers don't want me to drum for them," he announced.

"Then you aren't going to move!" cried Reddy.

"No!" Mr. Flicker replied. "And I don't intend there shall be any cyclone, either."
So at last Reddy Woodpecker felt better.

Day 83

1. Read chapter 7 of *The Tale of Reddy Woodpecker*.
2. Tell someone what happened in the chapter.

Chapter 7, VII THE TWO NEIGHBORS

WHILE Reddy Woodpecker and his cousin were getting acquainted their wives became quite friendly. Living as they did, each in an old apple tree at the lower end of the orchard, they often met. And since their doorways were almost opposite each other Mrs. Woodpecker and Mrs. Flicker didn't even have to leave their homes to enjoy a neighborly chat.

If one of them had something specially interesting to say, all she had to do was to stick her head out of the hole in the trunk of her tree and call. And if the other happened to be at home it was never more than a second before her head popped forth from her doorway. It was all very simple and most convenient.

Everything was pleasant until one day something happened. Something changed the friendly feelings between the two ladies. When Reddy Woodpecker peered out of his doorway one morning Mrs. Flicker called to him, "Good morning, my dear!"

He was so surprised he didn't know what to say.

But Mrs. Woodpecker knew what to say. It chanced that she was clinging to a limb above their home, so screened by some leaves that Mrs. Flicker couldn't see her. She quickly made known her presence. And she said so much that Mrs. Flicker soon withdrew her head. She hadn't answered Mrs. Woodpecker. Indeed she had had no opportunity; for Mrs. Woodpecker talked fast and furiously.

"It's no wonder she hides!" Mrs. Woodpecker spluttered. "I'd like to know what she means by calling my husband her 'dear!'"

Well, Reddy Woodpecker felt just as uncomfortable as Mrs. Flicker must have felt. But he didn't hide. He didn't dare to hide.

"What had you said to her?" Mrs. Woodpecker demanded.

"Honestly," Reddy replied, "I hadn't said a word. I had just stuck my head out. And the first thing I knew Mrs. Flicker called to me. You heard what she said."

"I certainly did!" was his wife's grim response. "It was a very queer way for her to speak to you."

"It was nothing," Reddy assured her, "nothing at all. She made a mistake."

"She certainly did!" cried Mrs. Woodpecker. "She didn't know I was right here where I could hear her. She should have been more careful. That's where she made a serious blunder."

"Oh, my goodness!" said Reddy. "I didn't mean that. It wasn't that sort of mistake. It was this sort: Mrs. Flicker..."

"Don't mention her name to me again!" shrilled Mrs. Woodpecker.

"Well, how can I talk about her, then?" Reddy asked his wife.

"If you feel that you must talk about her," said Mrs. Woodpecker, "call her she."

"All right! She made this mistake: She thought she was talking to you."

Mrs. Woodpecker laughed bitterly at that.

"You'll have hard work making me believe it," she told her husband.

"Well, you ask her if it isn't the truth," Reddy urged.

"I will!" his wife promised. "Don't worry! I'll ask her. . . . And now," she added," you'd better go and find some breakfast for the children. We can get along without any early tattoo this morning."

He went.

Day 84

1. Read chapter 8 of *The Tale of Reddy Woodpecker*.
2. Tell someone what happened in the chapter.

Chapter 8, VIII AN EARLY CALL

MRS. WOODPECKER flew to her neighbor Mrs. Flicker's tree and rapped, tap-tap-tap-tap. She didn't rap gently, either. She was not in a gentle mood. She intended to find out why Mrs. Flicker had called to Reddy Woodpecker, "Good morning, my dear!"

Mrs. Flicker promptly stuck her head out of her door.

"My husband is not at home," she said. And then she vanished.

"Well, the very idea! What a remark to make to me!" cried Mrs. Woodpecker. "As if I'd call on a gentleman!" Being angrier than ever, she rapped harder than before.

Again Mrs. Flicker peered out. Again she spoke. "Did you wish to leave a message, Mr. Woodpecker?" she inquired.

"I'm not Mr. Woodpecker! I'm Mrs. Woodpecker!" shrieked the caller.

"Oh! Oh! Oh! My! My! My!" exclaimed Mrs. Flicker, who was greatly astonished. "I beg your pardon! Excuse me! It's my mistake."

"It certainly isn't mine," said Mrs. Reddy Woodpecker. "It seems to me you're making a good many mistakes this morning, madam."

Mrs. Flicker looked very unhappy. She wasn't used to being called 'madam.' She could see that Mrs. Woodpecker was furious. She wanted to be friends with Mrs. Woodpecker.

"You and Mr. Woodpecker look very much alike," Mrs. Flicker said to her angry caller. "When one of you peeps out of your house it's hard to tell who's who. Just now when I came to my doorway I could see only your head. And I thought it was your husband. When I spoke to your husband a few minutes ago I thought it was you."

Mrs. Woodpecker stared at her neighbor for a few moments. Somehow she thought Mrs. Flicker must be telling the truth.

"It's your red caps, I think," Mrs. Flicker went on. "They make you look like twins."

"Dear me!" said Mrs. Woodpecker. "I hadn't thought of that. What can we do?" Her anger had suddenly left her.

"My husband and I have things nicely arranged," Mrs. Flicker told her caller.

"Now, you never have mistaken him for me, have you?"

"No!"

"Nor me for him?"

"No!"

"Do you know the reason?" Mrs. Flicker asked.

"No! No! I can't say I do," replied Mrs. Woodpecker eagerly.

"Well," said Mrs. Flicker, "my husband wears a black mustache.... And of course I don't," she added.

"That's it!" cried Mrs. Woodpecker. "I hadn't realized it. But it's so. And I must tell my husband to wear a mustache. It's the only safe way to avoid trouble. Then people can tell us apart."

Then Mrs. Woodpecker hurried away to speak to her husband. She was surprised that he didn't take kindly to her suggestion.

"I don't want to wear a mustache," he objected.

"But you must!" she insisted.

"Why don't you wear one?" he inquired. "It would do just as well."

"Don't be silly!" she snapped. "Ladies never wear mustaches."

"Yes, they do," he replied.

"No, they don't!" she disputed.

Well, he saw at once that it was useless to argue with her.

"Come with me a moment, my dear!" Reddy begged her.

She thought he was going somewhere to get a mustache. So of course she hurried after him.

Reddy Woodpecker stopped beside Farmer Green's barn.

"There!" he said, as he waved a wing towards a great poster that was pasted upon the side of the barn. "Do you see that lady? She has a mustache and a beard, too!"

It was just as he said. Mrs. Woodpecker couldn't help admitting that, to herself. And though she didn't speak to Reddy the rest of that day, he was satisfied. For she didn't mention mustaches to him again.

"It was lucky for me," he thought, "that the circus came to these parts this Summer."

Day 85

1. Read chapter 9 of *The Tale of Reddy Woodpecker*.
2. Tell someone what happened in the chapter.

Chapter 9, IX MRS. ROBIN WORRIES

THOUGH the Flickers welcomed Reddy Woodpecker when he came to live in Pleasant Valley there was hardly another bird family that wasn't sorry to see him settle there. Among all the feathered folk on Farmer Green's place the Robin family was perhaps the sorriest. They had a nest of eggs in the orchard, in a crotch of an old apple tree. And it was on just such trees that Reddy Woodpecker spent a great deal of his time, hunting for grubs. Jolly Robin himself might not have paid much heed to Reddy. But Mrs. Robin was a great worrier. Often she worried over nothing at all. And now that she had had a few talks with timid little Mrs. Chippy about the newcomer, Reddy Woodpecker, Mrs. Robin firmly believed that he had come to the farm expressly to rob her of her four greenish-blue eggs. After each talk with Mrs. Chippy Mrs. Robin came home all aflutter.

"We'll have to watch sharp!" she said to Jolly Robin again and again. "This Woodpecker person is a rascal. It's a pity we built here in the orchard. We'd have been safer on top of one of the posts under Farmer Green's porch."

"I mentioned that very place," Jolly reminded her. "But you were afraid of Miss Kitty Cat."

Not a day passed without some such words between them. Jolly did what he could to calm his wife's fears. He stayed near home all the time, when often he would have liked to fly across the meadow to chat with friends who lived on the edge of the woods.

Reddy Woodpecker never started to rap on a tree but Mrs. Robin set up a loud twitter, begging Jolly to hurry back to the nest.

He was wonderfully patient with her. Yet he couldn't help hoping, secretly, for the day when his family should be grown up and able to look out for themselves.

But if Mrs. Robin was anxious about her eggs her worry was nothing compared with what it became when the nestlings broke through their shells.

"This is the finest family in the whole valley," she confided to her husband. "I know that terrible Woodpecker person will steal these children if he can."

If the youngsters didn't peep for food their mother feared they were ill. If they did peep she feared Reddy Woodpecker would hear them. "He's such a dangerous person!" she would exclaim. "I wonder if he ever eats anything except eggs and nestlings."

"Yes, indeed!" Jolly assured her again and again. "He eats grubs, which he finds on the trees. And he eats insects, which he catches in the air."

"Thank goodness!" Mrs. Robin murmured. But her relief was short-lived. For she happened to meet little Mrs. Chippy one day and learned another bit of distressing news about Reddy Woodpecker. "He's a fruit eater!" Mrs. Robin told Jolly. "And you know we've been depending on the raspberries for our children."

A few days later she came home in a dreadful state of mind. "I went to take a look at the raspberry patch," she explained to her good husband. "I knew the berries would soon be ripe. In fact I've had my eye on one that was almost ready to be picked. And what do you think? Right before my own eyes that ruffian Reddy Woodpecker picked it and ate it himself!"

"Don't worry about that!" said Jolly Robin.

But Mrs. Robin insisted on worrying; nothing he said could stop her.

"Reddy Woodpecker is taking the food out of our children's mouths!" she wailed. "You'll have to drive him away from the raspberry patch! You'll have to fight him!"

Now, Jolly Robin hardly thought that he was a match for Reddy Woodpecker. So when his wife gave him those orders he began to worry, himself.

Day 86

1. Read chapter 10 of *The Tale of Reddy Woodpecker*.
2. Tell someone what happened in the chapter.

Chapter 10, X OBEYING ORDERS

JOLLY ROBIN's worrying wife wouldn't give him a moment's peace. "You'd better get along over to the raspberry patch," she kept telling him. "If you don't hurry that terrible Reddy Woodpecker will eat every berry. He'll snatch each one as it ripens and we shall not have any to feed our children."
Now, Jolly Robin didn't care to have any trouble with Reddy Woodpecker. But he soon saw that if he avoided Reddy he would only have trouble with Mrs. Robin. So at last he said, "Very well! I'll attend to him, my love." And off he flew, looking much braver than he

felt. You'd have thought, to see him, that he longed to find Reddy Woodpecker. Really he hoped that he wouldn't find Reddy anywhere.

Much to Jolly Robin's dismay he met Reddy Woodpecker among the raspberry bushes. Jolly jumped when he saw that dashing newcomer. But it was too late to dodge out of sight. Reddy Woodpecker saw him. So Jolly Robin made up his mind to put on a bold front. Sitting on a fence post that overlooked the raspberry patch he stared hard at Reddy Woodpecker. He thought perhaps he could frighten him away.

He might as well have stared at the barn door. To his great distress Reddy Woodpecker picked a berry and flew to a near-by post, where he sat and ate the fruit with relish. When he had finished the dainty he pretended to notice Jolly Robin for the first time and he bowed and scraped in the politest fashion.

Still Jolly Robin did not utter a word. Nor did he return any of Reddy's bows. But he began to feel himself swelling; he began to feel his feathers ruffle up. And he knew then that he must speak soon or burst. For there was no doubt that he was growing angry. So presently he cried: "Was that raspberry ripe?"

"Yes," replied Reddy Woodpecker, "and very juicy."

Now, Jolly Robin hadn't meant to ask any such question as that. He had meant to make some cutting remark. But he was so in the habit of being pleasant to everybody that it was very hard for him to be disagreeable.

"A-ahem!" he said. "Pardon me, sir!"

"Did did you know that my wife and I have been expecting to pick these raspberries for our children?"

But he might as well have said nothing at all. For Reddy Woodpecker only laughed and exclaimed, "You're a joker, aren't you?"

"No, I'm not," Jolly replied.
"Yes, you are," said Reddy Woodpecker. "You can't fool me. I know well enough that you don't intend to bring your children up on berries. I've seen you pulling angleworms for

them too many times." Then Reddy dropped off his post and clung to a bush while he picked another berry that seemed redder than the rest.

"Well," Jolly thought, "I've talked to him anyhow. At least I can tell my wife that." So he left Reddy to enjoy the fruit and sailed away to his home.

"You're back very quickly," Mrs. Robin remarked when she saw him. "Didn't you find that Woodpecker person?"

"Oh, yes! I found him," Jolly explained. "I found him and I talked with him, too."

Mrs. Robin cast a sharp glance at her husband.

"Where is he now?" she inquired.

"He's eating raspberries in the berry patch," Jolly told her. "When I talked with him I said…"

"You said!" Mrs. Robin interrupted. "You said! The question is, what did you do? If you didn't fight him you must go back and do your duty."

There was nothing he could do except obey her. So, feeling very desperate, Jolly Robin hurried back to the place where the raspberry bushes grew by the fence. He gave three loud chirps, to encourage himself. And then he darted down and sailed very close to Reddy Woodpecker's head. He didn't pause an instant to see what effect this action had on Reddy Woodpecker, but flew away as quickly as he could. "I guess I scared him that time," he muttered.

Meanwhile Reddy Woodpecker stared after him and watched him as he disappeared among the apple tree tops.

"Well, what do you think of that?" he said to himself with a grin.

Day 87

1. Read chapter 11 of *The Tale of Reddy Woodpecker*.
2. Tell someone what happened in the chapter.

Chapter 11, XI A VERY SHORT FIGHT

JOLLY ROBIN told his wife how he swooped down over Reddy Woodpecker's head. And he assured her that he had no doubt that Mr. Woodpecker would not be seen among the raspberry bushes again.

Jolly had felt quite pleased with himself. His threatened attack on Reddy had seemed to him to be very daring. So he was disappointed when his wife did not praise him.

"You ought to have stuck that rascal with your bill," Mrs. Robin complained. "If he's the sort of person I think he is he'll pay no heed to your warning."

As usual, Mrs. Robin proved to be right. That very day she herself beheld Reddy Woodpecker eating more raspberries. He had stolen every ripe berry. Though Mrs. Robin had hoped to find four (one for each of her nestlings) she didn't pick even one. They were all too hard and sour.

"It's a pity," she said to Jolly. "Everybody knows now-a-days that children need fruit. The day is past when you can bring them up on nothing but angleworms. You'll have to go back there to the raspberry patch and fight Reddy. You can't escape a fight any longer."

Well, what could he do? What could Jolly Robin do but obey his wife? He asked himself that question. And he could find only one answer. It was "Nothing!" There was nothing he could think of that would satisfy Mrs. Robin except a real battle. So he went forth.

Yes! Jolly Robin went forth very bravely to find Reddy Woodpecker. He meant to surprise him. But it was Jolly who received the surprise.

Reddy Woodpecker attacked first! The moment he spied Jolly Robin Reddy hurled himself at him. He skimmed so near to Jolly's head that that astonished little fellow ducked and hurried away. Yes! Jolly Robin retreated. It wasn't that Reddy Woodpecker was bigger than he was. To tell the truth, Reddy wasn't quite so big. But he liked to fight. And Jolly Robin loved peace.

Jolly hid in the midst of a thick hedge that grew beyond the fence. "Well," he muttered, "that fight was soon over. There's no use of telling Mrs. Robin about it. She would only worry." He sat there a long time. He didn't want to go home. He didn't know what to do. So he thought and thought; until at last a happy idea popped into his head. "I'll get help!" he exclaimed. "I'll get my friends from the other side of the meadow to come and help me fight Reddy."

Mrs. Robin was worrying terribly when Jolly reached home.

"You've been gone a long time," she complained. "Did you chase that Woodpecker person out of the valley?"

"No!" said Jolly. "But I expect to tomorrow."

"I thought I told you to fight him today," said his wife somewhat tartly.

"Yes! Yes!" he replied hastily. "We had a set-to Mr. Woodpecker and I. But the real fight will take place tomorrow."

"I'm glad to hear you talk that way at last," she told him. "It's high time something was done."

Day 88

1. Read chapter 12 of *The Tale of Reddy Woodpecker*.
2. Tell someone what happened in this chapter.

Chapter 12, XII JOLLY ROBIN'S HELPER

THE next morning Jolly Robin told his wife that she would have to do all the work of gathering the children's breakfast. "You know, my love," he explained, "I have important business to attend to today." And before she had time to object he left her.

Over near the garden fence he met three plump Robins who had flown across the meadow to help him fight Reddy Woodpecker. And soon the four had dropped down into the raspberry patch.

Reddy Woodpecker had not arrived. So, while they were waiting Jolly Robin's friends helped themselves to berries. Under the hot sun the fruit had ripened fast. Finding it both sweet and juicy they ate of it freely. And Jolly Robin could think of no reason why he should not do likewise.

By the time Reddy Woodpecker came, all the Robins from over the meadow were feeling so well fed and good-natured that they were in anything but a fighting mood.

"Let that Woodpecker enjoy this fruit if he likes it," they said to Jolly in an undertone. "There's more than enough for everybody. And now," they told him, "we must go home, because we have to help our wives feed our children."

Off they flew. And Jolly Robin found himself alone with Reddy Woodpecker.

"Ahem!" exclaimed Jolly Robin. "It's a fine morning, isn't it?"

"Delightful!" said Reddy Woodpecker.

"It looks as if you and I were going to have this raspberry patch all to ourselves, doesn't it?" Jolly continued.

Reddy Woodpecker agreed with him.

"We ought to keep others out of it," said Jolly.

Again Reddy Woodpecker was of the same mind as he.

"Then this is a bargain!" cried Jolly Robin. "I'll ask you to guard the place alone for a few minutes while I go home and speak to my wife."

Reddy Woodpecker grinned as he watched Jolly Robin winging his way homeward.

"Humph!" he grunted. "I may as well let that Robin have a taste of these berries. I certainly can't eat them all, nor carry them all home to my family."

Jolly Robin found his wife anxiously awaiting his return.

"Have you chased that Woodpecker person away?" she demanded.

"No, my love," he replied. "I've made other arrangements. Mr. Woodpecker is working for me now. So of course I don't want to scare him off the farm. He's helping me at the raspberry patch. He's helping me to guard the fruit. In fact I couldn't have come back to speak to you now if it wasn't for him. He's watching the berries for me now."

"Nonsense!" cried Mrs. Robin. "If that Woodpecker person is in the raspberry patch you may be sure he's eating berries as fast as he can."

"Only a few!" Jolly assured her. "There's more than enough for our family and his."

"How do you know that?" she demanded. "Did you count the berries?"

"No!" he replied.

"Go back and count them at once!" she commanded.

"Yes, my love!" Jolly answered.

He really did try to count the berries. But he soon found it to be an impossible task. Reddy Woodpecker ate so many raspberries and carried so many home to his children that Jolly Robin despaired of ever settling upon the correct number.

He felt very unhappy over the matter. And he even asked Reddy Woodpecker what he ought to do.

"Oh, tell your wife there are a million," Reddy Woodpecker suggested. "If she doesn't believe you, let her count them herself!"

"Oh, I couldn't do that," said Jolly Robin.

"Well, I say there are a million," Reddy declared. Then he picked and ate another berry. "Now there are nine hundred and ninety-nine thousand nine hundred and ninety-nine," he announced. "Go home and tell your wife I said so."

So Jolly Robin went. He went and told Mrs. Robin what Reddy Woodpecker had said.

She turned her back on him and exclaimed, "Fiddlesticks!"

Day 89

1. Read chapter 13 of *The Tale of Reddy Woodpecker*.
2. Tell someone what happened in the chapter.

Chapter 13, XIII THE CARPENTER

ONE day Reddy Woodpecker was tap, tap, tapping on a tall poplar that grew beside the brook. He had discovered a tiny opening in the bark and he wanted to see what was at the further end of it.

Suddenly a voice called out, "Well, well, well! What is it?" And a pale-faced person not unlike Buster Bumble-bee peered out at Reddy Woodpecker. He was careful to keep safely out of reach of Reddy's horny tongue. "I hope," said the dweller in the poplar, "you're not wanting me to build you a house. I can't work for you just now. I'm very busy today, making an addition to my own house."

Reddy stared at the speaker.

"I've already built my house with my wife's help," he replied. "Why should you think I needed your assistance?"

"Because," said the other, "I'm Whiteface, the Carpenter Bee. The neighbors are always pestering me to help them."

Then Reddy Woodpecker noticed that Whiteface was covered with sawdust. But before he could examine him very closely the carpenter vanished.

"I must have another look at that queer person," Reddy thought. So he began to rap once more.

Again the carpenter peeped forth.

"If you're out of work," he said, "I'll tell you plainly that you can't find it here. I never employ strangers to work for me, for I'm very particular." Then he was gone.

Tap, tap, tap! This time, when the carpenter answered Reddy's knocking, he was most impatient.

"Go away!" he cried. "You're shaking my whole house. I don't like it."

"Not so fast!" said Reddy Woodpecker. "I'm only making a friendly call. You and I are neighbors. But how am I ever going to get acquainted with you if you won't stop for a short chat?"

"I can't stand here idling my time away," the carpenter replied. "I'm a busy bee. Come inside if you want to see me!" And he disappeared again.

How could Reddy Woodpecker accept his invitation to enter? The carpenter's doorway was too small for him. And the wood was not the sort that Reddy liked to chisel away with his bill. It wasn't brittle enough to suit him. So he knocked again.

When the carpenter came rushing back to his doorway his pale face wore an anxious look.

"Oh!" he said. "I thought it was a fire. I thought somebody wanted to tell me my house was on fire. But it's only you. What do you want now?"

"I know you'd like to learn my name," Reddy Woodpecker began.

"Just leave your card!" the carpenter told him. "I'll look at it later when I have more time."

"When will that be?" Reddy demanded.

"I don't know," the odd person confessed. "It seems as if I never would get my house finished."

"Then," said Reddy, "there can't be any use in my leaving my card. Probably when you found time to look at it you wouldn't remember who left it."

"Probably not!" the carpenter admitted. "Good day, sir!" And he dodged out of sight.

Still Reddy Woodpecker was not discouraged. He knocked a fifth time.

"What!" exclaimed the carpenter when he answered Reddy's tapping. "Haven't you gone yet?"

"No!" Reddy replied. "I want to say..."

"If you have anything more to tell me, write me a letter!" said the pale-faced carpenter. And he set up a sign where Reddy Woodpecker could see it: "This Is My Busy Day!" Then he passed from view.

Reddy Woodpecker stayed a long time at the poplar tree beside the brook. He knocked and knocked and knocked until at last his head began to ache. But the sawdust-covered carpenter never showed his pale face again.

Day 90

1. Read chapter 14 of *The Tale of Reddy Woodpecker*.
2. Tell someone what happened in the chapter.

Chapter 14, XIV MR. CROW'S QUESTIONS

IF people snubbed Reddy Woodpecker he never cared. When the members of the Pleasant Valley Singing Society wouldn't let him join them he only smiled and said he intended to form a club of his own.

As soon as the bird neighbors heard of Reddy's plan they were all very curious to know more about it. But whenever anybody asked him questions he had little to say.

"You'll learn all about it later," he told them. "Please don't bother me now, for I'm a busy bird. I'm starting my club."

It was easy for Reddy Woodpecker to keep his secrets from such small feathered folk as little Mr. Chippy. But there was one that couldn't rest until he found out what he wanted to know. This was old Mr. Crow. He shot question after question at Reddy Woodpecker. At last Reddy just had to tell him something in order to gain a little peace. Reddy knew that Mr. Crow would leave him as soon as he had picked up a bit of news. The old gentleman would hurry away to tell it to everybody in the valley.

"What's your club going to be named?" Whenever Mr. Crow talked with Reddy Woodpecker that was his favorite question. He asked it so many times and so loudly that just to get rid of him Reddy finally told him.

"I'm going to call my club 'The Redcaps,'" he said.

Old Mr. Crow didn't tarry an instant longer. With an eager look in his snapping black eyes he went flapping off on his broad wings, far down the valley.

Now, Mr. Crow was a fast worker. In an hour's time he had zigzagged back again, having spread his bit of news far and wide.

And when he had repeated it to the last neighbor he could find he hurried to the orchard to ask Reddy Woodpecker more questions.

The moment he found Reddy Mr. Crow began to put one question after another so fast that you couldn't have told where one ended and the next one began.

Reddy Woodpecker pretended to be busier than ever.

"I can't stop now," he told Mr. Crow. "You'll have to see my secretary."

"Where is he? Who is he?" Mr. Crow inquired hoarsely.

"I can't answer those questions," Reddy replied. "Why not?" demanded Mr. Crow.

"Because I haven't a secretary yet," Reddy explained.

"Why should you have a secretary?" Mr. Crow asked him.

"Why shouldn't I?" Reddy retorted. "I guess, Mr. Crow, you don't know much about clubs. I guess you don't know that the president of a club always has a secretary."

"Are you president of the Redcaps?" Mr. Crow cried breathlessly.

"Well yes, I am!" Reddy admitted. "I didn't mean to tell you that today. But I can't deny it."

Mr. Crow was off like a shot. You'd have thought he had just spied Farmer Green with a gun in his hands. His caw, caw, caw told everybody in Pleasant Valley that he was going somewhere on important business.

Reddy Woodpecker pulled a fat grub from its hiding place in the old apple tree. He could still hear Mr. Crow squawking when the old gentleman was half a mile away. And Reddy smiled as he swallowed the grub.

"That's better than putting the news in a newspaper," he said with a chuckle.

Day 91

1. Read chapter 15 of *The Tale of Reddy Woodpecker*.
2. Tell someone what happened in the chapter.

Chapter 15, XV THE REDCAPS

REDDY WOODPECKER knew that Mr. Crow would come back to the orchard to ask him another question. The old gentleman simply had to learn more about Reddy's club.

"I'd like to know," said Mr. Crow. "I'd like to know why you are the president of The Redcaps."

"That's easily answered," Reddy replied. "It's because I wear the biggest and reddest cap of all the birds in the neighborhood."

Mr. Crow puzzled over the matter for a time.

"I don't understand what difference your cap makes," he said at last. "I've been thinking about joining the club. And I have no red cap."

"That's true, Mr. Crow," Reddy agreed. "And that's the reason why you can't join my club. Nobody that doesn't wear a red cap can be a member of The Redcaps."

Mr. Crow looked daggers at him.

"Humph!" cried the old gentleman. "I've been thinking about joining the club. But I've decided not to do it."

Reddy Woodpecker smiled at him. And for some reason Mr. Crow became angry.

"How many members has your club?" he squawked.

"One!" Reddy told him.

"Ha!" the old fellow exclaimed. "You can't have a club with only one member."

"I expect that several of the neighbors will join The Redcaps tomorrow," said Reddy Woodpecker. "They're only waiting for an invitation."

"Let me see," Mr. Crow murmured. "There's your cousin Mr. Flicker. He wears a red patch on the back of his head. But you can't call it a cap."

"I call it a cap," Reddy Woodpecker told him. "Mr. Flicker is going to get an invitation."

Mr. Crow then muttered something about cousins, and added something more about birds of a feather flocking together. And then he said, "There's the Downy Woodpecker and there's the Hairy Woodpecker both cousins of yours, too. They've only what you might call a touch of red on the backs of their necks; but I suppose..."

"Yes! I'm going to invite them to join The Redcaps," Reddy interrupted.

Mr. Crow looked terribly upset, though he claimed it was no more than he had expected. "That will be about all the members you will get," he added.

"Oh, no!" Reddy exclaimed. "You forget Mr. Sapsucker. He has a scarlet crown. I'll want him."

Mr. Crow swallowed hard a few times but said nothing.

"Then there's the Ruby-crowned Kinglet," Reddy went on. "He's going to have an invitation. And so is Mr. Kingbird."

"Not Mr. Kingbird!" spluttered old Mr. Crow. "His crown is orange-colored."

"It's red enough for me," Reddy retorted. "And of course I'll ask little Mr. Chippy to join us."

"Nonsense!" cried Mr. Crow. "His cap is only chestnut-colored."

"It's red enough for me," Reddy Woodpecker repeated in a firm voice.

"My goodness!" Mr. Crow squalled. "I suppose you'll ask the whole Wood Thrush family too and their cousin Mr. Veery. Their heads are reddish."

"No! They're too brown for me," Reddy Woodpecker decided, to Mr. Crow's great relief.

"What about Buddy Brown Thrasher?" Mr. Crow inquired. "What about his head?"

"Too brown!"

"Well," said old Mr. Crow, "I'm glad to see you have a little sense. But on the whole these Redcaps are going to be a queer lot."

Day 92

1. Read chapter 16 of *The Tale of Reddy Woodpecker*.
2. The chapter is called *A Sly Trick*. What was the trick? Why was it sly? What does sly mean? (Answers)

Chapter 16, XVI A SLY TRICK

THIS was the truth of the matter: Old Mr. Crow was jealous because he couldn't join Reddy Woodpecker's new club, The Redcaps. For days the old gentleman could speak of nothing else. He went grumbling and sneering up and down Pleasant Valley, stopping to talk with anybody he happened to see. It must be confessed that the neighbors found his ill humor very tiresome.

Meanwhile Reddy Woodpecker's club grew in numbers daily. It made Mr. Crow snort when anybody told him that The Redcaps had another new member.

Then all at once Mr. Crow's manner changed. He became quite sprightly and even winked an eye and cracked a joke now and then. His neighbors wondered what had happened to him.

They soon found out. For Mr. Crow announced that he had discovered a new member for Reddy Woodpecker's club. Strange to say, the old gentleman seemed to take great pride in helping The Redcaps.

"I'm going to take my find to the meeting of the club this afternoon," Mr. Crow told everybody.

"But you're not a member. You can't go to a meeting," his friends objected.

"Can't I?" said Mr. Crow wisely. "The air is free. I can go anywhere I please."

So that afternoon Mr. Crow flew down to the lower end of the meadow, where The Redcaps were gathering. He took a friend with him, whom he left hidden in some reeds at the edge of the swamp.

To Reddy Woodpecker Mr. Crow said, "You'd like another member, I dare say."

"Certainly!" Reddy replied. "The more the merrier provided they wear red caps."

"I think," said Mr. Crow, "when you see the gentleman I have in mind you'll say he has a red cap."

"Bring him up!" Reddy Woodpecker ordered.

"I can't. He's shy," Mr. Crow explained. "But if you'll come with me you can take a look at him."

So Reddy Woodpecker followed Mr. Crow down to the place where the reeds grew, near the swamp. And there Mr. Crow pointed out a gentleman who did indeed appear to be wearing a red cap.

"Good!" exclaimed Reddy Woodpecker. And to the stranger he called, "I don't know you. But I invite you, sir, to join The Redcaps."

The stranger answered in a muffled voice, "I accept."

Then Reddy took another and closer look at him. Reddy couldn't help feeling there was something queer about the fellow. Half hidden as he was among the reeds the stranger was not easy to see.

Suddenly Reddy Woodpecker turned upon Mr. Crow and called him a fraud.

"This person hasn't a red cap," Reddy declared. "I won't have him in my club. I know him now. He's hiding his head under his wing. That patch of scarlet isn't on his head. It's on his shoulder. He's one of that Red-winged Blackbird family that lives in the swamp. And his head is as black as your own, Mr. Crow."

By this time Mr. Crow was dancing up and down and cawing at the top of his lungs. "He's a member of The Redcaps!" he cried with great glee. "You invited him. And he accepted the invitation."

"Very well!" said Reddy Woodpecker. "But if he belongs to my club he'll have to keep his head under his wing."

"Then I resign!" cried the Red-winged Blackbird.

"Oh, don't do that!" Mr. Crow begged him.

"It's too late," Reddy told the old gentleman. "Your friend is a member of The Redcaps no longer."

Day 93

1. Read chapter 17 of *The Tale of Reddy Woodpecker*.
2. Tell someone what happened in the chapter.

Chapter 17, XVII A HUNTING PARTY

CUFFY BEAR was one of those lucky people that eat almost everything. He liked blueberries and he liked honey; he liked maple sugar and he liked baked beans. When he was eating he never complained about his food if only there was enough. Whatever he had, he wanted a plenty of it.

He was wandering through the woods one day when he heard a tap, tap, tapping a little way off. He stopped and listened and sniffed. And then he said, "Woof! It isn't a man. Unless I'm mistaken it's a Woodpecker."

Cuffy Bear turned aside and plunged through the bushes until he came into a little clearing. There, working away upon a dead tree, was Reddy Woodpecker. One couldn't help seeing his bright red cap.

"I say," Cuffy Bear called to him, "let's go hunting!"

Reddy looked around at Cuffy Bear.

"Hunting!" he echoed. "What sort of hunting?"

"Let's go hunting for grubs!" said Cuffy Bear. "I'm very fond of grubs. And I know you are, too."

Now, Reddy Woodpecker never had dreamed that Cuffy Bear would ever invite so small a person as he was to go hunting with him. So it was only to be expected that Reddy should be pleased and even somewhat flattered.

"All right!" he agreed. "When you're ready, say the word."

"There's no time like the present," Cuffy declared. And he went on to explain how they could help each other. "You can scout around for old stumps and fallen trees. And when you find one with plenty of grubs, come right back here at once and lead me to it. I'll tear it open so we can get more grubs in a minute than you can reach in a day by drilling for them one at a time with your bill. I'll show you how to gather grubs in quantities. You'll always want to hunt with me, after you see the way I find 'em."

Reddy Woodpecker nodded his head to show that he understood. Then he started to fly away. But Cuffy Bear called him back.

"One thing more!" he said. "Promise me that when you find a likely tree or stump you won't stop to eat any grubs. You mustn't eat any until I come. It wouldn't be fair."

Reddy Woodpecker promised. Cuffy Bear waved a paw at him to hurry him on his way. And off Reddy flew. He was back again in a few minutes. "I've found one," he said. "Follow me!"

"All right!" Cuffy Bear squealed. He went lumbering through the woods, trying to keep Reddy Woodpecker in sight. In a few moments he gave a frantic roar. "Come back!" he thundered.

Reddy Woodpecker returned.

"Don't fly so fast," Cuffy ordered. "I can't keep up with you. Fly slowly!"

"I can't fly slowly" Reddy retorted. "I don't know how."

"Then go a little way and sit down on a tree and wait for me," Cuffy directed. "But don't go out of my sight!"

Reddy Woodpecker did exactly as he was told. And in that manner they soon came to an old stump which was half crumbled away. "Ah!" cried Cuffy Bear. "This looks like a good one. ... I'll show you how to get the grubs." With a few sweeps of his great paws he quickly tore the old stump to pieces.

Reddy Woodpecker gasped at the huge number of lovely fat grubs that Cuffy had uncovered. He gasped again when he saw how fast Cuffy Bear ate them. They were gone in no time.

Licking his chops, Cuffy Bear stepped back and said, "That's the way to do it."

Reddy alighted on what was left of the old stump. He looked at it closely. And at last he actually found one grub that Cuffy Bear hadn't noticed. This Reddy ate, making a wry face.

"What's the matter?" Cuffy Bear inquired. "Isn't it good?"

"It's good enough what there is of it," Reddy Woodpecker replied.

Day 94

1. Read chapter 18 of *The Tale of Reddy Woodpecker*.
2. Tell someone what happened in the chapter.

Chapter 18, XVIII A BIG APPETITE

"COME, now!" cried Cuffy Bear to Reddy Woodpecker. "We've only begun our hunt. Hurry and find another old, grubby stump!"

Having eaten only one grub, while Cuffy Bear had bolted dozens, Reddy Woodpecker was not feeling very happy. However, he went flying off to search the woods. And it wasn't long before he discovered another stump that looked even more promising than the first one.

Then well! Reddy must have forgotten his promise that he wouldn't stop to eat a single grub, but would fly straight back to the spot where he had left Cuffy Bear. He clung to the side of the stump with his odd feet, which were made expressly for work of that sort. And he began to drill a hole with his bill. He was sure there was a grub lurking just beneath the brittle bark.

Tap, tap, tap! sounded his bill against the stump. Tap, tap, tap!

Before Reddy reached the grub he heard a great crash in the bushes. He knew at once that Cuffy Bear had heard the sound of his drilling and had come hurrying after him. "I heard you signaling to me," Cuffy grunted.

He tore that stump open in a twinkling. Reddy Woodpecker had to stand aside and look on while Cuffy Bear devoured every grub in sight. When at last Cuffy drew back and allowed him to search the ruin Reddy couldn't find even one grub.

"Come on!" Cuffy urged him. "Let's get on with our hunting!"

But this time Reddy hung back.

"What! Haven't you had enough grubs?" he asked none too pleasantly.

"Enough!" Cuffy repeated. "Why, I'm only beginning to feel hungry. These few grubs that I've eaten have just stirred up my appetite."

Reddy Woodpecker was astonished.

"Well, if you're hungry, what do you think of me?" he wanted to know.

And now Cuffy Bear was amazed.

"You!" he cried. "Haven't you had a good meal? Didn't you eat a grub off that first stump we found?"

"One grub!" Reddy Woodpecker exclaimed scornfully. "What's one grub?"

"I should think," Cuffy Bear answered, "one grub was a good meal for anybody of your size."

"It's not," Reddy declared. He looked very sullen and glum.

Cuffy Bear was sure that Reddy was mistaken. He even tried to show Reddy that he was wrong.

"One ought to be a big meal for you," he insisted. "Why, last week I went out for my supper one night and I ate only one. And it was all I wanted."

"Then you had already had a big dinner," said Reddy Woodpecker.

"I hadn't had any dinner at all!"

Reddy Woodpecker stared at him. He couldn't believe it. There must be something queer about that story, somewhere. At last he asked Cuffy a blunt question.

"You say you ate one," he observed. "One what?"

"Let me see," said Cuffy Bear. "Let me think a moment. . . . Oh, yes! Now I remember. It was one pig!"

Day 95

1. Read chapter 19 of *The Tale of Reddy Woodpecker*.
2. What do you think is the answer to the question in the chapter title?

Chapter 19, XIX WHO WAS GREEDY?

REDDY WOODPECKER was very angry with Cuffy Bear. He thought that when they hunted grubs together it was only fair that they should divide the game. So far Cuffy had taken all but one. And that was one that he had overlooked.

"I don't believe I'll hunt with you any more," Reddy Woodpecker told Cuffy.

That news surprised Cuffy Bear. "Why, what's the matter?" he inquired. "Haven't we had good luck?"

Reddy Woodpecker sniffed.

"You have had fine luck," he replied.
"But I certainly haven't. When you asked me to hunt grubs with you I expected we would divide the grubs."

Cuffy Bear shook his head doubtfully.

"It's not easy to divide a grub," he said. "That's why I let you have all of that one that you found a while ago."

"You don't understand me," Reddy went on. "What I mean is this: If we find two dozen grubs in a stump you should have one dozen and I should have one dozen."

"I've never hunted in that way before," Cuffy told him. "But since you insist, I'm willing to try it. And maybe it would be only fair if I found the next stump and let you open it."

Now, this was a much better offer than Reddy Woodpecker had expected, so he made haste to accept it.

Then Cuffy Bear went wandering away into the woods. He was gone a long time. But at last he came back and said gruffly, "Follow me!"

They reached, after a while, a spot where Cuffy Bear stopped and pointed a paw towards an old stump. "There it is," he said. "Now you tear it open."

Reddy Woodpecker alighted upon the stump and clung to it while he drilled into it with his bill, tap, tap, tap!

Meanwhile Cuffy Bear watched him impatiently.

"My goodness!" he muttered. "That fellow is slow! I'll never get another grub if I wait for him."
At last, however, Reddy pulled out a grub and ate it.

"My turn next!" growled Cuffy Bear as Reddy Woodpecker promptly went after another.

Well, very soon Reddy thrust his tongue into another hole that he drilled and drew out another grub.
"That's mine!" cried Cuffy Bear.

Reddy Woodpecker tried to let it fall upon the ground. He did not find it easy to drop the grub. His horny tongue had pierced it. And in trying to let go of it he had a mishap. He swallowed the grub.

When Cuffy Bear saw what had happened he let out a frightful roar.

"That was an accident," Reddy explained over his shoulder.

To Cuffy Bear's dismay the same accident happened over and over again. Finally Cuffy couldn't wait another moment. With a terrible growl he rushed up to the stump, while Reddy Woodpecker slipped out of his way just in time. In another instant Cuffy had split the old stump wide open and had his head buried in it.

"Here!" cried Reddy Woodpecker. "How many grubs do you want?"

"Only about a hundred dozen!" Cuffy Bear mumbled.

When he heard that, Reddy Woodpecker shrieked. "One hundred dozen would feed my whole family," he declared. "I shall never hunt grubs with you again."

"That's a pity," said Cuffy Bear. "But won't you join me tonight? I'm going after different game."

"What's that?" Reddy asked him.

"Pigs!" Cuffy replied.

He couldn't understand why Reddy Woodpecker went off without saying another word.

"He's a queer one," Cuffy muttered. "I don't care if he doesn't hunt with me. He's too greedy."

Day 96

1. Read chapter 20 of *The Tale of Reddy Woodpecker*.
2. Tell someone what happened in the chapter.

Chapter 20, XX CATCHING FLIES

AFTER his children were grown up Reddy Woodpecker had plenty of time to wander about and see all the sights in Pleasant Valley. He had often heard that one of the most curious sights was an odd person known as Ferdinand Frog. So one day Reddy flew down to Black Creek, where this nimble gentleman lived.

Unseen by Mr. Frog, Reddy Woodpecker clung to an old stump that leaned over the water, as if it wanted to enjoy a swim but didn't quite dare take the first plunge. Keeping most of himself hidden, Reddy peeped around the stump and watched Ferdinand Frog as he sat on a flat rock near the bank and caught flies.

Mr. Frog was an expert at that sport. Whenever a fly ventured near enough to him his long tongue darted out of his wide mouth so quickly you could hardly see it. And it darted back again just as fast, bearing the fly upon the end of it.

"I don't see how he spears 'em like that," thought Reddy Woodpecker, "with nothing but air behind them." Mr. Frog's knack was so unusual that at last Reddy Woodpecker couldn't keep silent any longer.

So he called to Mr. Frog, "How do you do?"

"I'm very well, thank you!" cried Fedinand Frog instantly. "How are you?"

Reddy Woodpecker had to explain that Mr. Frog hadn't understood him.

"What I was going to ask you," he said, "was not 'How do you do?" It was "How do you do that?'"

"That what?" Ferdinand Frog inquired.

"How do you spear flies with your tongue when they're in the air?" Reddy Woodpecker asked. "I can spear grubs and things with my tongue when they're on a tree. And I can catch flies in my mouth when I'm flying. But I've never learned your trick."

"I don't spear flies," said Mr. Frog.

Of course Reddy Woodpecker thought that Mr. Frog had told a whopper. Hadn't he been watching him?

"I don't spear flies with my tongue," Ferdinand Frog went on. "My tongue is sticky. When it touches a fly, he's caught. It's very simple."

"That's an elegant way to catch 'em," Reddy remarked.

"Yes," said Mr. Frog; "and that's an elegant suit you're wearing. Would you mind if I copied it? You know, I'm the well known tailor of Pleasant Valley. And I'm always on the lookout for something different. Your clothes are different from any I've ever seen before. I dare say they'll become quite fashionable in about ten years."

Well, Reddy Woodpecker didn't know whether to be angry or pleased. He had heard that Mr. Frog was queer. But he hadn't supposed Mr. Frog could be as queer as he seemed.

"You may copy my suit if you wish," Reddy blurted at last.

"Good!" the tailor exclaimed. "Come with me to my shop and I'll make some notes."

This was more than Reddy Woodpecker cared to do. "I won't!" he said flatly.

"Tut! Tut!" cried Mr. Frog. "You promised I might copy your suit. You mustn't break your promise."

"I'm not going inside any shop," Reddy declared very firmly.

"Of course not!" said Mr. Frog. "I'll go inside. You can stay outside. And I'll look you over through the doorway and jot down what I need."

"All right!" said Reddy Woodpecker.

So Mr. Frog leaped ashore and gayly led the way to his shop nearby.

Day 97

1. Read chapter 21 of *The Tale of Reddy Woodpecker*.
2. Tell someone what happened in the chapter.

Chapter 21, XXI THE ODD MR. FROG

REDDY WOODPECKER stood on the doorstep of Mr. Frog's shop. And inside the tiny building Mr. Frog the tailor squatted cross-legged and scratched upon a flat stone. Now and then he glanced up to look closely at Reddy Woodpecker.

"Colors: red, white and yes! blue!" Mr. Frog murmured, blinking his bulging eyes at Reddy Woodpecker. "It's a little too blackish for my taste, but it's certainly blue. ... A good suit for the Fourth of July!" he muttered. "Just the thing for a clown to wear in a parade of Horribles!"

Mr. Frog's remarks did not please Reddy Woodpecker. In fact they made him very angry. But Mr. Frog didn't appear to notice that. He went right on talking to himself.

"Red head and black tail!" he said, scratching upon his stone all the while. "Black head and red tail would be much better."

"I didn't come here to be abused!" Reddy Woodpecker spluttered.

The tailor paid no heed to Reddy's protest.

"Too much stiffening in the tail!" Mr. Frog mumbled. "Colors too gay for everyday wear! Too loud for the best taste!"

By this time Reddy Woodpecker had become so furious that he couldn't speak.

Meanwhile Mr. Frog continued to look him over calmly, and as his gaze fell at last upon Reddy's feet he began to titter.

"This person's feet are all wrong," he chanted, scratching like mad upon his flat stone. "Never saw a bird before with toes like his. The rule for birds is: three toes in front, one toe in back. This person has two in front and two in back. I thought there was something queer about him."

"Look here!" Reddy Woodpecker burst forth. "I won't stay here any longer. You're making fun of me. I don't care if I did promise. If my clothes are so queer why do you want to copy them?"

"I don't want to copy them," Mr. Frog replied. "I'd hate to copy them."

"Then why did you ask me to stand here in front of your shop while you wrote down all this nonsense?"

"You're mistaken," Mr. Frog told him. "I haven't written a word. I asked you to come here because you look like a customer. It's good business to have customers seen about my shop. I haven't had a real customer this season," he added somewhat sadly. "So you can't blame me if I want people to think I have one at last now can you?"

Reddy Woodpecker had no patience with him. "I think you're nothing but a fraud," he declared. "I don't believe you're a tailor at all."

"Dear me!" said Mr. Frog. "Maybe I'm not. Sometimes I've wondered if I wasn't fooling myself."

"You'd better stick to catching flies," Reddy advised him. "That's all you're good for."

"Perhaps you're right," Mr. Frog replied. He seemed quite meek and mournful. But all at once he smiled. "Anyhow," he remarked, "it's lucky that the flies stick to me now isn't it?"

Day 98

1. Read chapter 22 of *The Tale of Reddy Woodpecker*.
2. Tell someone what happened in the chapter.

Chapter 22 XXII DODGING DANGER

SOON after Reddy Woodpecker settled in Farmer Green's orchard he noticed that a certain person often followed him. The stranger wore gray fur and always flourished a long, bushy tail behind him. He could climb trees as well as Reddy Woodpecker himself. And though he couldn't fly, he was very skillful at leaping from one tree top into another.

Whenever Reddy Woodpecker happened to turn around and spy this lurking stranger the fellow acted as if he hadn't seen Reddy Woodpecker. He would pretend to whisk a bit of bark off the tip of his tail, or arrange his mustache. But the moment Reddy turned his back upon him the stranger would creep a little nearer.

At last this sly person made a quick dash at Reddy Woodpecker one day. He discovered, then, that Reddy was both wide awake and spry. For Reddy slipped off the tree trunk where he had been clinging and easily escaped the greedy clutches of the stranger.

It's no wonder that Reddy was angry. No one would care to have his breakfast interrupted in such a fashion.

"I knew that sneak meant to catch me if he could," Reddy muttered to himself as he went on with his breakfast.

A few moments later his cousin Mr. Flicker settled upon an ant hill below him.

"Who is that stranger?" Reddy Woodpecker asked Mr. Flicker.

Mr. Flicker glanced at the sly person who was just dodging behind a limb. "He's no stranger," said Mr. Flicker. "He has lived here a good deal longer than you have. That's Frisky Squirrel."

"Well, he's a little too frisky," Reddy Woodpecker scolded. "He just jumped at me. He has been trying to catch me ever since I came to the farm."

Mr. Flicker laughed. "That's a regular trick of his," he remarked. "He's always jumping off a fence post at me. But I have no trouble dodging him."

"I don't see why he wants to catch me," Reddy grumbled. "He can't know yet that I'm fond of nuts. But in the fall, when the nuts are ripe, I expect I'll make him almost crazy."

The next time Reddy met his tormentor he called to him as pleasantly as if there'd never been any trouble between them.

"How's this place for nuts?"

"Fine!" cried Frisky Squirrel. "The woods beyond the meadow are famous for their beechnuts."

"That's good news," said Reddy. "I'm glad I settled here."

Frisky gave him a sharp look. "You don't like beechnuts, do you?" he asked.

"Don't I? Oh, don't I?" Reddy cried.

Strange to say Frisky Squirrel knew the answer to that question.

"Oh! You do like them!" he chattered. "Well, maybe there aren't as many beechnuts as I thought. Maybe the beechnutting is poor here. No doubt I'm mistaken about it. Why don't you go over on the other side of Blue Mountain to live? You're sure to find plenty of beechnuts over there next fall."

Reddy Woodpecker laughed heartily. Frisky Squirrel could not deceive him.

Day 99

1. Read chapter 23 of *The Tale of Reddy Woodpecker*.
2. Tell someone what happened in the chapter.

Chapter 23 XXIII BEECHNUTS

"I'm going to stay right here on this farm," Reddy Woodpecker declared. "I like this place."

"Perhaps you expect to leave for the South before the beechnuts are ripe," Frisky Squirrel suggested hopefully.

"Not I!" replied Reddy Woodpecker. "If I leave, I shall wait until the last beechnut is eaten. And no doubt I shall not leave at all. This looks to me like a good place to spend the winter."

Now that Frisky Squirrel knew Reddy Woodpecker ate beechnuts he was more determined than ever to catch him. He had hunted Reddy before. Now he haunted him. He dogged Reddy Woodecker's footsteps. He crept up behind him and jumped at him a dozen times a day.

Though Frisky didn't know it, he couldn't have captured Reddy Woodpecker in a thousand years. Reddy was too wary to be caught. He always chuckled after dodging. And he always called mockingly, "Not this time, young fellow!"

All summer long the chase went on. Frisky Squirrel seemed to think that if only he hunted Reddy long enough there would come a time when he would catch him napping.

Now, every year as fall drew near it was Frisky's custom to go each day to the woods, to inspect the beechnuts. He went very slyly. It was a business of great importance. Of course he didn't care to have everybody know what he was doing.

Imagine his annoyance, then, on his first trip to the beech grove, to hear Reddy Woodpecker call out to him, "What do you think of 'em? Will they be ready to eat soon?"

Reddy was high up in a beech tree. And Frisky Squirrel was so angry that he could only look up at him and chatter.

"You haven't answered my questions," Reddy observed presently. "Perhaps you aren't a good judge of beechnuts. Perhaps I'd better ask Jasper Jay."

That threat made Frisky Squirrel angrier than ever. He darted up the tree as fast as he could scramble. If he hadn't been so angry he would have known how utterly useless it was to try to catch Reddy Woodpecker when Reddy was looking right at him.

Reddy calmly moved to another tree. Frisky Squirrel leaped into the top of it. Again Reddy moved.

Then Frisky sat up on a limb and glared at him.

"Don't mention these nuts to Jasper Jay!" he cried. "I've been hoping he'd forget about them. Eat what you want if you must. But for goodness' sake don't go and tell the whole neighborhood about them. Just between you and me, these nuts will be ready to eat as soon as there's a frost to sweeten them."

"You're very kind," Reddy Woodpecker told him. "Very kind indeed!"

Well, in about two weeks there was a frost. When Reddy Woodpecker awoke one morning the fields were white and a thin coating of ice covered the watering trough in the barnyard.

Some of the birds in Pleasant Valley had long since left for the South. And many of those that hadn't announced that they expected to start for a milder climate that very evening.

The weather soon grew warmer. And on the following day Reddy Woodpecker and Frisky Squirrel met at the beech grove.

"These are good nuts, eh?" called Reddy.

"They'd taste sweeter if you weren't here," Frisky Squirrel mumbled out of a full mouth.

Day 100

1. Read chapter 24 of *The Tale of Reddy Woodpecker*.
2. Tell someone what happened in the chapter.

Chapter 24 XXIV THE WINTER'S STORE

AFTER Frisky Squirrel had enjoyed a hearty meal of beechnuts he began to make hurried trips to a hollow tree nearby. He lived in that tree. It had a fine big storeroom. And there he carried beechnuts in his cheeks. Frisky did not intend to go hungry when winter came.

Meanwhile he watched Reddy Woodpecker out of the corner of his eye. He still hoped to catch Reddy unawares. And at last Frisky saw something that he hadn't expected to see. It made him stop short and stare.

He saw Reddy Woodpecker loosen a bit of bark and hide a beechnut under it.

Soon he beheld Reddy stowing beechnuts away in a hole in an old stump.

Frisky Squirrel was wild with rage.

"I told you might eat as many nuts as you pleased, if only you wouldn't mention beechnuts to Jasper Jay. I didn't say you might hide beechnuts. But I've caught you hoarding them!"

Reddy Woodpecker was not ruffled not even a single feather.

"I'm putting away a few nuts," he admitted. "I expect to spend the winter here. And of course I shall need something to eat."

"Don't you dare hide another nut!" Frisky Squirrel scolded.

"You're hoarding nuts yourself!"

"That's different," Frisky blustered.

All at once a loud, harsh voice squalled right above their heads. It belonged to Jasper Jay. "A quarrel!" he bawled.

"A quarrel over beechnuts! I must do what I can to stop it. I'll gather as many beechnuts as I can; because when they're all gone there won't be anything to quarrel about."

"Another hoarder!" chattered Frisky.

And Jasper Jay was not the last to appear. For Johnnie Green soon came hurrying up with a basket. And Frisky regarded him with great disfavor.

"Another hoarder!" Frisky groaned. And he began to scold Johnnie. "Go away!" he cried. "We don't want you here." To his great disgust Johnnie Green shied a stone at him and told him not to be saucy.

Jasper Jay jeered loudly at Frisky.

"That's what you get for being a pig," he told him. And turning to Reddy Woodpecker, Jasper added, "You see the pigs aren't all in the pigsty!"

Frisky Squirrel pretended that he didn't hear any of Jasper Jay's remarks. He set to work again to gather beechnuts enough to last him all winter and never once stopped to dash at Reddy Woodpecker nor even look at him.

That was only the first of many busy days for Reddy. Having made up his mind to spend the winter at Farmer Green's place he hid nuts everywhere.

No doubt he never could remember all of his hiding places. But he found enough of them when winter came. And though Frisky Squirrel had stowed away all the nuts he could possibly need, he never could bear to watch Reddy Woodpecker pull out a beechnut from beneath a strip of bark.

He said he never did like to see a bird eat nuts.

THE END

Day 101

1. Write a book report for *The Tale of Reddy Woodpecker*.
2. Write on a page the title of the book, the author, the characters (who the story was about), what happened to them and your favorite part. Then you can add a picture.
3. You could give this to a parent to add to your portfolio.

Day 102

1. Before we start reading our next book, we're going to play some reading games. This one is to practice the different sounds that one letter combination can make.
2. You are going to figure out what same two letters are missing from the words in each group. (Answers)
3. After you know what goes in the blanks, read out loud the words in each group. What sound do the letters in the blanks make in each group?

Group 1: b _ _ k   f _ _ t   w _ _ d   t _ _ k

Group 2: t _ _ l   l _ _ se   p _ _ dle   sch _ _ l

Group 3: d _ _ r   fl _ _ r

Hint if you need it: (All of the blanks are filled in with the same letter!)

Day 103

1. This game will help you think about words as families. When you can read one word in the family, you can read them all! When you come across a word you don't know, look for familiar pieces in the word.
2. For the activity below, think of as many words as you can that end with each of the given endings. All of your words will rhyme! (Answers)
3. Here's an example. If I give you AT, you can think of bat, cat, fat, hat, mat, Nat, sat, and vat. If you can read bat, you can read cat because you know AT and you know what a C sounds like. These are word families, words that go together. Now it's your turn. Come up with as many words as you can for each word family.

_ _ED   _ _ IG   _ _AN   _ _OT   _ _UN

Day 104

1. Read *One Inside the Other.*

You are in your family. Your family is in your community. Your community is in a county or city. Your county or city is in a state. Your state is in a country. Your country is in a continent. Your continent is in the world.

A period is in a sentence. A sentence is in a story. A story is in a book. A book is in a library. A library is in a community. A community is in a county. A county is in a state. A state is in a country. A country is in a continent. A continent is in the world.

A seed is in a plant. A plant is in a garden. A garden is in a yard. A yard is in a community. A community is in a county. A county is in a state. A state is in a country. A country is in a continent. A continent is in the world.

A crumb is in a cabinet. A cabinet is in a kitchen. A kitchen is in a home. A home is in a community. A community is in a county. A county is in a state. A state is in a country. A country is in a continent. A continent is in the world.

A star is in the universe. The universe is too big to fit in anything!

Day 105

1. Read *What's for Breakfast?*

What did you have for breakfast today?

If you were in America, maybe you had cereal, a big bowl of sweet cereal with milk.

If you were in Greece, maybe you had olives and crumbly white cheese.

If you were in Turkey, maybe you had circle-shaped bread covered in sesame seeds.

If you were in Columbia, maybe you had a cheesy soup.

If you were in Uganda, maybe you had a stew with bananas.

If you were in Kenya, maybe you had cornmeal mush.

What did you have for breakfast today?

Day 106

1. Read chapter 1 of *The Adventures of Danny Meadow Mouse*. This book is by a different author.
2. Tell someone what happened in the chapter.

<u>THE ADVENTURES OF DANNY MEADOW MOUSE</u> by THORNTON W. BURGESS

CHAPTER I Danny Meadow Mouse Is Worried

Danny Meadow Mouse sat on his door-step with his chin in his hands, and it was very plain to see that Danny had something on his mind. He had only a nod for Jimmy Skunk, and even Peter Rabbit could get no more than a grumpy "Good morning." It wasn't that he had been caught napping the day before by Reddy Fox and nearly made an end of. No, it wasn't that. Danny had learned his lesson, and Reddy would never catch him again. It wasn't that he was all alone with no one to play with. Danny was rather glad that he was alone. The fact is, Danny Meadow Mouse was worried.

Now worry is one of the worst things in the world, and it didn't seem as if there was anything that Danny Meadow Mouse need worry about. But you know it is the easiest thing in the world to find something to worry over and make yourself uncomfortable about. And when you make yourself uncomfortable, you are almost sure to make everyone around you equally uncomfortable. It was so with Danny Meadow Mouse. Striped Chipmunk had twice called him "Cross Patch" that morning, and Johnny Chuck, who had fought Reddy Fox for him the day before, had called him "Grumpy." And what do you think was the matter with Danny Meadow Mouse? Why, he was worrying because his tail was short. Yes, sir, that is all that ailed Danny Meadow Mouse that bright morning.

You know some people let their looks make them miserable. They worry because they are homely or freckled, or short or tall, or thin or stout, all of which is very foolish. And Danny Meadow Mouse was just as foolish in worrying because his tail was short.

It is short! It certainly is all of that! Danny never had realized how short until he chanced to meet his cousin Whitefoot, who lives in the Green Forest. He was very elegantly dressed, but the most imposing thing about him was his long, slim, beautiful tail. Danny had at once become conscious of his own stubby little tail, and he had hardly had pride enough to hold his head up as became an honest Meadow Mouse. Ever since he had been thinking and thinking, and wondering how his family came to have such short tails. Then he grew envious and began to wish and wish and wish that he could have a long tail like his cousin Whitefoot.

He was so busy wishing that he had a long tail that he quite forgot to take care of the tail he did have, and he pretty nearly lost it and his life with it. Old Whitetail the Marsh Hawk spied Danny sitting there moping on his doorstep, and came sailing over the tops of the meadow grasses so softly that he all but caught Danny. If it hadn't been for one of the Merry Little Breezes, Danny would have been caught. And all because he was envious. It's a bad, bad habit.

Day 107

1. Read chapter 2 of *The Adventures of Danny Meadow Mouse*.
2. Tell someone what happened in the chapter.

CHAPTER II Danny Meadow Mouse and His Short Tail

All Danny Meadow Mouse could think about was his short tail. He was so ashamed of it that whenever anyone passed, he crawled out of sight so that they should not see how short his tail was. Instead of playing in the sunshine as he used to do, he sat and sulked. Pretty soon his friends began to pass without stopping. Finally one day old Mr. Toad sat down in front of Danny and began to ask questions.

"What's the matter?" asked old Mr. Toad.

"Nothing," replied Danny Meadow Mouse.

"I don't suppose there really is anything the matter, but what do you think is the matter?" said old Mr. Toad.

Danny fidgeted, and old Mr. Toad looked up at jolly, round, red Mr. Sun and winked. "Sun is just as bright as ever, isn't it?" he inquired.

"Yes," said Danny.

"Got plenty to eat and drink, haven't you?" continued Mr. Toad.
"Yes," said Danny.

"Seems to me that that is a pretty good-looking suit of clothes you're wearing," said Mr. Toad, eyeing Danny critically. "Sunny weather, plenty to eat and drink, and good clothes-- must be you don't know when you're well off, Danny Meadow Mouse."

Danny hung his head. Finally he looked up and caught a kindly twinkle in old Mr. Toad's eyes. "Mr. Toad, how can I get a long tail like my cousin Whitefoot of the Green Forest?" he asked.

"So that's what's the matter! Ha! ha! ha! Danny Meadow Mouse, I'm ashamed of you! I certainly am ashamed of you!" said Mr. Toad. "What good would a long tail do you? Tell me that."

For a minute Danny didn't know just what to say. "I--I--I'd look so much better if I had a long tail," he ventured.

Old Mr. Toad just laughed. "You never saw a Meadow Mouse with a long tail, did you? Of course not. What a sight it would be! Why, everybody on the Green Meadows would laugh themselves sick at the sight! You see you need to be slim and trim and handsome to carry a long tail well. And then what a nuisance it would be! You would always have to be thinking of your tail and taking care to keep it out of harm's way. Look at me. I'm homely. Some folks call me ugly to look at. But no one tries to catch me as Farmer Brown's boy does Billy Mink because of his fine coat; and no one wants to put me in a cage because of a fine voice. I am satisfied to be just as I am, and if you'll take my advice, Danny Meadow Mouse, you'll be satisfied to be just as you are."

"Perhaps you are right," said Danny Meadow Mouse after a little. "I'll try."

Day 108

1. Read chapter 3 of *The Adventures of Danny Meadow Mouse*.
2. Tell someone what happened in the chapter.

CHAPTER III Danny Meadow Mouse Plays Hide and Seek

Life is always a game of hide and seek to Danny Meadow Mouse. You see, he is such a fat little fellow that there are a great many other furry-coated people, and almost as many who wear feathers, who would gobble Danny up for breakfast or for dinner if they could. Some of them pretend to be his friends, but Danny always keeps his eyes open when they are around and always begins to play hide and seek. Peter Rabbit and Jimmy Skunk and Striped Chipmunk and Happy Jack Squirrel are all friends whom he can trust, but he always has a bright twinkling eye open for Reddy Fox and Billy Mink and Shadow the Weasel and old Whitetail the Marsh Hawk, and several more, especially Hooty the Owl at night.

Now Danny Meadow Mouse is a stout-hearted little fellow, and when rough Brother North Wind came shouting across the Green Meadows, tearing to pieces the snow clouds and shaking out the snowflakes until they covered the Green Meadows deep, deep, deep, Danny just snuggled down in his warm coat in his snug little house of grass and waited. Danny liked the snow. Yes, sir, Danny Meadow Mouse liked the snow. He just loved to dig in it and make tunnels. Through those tunnels in every direction he could go where he pleased and when he pleased without being seen by anybody. It was great fun!

Every little way he made a little round doorway up beside a stiff stalk of grass. Out of this he could peep at the white world, and he could get the fresh cold air. Sometimes, when he was quite sure that no one was around, he would scamper across on top of the snow from one doorway to another, and when he did this, he made the prettiest little footprints.

Now Reddy Fox knew all about those doorways and who made them. Reddy was having hard work to get enough to eat this cold weather, and he was hungry most of the time.

One morning, as he came tiptoeing softly over the meadows, what should he see just ahead of him but the head of Danny Meadow Mouse pop out of one of those little round doorways. Reddy's mouth watered, and he stole forward more softly than ever. When he got within jumping distance, he drew his stout hind legs under him and made ready to spring. Presto! Danny Meadow Mouse had disappeared! Reddy Fox jumped just the same and began to dig as fast as he could make his paws go. He could smell Danny Meadow Mouse and that made him almost frantic.

All the time Danny Meadow Mouse was scurrying along one of his little tunnels, and when finally Reddy Fox stopped digging because he was quite out of breath, Danny popped his head out of another little doorway and laughed at Reddy. Of course Reddy saw him, and of course Reddy tried to catch him there, and dug frantically just as before. And of course Danny Meadow Mouse wasn't there.

After a while Reddy Fox grew tired of this kind of a game and tried another plan. The next time he saw Danny Meadow Mouse stick his head out, Reddy pretended not to see him. He stretched himself out on the ground and made believe that he was very tired and sleepy. He closed his eyes. Then he opened them just the tiniest bit, so that he could see Danny Meadow Mouse and yet seem to be asleep. Danny watched him for a long time. Then he chuckled to himself and dropped out of sight.

No sooner was he gone than Reddy Fox stole over close to the little doorway and waited. "He'll surely stick his head out again to see if I'm asleep, and then I'll have him," said Reddy to himself. So he waited and waited and waited. By and by he turned his head. There was Danny Meadow Mouse at another little doorway laughing at him!

Day 109

1. Read chapter 4 of *The Adventures of Danny Meadow Mouse*.
2. Tell someone what happened in the chapter.

CHAPTER IV Old Granny Fox Tries for Danny Meadow Mouse

Danny Meadow Mouse had not enjoyed anything so much for a long time as he did that game of hide and seek. He tickled and chuckled all the afternoon as he thought about it.

Of course Reddy had been "it." He had been "it" all the time, for never once had he caught Danny Meadow Mouse. If he had--well, there wouldn't have been any more stories about Danny Meadow Mouse, because there wouldn't have been any Danny Meadow Mouse any more.

But Danny never let himself think about this. He had enjoyed the game all the more because it had been such a dangerous game. It had been such fun to dive into one of his little round doorways in the snow, run along one of his own little tunnels, and then peep out at another doorway and watch Reddy Fox digging as fast as ever he could at the doorway Danny had just left. Finally Reddy had given up in disgust and gone off muttering angrily to try to find something else for dinner. Danny had sat up on the snow and watched him go. In his funny little squeaky voice Danny shouted:

"Though Reddy Fox is smart and sly,
  Hi-hum-diddle-de-o!
I'm just as smart and twice as spry.
  Hi-hum-diddle-de-o!"

That night Reddy Fox told old Granny Fox all about how he had tried to catch Danny Meadow Mouse. Granny listened with her head cocked on one side. When Reddy told how fat Danny Meadow Mouse was, her mouth watered. You see now that snow covered the Green Meadows and the Green Forest, Granny and Reddy Fox had hard work to get enough to eat, and they were hungry most of the time. "I'll go with you down on the meadows to-morrow morning, and then we'll see if Danny Meadow Mouse is as smart as he thinks he is," said Granny Fox.

So, bright and early the next morning, old Granny Fox and Reddy Fox went down on the meadows where Danny Meadow Mouse lives. Danny had felt in his bones that Reddy would come back, so he was watching, and he saw them as soon as they came out of the Green Forest. When he saw old Granny Fox, Danny's heart beat a little faster than before, for he knew that Granny Fox is very smart and very wise and has learned most of the tricks of all the other little meadow and forest people.

"This is going to be a more exciting game than the other," said Danny to himself, and scurried down out of sight to see that all his little tunnels were clear so that he could run fast through them if he had to. Then he peeped out of one of his little doorways hidden in a clump of tall grass.

Old Granny Fox set Reddy to hunting for Danny's little round doorways, and as fast as he found them, Granny came up and sniffed at each. She knew that she could tell by the smell which one he had been at last. Finally she came straight towards the tall bunch of grass. Danny ducked down and scurried along one of his little tunnels. He heard Granny Fox sniff at the doorway he had just left. Suddenly something plunged down through the snow right at his very heels. Danny didn't have to look to know that it was Granny Fox herself, and he squeaked with fright.

Day 110

1. Read chapter 5 of *The Adventures of Danny Meadow Mouse.*
2. Tell someone what happened in the chapter.

CHAPTER V What Happened on the Green Meadows

Thick and fast things were happening to Danny Meadow Mouse down on the snow-covered Green Meadows. Rather, they were almost happening. He hadn't minded when Reddy Fox all alone tried to catch him. Indeed, he had made a regular game of hide and seek of it and had enjoyed it immensely. But now it was different. Granny Fox wasn't so easily fooled as Reddy Fox. Just Granny alone would have made the game dangerous for Danny Meadow Mouse. But Reddy was with her, and so Danny had two to look out for, and he got so many frights that it seemed to him as if his heart had moved right up into his mouth and was going to stay there. Yes, sir, that is just how it seemed.

Down in his little tunnels underneath the snow Danny Meadow Mouse felt perfectly safe from Reddy Fox, who would stop and dig frantically at the little round doorway where he had last seen Danny. But old Granny Fox knew all about those little tunnels, and she didn't waste any time digging at the doorways. Instead she cocked her sharp little ears and listened with all her might. Now Granny Fox has very keen ears, oh, very keen ears, and she heard just what she hoped she would hear. She heard Danny Meadow Mouse running along one of his little tunnels under the snow.

Plunge! Old Granny Fox dived right into the snow and right through into the tunnel of Danny Meadow Mouse. Her two black paws actually touched Danny's tail. He was glad then that it was no longer.

"Ha!" cried Granny Fox, "I almost got him that time!"

Then she ran ahead a little way over the snow, listening as before. Plunge! Into the snow she went again. It was lucky for him that Danny had just turned into another tunnel, for otherwise she would surely have caught him.

Granny Fox blew the snow out of her nose. "Next time I'll get him!" said she.

Now Reddy Fox is quick to learn, especially when it is a way to get something to eat. He watched Granny Fox, and when he understood what she was doing, he made up his mind to have a try himself, for he was afraid that if she caught Danny Meadow Mouse, she would think that he was not big enough to divide. Perhaps that was because Reddy is very selfish himself. So the next time Granny plunged into the snow and missed Danny Meadow Mouse just as before, Reddy rushed in ahead of her, and the minute he heard Danny running down below, he plunged in just as he had seen Granny do. But he didn't take the pains to make sure of just where Danny was, and so of course he didn't come anywhere near him. But he frightened Danny still more and made old Granny Fox lose her temper.

Poor Danny Meadow Mouse! He had never been so frightened in all his life. He didn't know which way to turn or where to run. And so he sat still, which, although he didn't know it, was the very best thing he could do. When he sat still he made no noise, and so of course Granny and Reddy Fox could not tell where he was. Old Granny Fox sat and listened and listened and listened, and wondered where Danny Meadow Mouse was. And down under the snow Danny Meadow Mouse sat and listened and listened and listened, and wondered where Granny and Reddy Fox were.

"Pooh!" said Granny Fox after a while, "that Meadow Mouse thinks he can fool me by sitting still. I'll give him a scare."

Then she began to plunge into the snow this way and that way, and sure enough, pretty soon she landed so close to Danny Meadow Mouse that one of her claws scratched him.

Day 111

1. Read chapter 6 of *The Adventures of Danny Meadow Mouse.*
2. Tell someone what happened in the chapter.

CHAPTER VI Danny Meadow Mouse Remembers and Reddy Fox Forgets

"There he goes!" cried old Granny Fox. "Don't let him sit still again!"

"I hear him!" shouted Reddy Fox, and plunged down into the snow just as Granny Fox had done a minute before. But he didn't catch anything, and when he had blown the snow out of his nose and wiped it out of his eyes, he saw Granny Fox dive into the snow with no better luck.

"Never mind," said Granny Fox, "as long as we keep him running, we can hear him, and some one of these times we'll catch him. Pretty soon he'll get too tired to be so spry, and when he is--" Granny didn't finish, but licked her chops and smacked her lips. Reddy Fox grinned, then licked his chops and smacked his lips. Then once more they took turns diving into the snow.

And down underneath in the little tunnels he had made, Danny Meadow Mouse was running for his life. He was getting tired, just as old Granny Fox had said he would. He was almost out of breath. He was sore and one leg smarted, for in one of her jumps old Granny Fox had so nearly caught him that her claws had torn his pants and scratched him.

"Oh, dear! Oh, dear! If only I had time to think!" panted Danny Meadow Mouse, and then he squealed in still greater fright as Reddy Fox crashed down into his tunnel right at his very heels. "I've got to get somewhere! I've got to get somewhere where they can't get at me!" he sobbed. And right that very instant he remembered the old fence-post!

The old fence-post lay on the ground and was hollow. Fastened to it were long wires with sharp cruel barbs. Danny had made a tunnel over to that old fence-post the very first day after the snow came, for in that hollow in the old post he had a secret store of seeds. Why hadn't he thought of it before? It must have been because he was too frightened to think. But he remembered now, and he dodged into the tunnel that led to the old fence-post, running faster than ever, for though his heart was in his mouth from fear, in his heart was hope, and hope is a wonderful thing.

Now old Granny Fox knew all about that old fence-post and she remembered all about those barbed wires fastened to it. Although they were covered with snow she knew just about where they lay, and just before she reached them she stopped plunging down into the snow. Reddy Fox knew about those wires; too, but he was so excited that he forgot all about them.

"Stop!" cried old Granny Fox sharply.

But Reddy Fox didn't hear, or if he heard he didn't heed. His sharp ears could hear Danny Meadow Mouse running almost underneath him. Granny Fox could stop if she wanted to, but he was going to have Danny Meadow Mouse for his breakfast! Down into the snow he plunged as hard as ever he could.

"Oh! Oh! Wow! Wow! Oh, dear! Oh, dear!"

That wasn't the voice of Danny Meadow Mouse. Oh, my, no! It was the voice of Reddy Fox. Yes, sir, it was the voice of Reddy Fox. He had landed with one of his black paws right on one of those sharp wire barbs, and it did hurt dreadfully.

"I never did know a young Fox who could get into as much trouble as you can!" snapped old Granny Fox, as Reddy hobbled along on three legs behind her, across the snow-covered Green Meadows. "It serves you right for forgetting!"

"Yes'm," said Reddy meekly.

And safe in the hollow of the old fence-post, Danny Meadow Mouse was dressing the scratch on his leg made by the claws of old Granny Fox.

Day 112

1. Read chapter 7 of *The Adventures of Danny Meadow Mouse*.
2. Tell someone what happened in the chapter.

CHAPTER VII Old Granny Fox Tries a New Plan

Old Granny Fox kept thinking about Danny Meadow Mouse. She knew that he was fat, and it made her mouth water every time she thought of him. She made up her mind that she must and would have him. She knew that Danny had been very, very much frightened when she and Reddy Fox had tried so hard to catch him by plunging down through the snow into his little tunnels after him, and she felt pretty sure that he wouldn't go far away from the old fence-post, in the hollow of which he was snug and safe.

Old Granny Fox is very smart. "Danny Meadow Mouse won't put his nose out of that old fence-post for a day or two. Then he'll get tired of staying inside all the time, and he'll peep out of one of his little round doorways to see if the way is clear. If he doesn't see any danger, he'll come out and run around on top of the snow to get some of the seeds in the tops of the tall grasses that stick out through the snow. If nothing frightens him, he'll keep going, a little farther and a little farther from that old fence-post. I must see to it that Danny Meadow Mouse isn't frightened for a few days." So said old Granny Fox to herself, as she lay under a hemlock tree, studying how she could best get the next meal.

Then she called Reddy Fox to her and forbade him to go down on the meadows until she should tell him he might. Reddy grumbled and mumbled and didn't see why he shouldn't go where he pleased, but he didn't dare disobey. You see he had a sore foot. He had hurt it on a wire barb when he was plunging through the snow after Danny Meadow Mouse, and now he had to run on three legs. That meant that he must depend upon Granny Fox to help him get enough to eat. So Reddy didn't dare to disobey.

It all came out just as Granny Fox had thought it would. Danny Meadow Mouse did get tired of staying in the old fence-post. He did peep out first, and then he did run a little way on the snow, and then a little farther and a little farther. But all the time he took great care not to get more than a jump or two from one of his little round doorways leading down to his tunnels under the snow.

Hidden on the edge of the Green Forest, Granny Fox watched him. She looked up at the sky, and she knew that it was going to snow again. "That's good," said she. "Tomorrow morning I'll have fat Meadow Mouse for breakfast," and she smiled a hungry smile.

The next morning, before jolly, round, red Mr. Sun was out of bed, old Granny Fox trotted down onto the meadows and straight over to where, down under the snow, lay the old fence-post. It had snowed again, and all the little doorways of Danny Meadow Mouse were covered up with soft, fleecy snow. Behind Granny Fox limped Reddy Fox, grumbling to himself.

When they reached the place where the old fence-post lay buried under the snow, old Granny Fox stretched out as flat as she could. Then she told Reddy to cover her up with the new soft snow. Reddy did as he was told, but all the time he grumbled. "Now you go off to the Green Forest and keep out of sight," said Granny Fox. "By and by I'll bring you some Meadow Mouse for your breakfast," and Granny Fox chuckled to think how smart she was and how she was going to catch Danny Meadow Mouse.

Day 113

1. Read chapter 8 of *The Adventures of Danny Meadow Mouse.*
2. Tell someone what happened in the chapter.

CHAPTER VIII Brother North Wind Proves a Friend

Danny Meadow Mouse had seen nothing of old Granny Fox or Reddy Fox for several days. Every morning the first thing he did, even before he had breakfast, was to climb up to one of his little round doorways and peep out over the beautiful white meadows, to see if there was any danger near. But every time he did this, Danny used a different doorway. "For," said Danny to himself, "if any one should happen, just happen, to see me this morning, they might be waiting just outside my doorway to catch me tomorrow morning." You see there is a great deal of wisdom in the little head that Danny Meadow Mouse carries on his shoulders.

But the first day and the second day and the third day he saw nothing of old Granny Fox or of Reddy Fox, and he began to enjoy running through his tunnels under the snow and scurrying across from one doorway to another on top of the snow, just as he had before the Foxes had tried so hard to catch him. But he hadn't forgotten, as Granny Fox had hoped he would. No, indeed, Danny Meadow Mouse hadn't forgotten. He was too wise for that.

One morning, when he started to climb up to one of his little doorways, he found that it was closed. Yes, sir, it was closed. In fact, there wasn't any doorway. More snow had fallen from the clouds in the night and had covered up every one of the little round doorways of Danny Meadow Mouse.

"Ha!" said Danny, "I shall have a busy day, a very busy day, opening all my doorways. I'll eat my breakfast, and then I'll go to work."

So Danny Meadow Mouse ate a good breakfast of seeds which he had stored in the hollow in the old fence-post buried under the snow, and then he began work on the nearest doorway. It really wasn't work at all, for you see the snow was soft and light, and Danny dearly loved to dig in it. In a few minutes he had made a wee hole through which he could peep up at jolly, round Mr. Sun. In a few minutes more he had made it big enough to put his head out. He looked this way and he looked that way. Far, far off on the top of a tree he could see old Roughleg the Hawk, but he was so far away that Danny didn't fear him at all.

"I don't see anything or anybody to be afraid of," said Danny and poked his head out a little farther.

Then he sat and studied everything around him a long, long time. It was a beautiful white world, a very beautiful white world. Everything was so white and pure and beautiful that it didn't seem possible that harm or danger for anyone could even be thought of. But Danny Meadow Mouse learned long ago that things are not always what they seem, and so he sat with just his little head sticking out of his doorway and studied and studied. Just a little way off was a little heap of snow.

"I don't remember that," said Danny. "And I don't remember anything that would make that. There isn't any little bush or old log or anything underneath it. Perhaps rough Brother North Wind heaped it up, just for fun."

But all the time Danny Meadow Mouse kept studying and studying that little heap of snow. Pretty soon he saw rough Brother North Wind coming his way and tossing the snow about as he came. He caught a handful from the top of the little heap of snow that Danny was studying, and when he had passed, Danny's sharp eyes saw something red there. It was just the color of the cloak old Granny Fox wears.

"Granny Fox, you can't fool me! I see you plain as plain can be!" shouted Danny Meadow Mouse and dropped down out of sight, while old Granny Fox shook the snow from her red cloak and, with a snarl of disappointment and anger, slowly started for the Green Forest, where Reddy Fox was waiting for her.

Day 114

1. Read chapter 9 of *The Adventures of Danny Meadow Mouse*.
2. Tell someone what happened in the chapter.

CHAPTER IX Danny Meadow Mouse Is Caught at Last

"Tippy-toppy-tippy-toe,
Play and frolic in the snow!
Now you see me! Now you don't!
Think you'll catch me, but you won't!
Tippy-toppy-tippy-toe,
Oh, such fun to play in snow!"

Danny Meadow Mouse sang this, or at least he tried to sing it, as he skipped about on the snow that covered the Green Meadows. But Danny Meadow Mouse has such a little voice, such a funny little squeaky voice, that had you been there you probably would never have guessed that he was singing. He thought he was, though, and was enjoying it just as much as if he had the most beautiful voice in the world. You know singing is nothing in the world but happiness in the heart making itself heard.

Oh, yes, Danny Meadow Mouse was happy! Why shouldn't he have been? Hadn't he proved himself smarter than old Granny Fox? That is something to make anyone happy. Some folks may fool Granny Fox once; some may fool her twice; but there are very few who can keep right on fooling her until she gives up in disgust. That is just what Danny Meadow Mouse had done, and he felt very smart and of course he felt very happy.

So Danny sang his little song and skipped about in the moonlight, and dodged in and out of his little round doorways, and all the time kept his sharp little eyes open for any sign of Granny Fox or Reddy Fox. But with all his smartness, Danny forgot. Yes, sir, Danny forgot one thing. He forgot to watch up in the sky. He knew that of course old Roughleg the Hawk was asleep, so he had nothing to fear from him. But he never once thought of Hooty the Owl.

Dear me, dear me! Forgetting is a dreadful habit. If nobody ever forgot, there wouldn't be nearly so much trouble in the world. No, indeed, there wouldn't be nearly so much trouble. And Danny Meadow Mouse forgot. He skipped and sang and was happy as could be, and never once thought to watch up in the sky.

Over in the Green Forest Hooty the Owl had had poor hunting, and he was feeling cross. You see, Hooty was hungry, and hunger is apt to make one feel cross. The longer he hunted, the hungrier and crosser he grew. Suddenly he thought of Danny Meadow Mouse.

"I suppose he is asleep somewhere safe and snug under the snow," grumbled Hooty, "but he might be, he just might be out for a frolic in the moonlight. I believe I'll go down on the meadows and see."

Now Hooty the Owl can fly without making the teeniest, weeniest sound. It seems as if he just drifts along through the air like a great shadow. Now he spread his great wings and floated out over the meadows. You know Hooty can see as well at night as most folks can by day, and it was not long before he saw Danny Meadow Mouse skipping about on the snow and dodging in and out of his little round doorways. Hooty's great eyes grew brighter and fiercer. Without a sound he floated through the moonlight until he was just over Danny Meadow Mouse.

Too late Danny looked up. His little song ended in a tiny squeak of fear, and he started for his nearest little round doorway. Hooty the Owl reached down with his long cruel claws and--Danny Meadow Mouse was caught at last!

Day 115

1. Read chapter 10 of *The Adventures of Danny Meadow Mouse*.
2. Tell someone what happened in this chapter.

CHAPTER X A Strange Ride and How It Ended

Danny Meadow Mouse often had sat watching Skimmer the Swallow sailing around up in the blue, blue sky. He had watched Ol' Mistah Buzzard go up, up, up, until he was nothing but a tiny speck, and Danny had wondered how it would seem to be way up above the Green Meadows and the Green Forest and look down. It had seemed to him that it must be very wonderful and beautiful. Sometimes he had wished that he had wings and could go up in the air and look down. And now here he was, he, Danny Meadow Mouse, actually doing that very thing!

But Danny could see nothing wonderful or beautiful now. No, indeed! Everything was terrible, for you see Danny Meadow Mouse wasn't flying himself. He was being carried. Yes, sir, Danny Meadow Mouse was being carried through the air in the cruel claws of Hooty the Owl! And all because Danny had forgotten--forgotten to watch up in the sky for danger.

Poor, poor Danny Meadow Mouse! Hooty's great cruel claws hurt him dreadfully! But it wasn't the pain that was the worst. No, indeed! It wasn't the pain! It was the thought of what would happen when Hooty reached his home in the Green Forest, for he knew that there Hooty would gobble him up, bones and all. As he flew, Hooty kept chuckling, and Danny Meadow Mouse knew just what those chuckles meant. They meant that Hooty was thinking of the good meal he was going to have.

Hanging there in Hooty's great cruel claws, Danny looked down on the snow-covered Green Meadows he loved so well. They seemed a frightfully long way below him, though really they were not far at all, for Hooty was flying very low. But Danny Meadow Mouse had never in all his life been so high up before, and so it seemed to him that he was way, way up in the sky, and he shut his eyes so as not to see. But he couldn't keep them shut. No, sir, he couldn't keep them shut! He just had to keep opening them. There was the dear old Green Forest drawing nearer and nearer. It always had looked very beautiful to Danny Meadow Mouse, but now it looked terrible, very terrible indeed, because over in it, hidden away there in some dark place, was the home of Hooty the Owl.

Just ahead of him was the Old Briar-patch where Peter Rabbit lives so safely. Every old bramble in it was covered with snow and it was very, very beautiful. Really everything was just as beautiful as ever--the moonlight, the Green Forest, the snow-covered Green Meadows, the Old Briar-patch. The only change was in Danny Meadow Mouse himself, and it was all because he had forgotten.

Suddenly Danny began to wriggle and struggle. "Keep still!" snapped Hooty the Owl.

But Danny only struggled harder than ever. It seemed to him that Hooty wasn't holding him as tightly as at first. He felt one of Hooty's claws slip. It tore his coat and hurt dreadfully, but it slipped! The fact is, Hooty had only grabbed Danny Meadow Mouse by the loose part of his coat, and up in the air he couldn't get hold of Danny any better. Danny kicked, squirmed and twisted, and twisted, squirmed, and kicked. He felt his coat tear and of course the skin with it, but he kept right on, for now he was hanging almost free. Hooty had started down now, so as to get a better hold. Danny gave one more kick and then--he felt himself falling!

Danny Meadow Mouse shut his eyes and held his breath. Down, down, down he fell. It seemed to him that he never would strike the snow-covered meadows! Really he fell only a very little distance. But it seemed a terrible distance to Danny. He hit something that scratched him, and then plump! he landed in the soft snow right in the very middle of the Old Briar-patch, and the last thing he remembered was hearing the scream of disappointment and rage of Hooty the Owl.

Day 116

1. Read chapter 11 of *The Adventures of Danny Meadow Mouse*.
2. Tell someone what happened in this chapter.

CHAPTER XI Peter Rabbit Gets a Fright

Peter Rabbit sat in his favorite place in the middle of the dear Old Briar-patch, trying to decide which way he would go on his travels that night. The night before he had had a narrow escape from old Granny Fox over in the Green Forest. There was nothing to eat around the Smiling Pool and no one to talk to there any more, and you know that Peter must either eat or ask questions in order to be perfectly happy. No, the Smiling Pool was too dull a place to interest Peter on such a beautiful moonlight night, and Peter had no mind to try his legs against those of old Granny Fox again in the Green Forest.

Early that morning, just after Peter had settled down for his morning nap, Tommy Tit the Chickadee had dropped into the dear Old Briar-patch just to be neighborly. Peter was just dozing off when he heard the cheeriest little voice in the world. It was saying:

"Dee-dee-chickadee!
I see you! Can you see me?"

Peter began to smile even before he could get his eyes open and look up. There, right over his head, was Tommy Tit hanging head down from a nodding old bramble. In a twinkling he was down on the snow right in front of Peter, then up in the brambles again, right side up, upside down, here, there, everywhere, never still a minute, and all the time chattering away in the cheeriest little voice in the world.

"Dee-dee-chickadee!
I'm as happy as can be!
Find it much the better way
To be happy all the day.
Dee-dee-chickadee!
Everybody's good to me!"

"Hello, Tommy!" said Peter Rabbit. "Where'd you come from?"

"From Farmer Brown's new orchard up on the hill. It's a fine orchard, Peter Rabbit, a fine orchard. I go there every morning for my breakfast. If the winter lasts long enough, I'll have all the trees cleaned up for Farmer Brown."

Peter looked puzzled. "What do you mean?" he asked.

"Just what I say," replied Tommy Tit, almost turning a somersault in the air. "There's a million eggs of insects on those young peach trees, but I'm clearing them all off as fast as I can. They're mighty fine eating, Peter Rabbit, mighty fine eating!" And with that Tommy Tit had said good-by and flitted away.

Peter was thinking of that young orchard now, as he sat in the moonlight trying to make up his mind where to go. The thought of those young peach trees made his mouth water. It was a long way up to the orchard on the hill, a very long way, and Peter was wondering if it really was safe to go. He had just about made up his mind to try it, for Peter is very, very fond of the bark of young peach trees, when thump! something dropped out of the sky at his very feet.

It startled Peter so that he nearly tumbled over backward. And right at the same instant came the fierce, angry scream of Hooty the Owl. That almost made Peter's heart stop beating, although he knew that Hooty couldn't get him down there in the Old Briar-patch. When Peter got his wits together and his heart didn't go so jumpy, he looked to see what had dropped so close to him out of the sky. His big eyes grew bigger than ever, and he rubbed them to make quite sure that he really saw what he thought he saw. Yes, there was no doubt about it--there at his feet lay Danny Meadow Mouse!

Day 117

1. Read chapter 12 of *The Adventures of Danny Meadow Mouse.*
2. Tell someone what happened in the chapter.

CHAPTER XII The Old Briar-patch Has a New Tenant

Danny Meadow Mouse slowly opened his eyes and then closed them again quickly, as if afraid to look around. He could hear someone talking. It was a pleasant voice, not at all like the terrible voice of Hooty the Owl, which was the very last thing that Danny Meadow Mouse could remember. Danny lay still a minute and listened.

"Why, Danny Meadow Mouse, where in the world did you drop from?" asked the voice. It sounded like--why, very much like Peter Rabbit speaking. Danny opened his eyes again. It was Peter Rabbit.

"Where--where am I?" asked Danny Meadow Mouse in a very weak and small voice.

"In the middle of the dear Old Briar-patch with me," replied Peter Rabbit. "But how did you get here? You seemed to drop right out of the sky."

Danny Meadow Mouse shuddered. Suddenly he remembered everything: how Hooty the Owl had caught him in great cruel claws and had carried him through the moonlight across the snow-covered Green Meadows; how he had felt Hooty's claws slip and then had struggled and kicked and twisted and turned until his coat had torn and he had dropped down, down, down until he had landed in the soft snow and knocked all the breath out of his little body. The very last thing he could remember was Hooty's fierce scream of rage and disappointment. Danny shuddered again.

Then a new thought came to him. He must get out of sight! Hooty might catch him again! Danny tried to scramble to his feet.

"Ouch! Oh!" groaned Danny and lay still again.

"There, there. Keep still, Danny Meadow Mouse. There's nothing to be afraid of here," said Peter Rabbit gently. His big eyes filled with tears as he looked at Danny Meadow Mouse, for Danny was all torn and hurt by the cruel claws of Hooty the Owl, and you know Peter has a very tender heart.

So Danny lay still, and while Peter Rabbit tried to make him comfortable and dress his hurts, he told Peter all about how he had forgotten to watch up in the sky and so had been caught by Hooty the Owl, and all about his terrible ride in Hooty's cruel claws.

"Oh, dear, whatever shall I do now?" he ended. "However shall I get back home to my warm house of grass, my safe little tunnels under the snow, and my little store of seeds in the snug hollow in the old fence-post?"

Peter Rabbit looked thoughtful. "You can't do it," said he. "You simply can't do it. It is such a long way for a little fellow like you that it wouldn't be safe to try. If you went at night, Hooty the Owl might catch you again. If you tried in daylight, old Roughleg the Hawk would be almost sure to see you. And night or day old Granny Fox or Reddy Fox might come snooping around, and if they did, they would be sure to catch you. I tell you what, you stay right here! The dear Old Briar-patch is the safest place in the world. Why, just think, here you can come out in broad daylight and laugh at Granny and Reddy Fox and at old Roughleg the Hawk, because the good old brambles will keep them out, if they try to get you. You can make just as good tunnels under the snow here as you had there, and there are lots and lots of seeds on the ground to eat. You know I don't care for them myself. I'm lonesome sometimes, living here all alone. You stay here, and we'll have the Old Briar-patch to ourselves."

Danny Meadow Mouse looked at Peter gratefully. "I will, and thank you ever so much, Peter Rabbit," he said.

And this is how the dear Old Briar-patch happened to have another tenant.

Day 118

1. Read chapter 13 of *The Adventures of Danny Meadow Mouse*.
2. Tell someone what this chapter was about.

CHAPTER XIII Peter Rabbit Visits the Peach Orchard

"Don't go, Peter Rabbit! Don't go!" begged Danny Meadow Mouse.

Peter hopped to the edge of the Old Briar-patch and looked over the moonlit, snow-covered meadows to the hill back of Farmer Brown's house. On that hill was the young peach orchard of which Tommy Tit the Chickadee had told him, and ever since Peter's mouth had watered and watered every time he thought of those young peach trees and the tender bark on them.

"I think I will, Danny, just this once," said Peter. "It's a long way, and I've never been there before; but I guess it's just as safe as the Meadows or the Green Forest.

"Oh I'm as bold as bold can be!
 Sing hoppy-hippy-hippy-hop-o!
 I'll hie me forth the world to see!
 Sing hoppy-hippy-hippy-hop-o!
   My ears are long,
   My legs are strong,
   So now good day;
   I'll hie away!
 Sing hoppy-hippy-hippy-hop-o!"

(Note: Hie is a word we don't use now. It means to go quickly.)

And with that, Peter Rabbit left the dear safe Old Briar-patch, and away he went lipperty-lipperty-lip, across the Green Meadows towards the hill and the young orchard back of Farmer Brown's house.

Danny Meadow Mouse watched him go and shook his head in disapproval. "Foolish, foolish, foolish!" he said over and over to himself. "Why can't Peter be content with the good things that he has?"

Peter Rabbit hurried along through the moonlight, stopping every few minutes to sit up to look and listen. He heard the fierce hunting call of Hooty the Owl way over in the Green Forest, so he felt sure that at present there was nothing to fear from him. He knew that since their return to the Green Meadows and the Green Forest, Granny and Reddy Fox had kept away from Farmer Brown's, so he did not worry about them.

All in good time Peter came to the young orchard. It was just as Tommy Tit the Chickadee had told him. Peter hopped up to the nearest peach tree and nibbled the bark. My, how good it tasted! He went all around the tree, stripping off the bark. He stood up on his long hind legs and reached as high as he could. Then he dug the snow away and ate down as far as he could. When he could get no more tender young bark, he went on to the next tree.

Now though Peter didn't know it, he was in the very worst kind of mischief. You see, when he took off all the bark all the way around the young peach tree he killed the tree, for you know it is on the inside of the bark that the sap which gives life to a tree and makes it grow goes up from the roots to all the branches. So when Peter ate the bark all the way around the trunk of the young tree, he had made it impossible for the sap to come up in the spring. Oh, it was the worst kind of mischief that Peter Rabbit was in.

But Peter didn't know it, and he kept right on filling that big stomach of his and enjoying it so much that he forgot to watch out for danger. Suddenly, just as he had begun on another tree, a great roar right behind him made him jump almost out of his skin. He knew that voice, and without waiting to even look behind him, he started for the stone wall on the other side of the orchard. Right at his heels, his great mouth wide open, was Bowser the Hound.

Day 119

1. Read chapter 14 of *The Adventures of Danny Meadow Mouse*.
2. Tell someone what happened in this chapter.

CHAPTER XIV Farmer Brown Sets a Trap

Peter Rabbit was in trouble. He had got into mischief and now, like everyone who gets into mischief, he wished that he hadn't. The worst of it was that he was a long way from his home in the dear Old Briar-patch, and he didn't know how he ever could get back there again. Where was he? Why, in the stone wall on one side of Farmer Brown's young peach orchard. How Peter blessed the old stone wall in which he had found a safe hiding-place! Bowser had hung around nearly all night, so that Peter had not dared to try to go home. Now it was daylight, and Peter knew it would not be safe to put his nose outside.

Peter was worried, so worried that he couldn't go to sleep as he usually does in the daytime. So he sat hidden in the old wall and waited and watched. By and by he saw Farmer Brown and Farmer Brown's boy come out into the orchard. Right away they saw the mischief which Peter had done, and he could tell by the sound of their voices that they were very, very angry. They went away, but before long they were back again, and all day long Peter watched them work putting something around each of the young peach-trees. Peter grew so curious that he forgot all about his troubles and how far away from home he was. He could hardly wait for night to come so that he might see what they had been doing.

Just as jolly, round, red Mr. Sun started to go to bed behind the Purple Hills, Farmer Brown and his boy started back to the house. Farmer Brown was smiling now.

"I guess that will fix him!" he said.

"Now what does he mean by that?" thought Peter. "Whom will it fix? Can it be me? I don't need any fixing."

He waited just as long as he could. When all was still, and the moonlight had begun to make shadows of the trees on the snow, Peter very cautiously crept out of his hiding-place. Bowser the Hound was nowhere in sight, and everything was as quiet and peaceful as it had been when he first came into the orchard the night before. Peter had fully made up his mind to go straight home as fast as his long legs would take him, but his dreadful curiosity insisted that first he must find out what Farmer Brown and his boy had been doing to the young peach trees.

So Peter hurried over to the nearest tree. All around the trunk of the tree, from the ground clear up higher than Peter could reach, was wrapped wire netting. Peter couldn't get so much as a nibble of the delicious bark. He hadn't intended to take any, for he had meant to go right straight home, but now that he couldn't get any, he wanted some more than ever,--just a bite. Peter looked around. Everything was quiet. He would try the next tree, and then he would go home.

But the next tree was wrapped with wire. Peter hesitated, looked around, turned to go home, thought of how good that bark had tasted the night before, hesitated again, and then hurried over to the third tree. It was protected just like the others. Then Peter forgot all about going home. He wanted some of that delicious bark, and he ran from one tree to another as fast as he could go.

At last, way down at the end of the orchard, Peter found a tree that had no wire around it. "They must have forgotten this one!" he thought, and his eyes sparkled. All around on the snow were a lot of little, shiny wires, but Peter didn't notice them. All he saw was that delicious bark on the young peach tree. He hopped right into the middle of the wires, and then, just as he reached up to take the first bite of bark, he felt something tugging at one of his hind legs.

Day 120

1. Read chapter 15 of *The Adventures of Danny Meadow Mouse*.
2. Tell someone what happened in this chapter.

CHAPTER XV Peter Rabbit Is Caught in a Snare

When Peter Rabbit, reaching up to nibble the bark of one of Farmer Brown's young trees, felt something tugging at one of his hind legs, he was so startled that he jumped to get away. Instead of doing this, he fell flat on his face. The thing on his hind leg had tightened and held him fast. A great fear came to Peter Rabbit, and lying there in the snow, he kicked and struggled with all his might. But the more he kicked, the tighter grew that hateful thing on his leg! Finally he grew too tired to kick any more and lay still. The dreadful thing that held him hurt his leg, but it didn't pull when he lay still.

When he had grown a little calmer, Peter sat up to examine the thing which held him so fast. It was something like one of the blackberry vines he had sometimes tripped over, only it was bright and shiny, and had no branches or tiny prickers, and one end was fastened to a stake. Peter tried to bite off the shiny thing, but even his great, sharp front teeth couldn't cut it. Then Peter knew what it was. It was wire! It was a snare which Farmer Brown had set to catch him, and which he had walked right into because he had been so greedy for the bark of the young peach tree that he had not used his eyes to look out for danger.

Oh, how Peter Rabbit did wish that he had not been so curious to know what Farmer Brown had been doing that day, and that he had gone straight home as he had meant to do, instead of trying to get one more meal of young peach bark! Big tears rolled down Peter's cheeks. What should he do? What could he do? For a long time Peter sat in the moonlight, trying to think of something to do. At last he thought of the stake to which that hateful wire was fastened. The stake was of wood, and Peter's teeth would cut wood. Peter's heart gave a great leap of hope, and he began at once to dig away the snow from around the stake, and then settled himself to gnaw the stake in two.

Peter had been hard at work on the stake a long time and had it a little more than half cut through, when he heard a loud sniff down at the other end of the orchard. He looked up to see--whom do you think? Why, Bowser the Hound! He hadn't seen Peter yet, but he had already found Peter's tracks, and it would be but a few minutes before he found Peter himself.

Poor Peter Rabbit! There wasn't time to finish cutting off the stake. What could he do? He made a frightened jump just as he had when he first felt the wire tugging at his leg. Just as before, he was thrown flat on his face. He scrambled to his feet and jumped again, only to be thrown just as before. Just then Bowser the Hound saw him and opening his mouth sent forth a great roar. Peter made one more frantic jump. Snap! the stake had broken! Peter pitched forward on his head, turned a somersault, and scrambled to his feet. He was free at last! That is, he could run, but after him dragged a piece of the stake.

How Peter did run! It was hard work, for you know he had to drag that piece of stake after him. But he did it, and just in time he crawled into the old stone wall on one side of the orchard, while Bowser the Hound barked his disappointment to the moon.

Day 121

1.   Read chapter 16 of *The Adventures of Danny Meadow Mouse*.
2.   Tell someone what happened in this chapter.

CHAPTER XVI Peter Rabbit's Hard Journey

Peter Rabbit sat in the old stone wall along one side of Farmer Brown's orchard, waiting for Mrs. Moon to put out her light and leave the world in darkness until jolly, round, red Mr. Sun should kick off his rosy bedclothes and begin his daily climb up in the blue, blue sky. In the winter, Mr. Sun is a late sleeper, and Peter knew that there would be two or three hours after Mrs. Moon put out her light when it would be quite dark. And Peter also knew too that by this time Hooty the Owl would probably have caught his dinner. So would old Granny Fox and Reddy Fox. Bowser the Hound would be too sleepy to be on the watch. It would be the very safest time for Peter to try to get to his home in the dear Old Briar-patch.

So Peter waited and waited. Twice Bowser the Hound, who had chased him into the old wall, came over and barked at him and tried to get at him. But the old wall kept Peter safe, and Bowser gave it up. And all the time Peter sat waiting he was in great pain. You see that shiny wire was drawn so tight that it cut into his flesh and hurt dreadfully, and to the other end of the wire was fastened a piece of wood, part of the stake to which the snare had been made fast and which Peter had managed to gnaw and break off.

It was on account of this that Peter was waiting for Mrs. Moon to put out her light. He knew that with that stake dragging after him he would have to go very slowly, and he could not run any more risk of danger than he actually had to. So he waited and waited, and by and by, sure enough, Mrs. Moon put out her light. Peter waited a little longer, listening with all his might. Everything was still. Then Peter crept out of the old stone wall.

Right away trouble began. The stake dragging at the end of the wire fast to his leg caught among the stones and pulled Peter up short. My, how it did hurt! It made the tears come. But Peter shut his teeth hard, and turning back, he worked until he got the stake free. Then he started on once more, dragging the stake after him.

Very slowly across the orchard and under the fence on the other side crept Peter Rabbit, his leg so stiff and sore that he could hardly touch it to the snow, and all the time dragging that piece of stake, which seemed to grow heavier and harder to drag every minute. Peter did not dare to go out across the open fields, for fear some danger might happen along, and he would have no place to hide. So he crept along close to the fences where bushes grow, and this made it very, very hard, for the dragging stake was forever catching in the bushes with a yank at the sore leg which brought Peter up short with a squeal of pain.

This was bad enough, but all the time Peter was filled with a dreadful fear that Hooty the Owl or Granny Fox might just happen along. He had to stop to rest very, very often, and then he would listen and listen. Over and over again he said to himself:

"Oh, dear, whatever did I go up to the young peach orchard for when I knew I had no business there? Why couldn't I have been content with all the good things that were mine in the Green Forest and on the Green Meadows? Oh, dear! Oh, dear!"

Just as jolly, round, red Mr. Sun began to light up the Green Meadows, Peter Rabbit reached the dear Old Briar-patch. Danny Meadow Mouse was sitting on the edge of it anxiously watching for him. Peter crawled up and started to creep in along one of his little private paths. He got in himself, but the dragging stake caught among the brambles, and Peter just fell down in the snow right where he was, too tired and worn out to move.

Day 122

1. Read chapter 17 of *The Adventures of Danny Meadow Mouse*.
2. Tell someone what happened in this chapter.

CHAPTER XVII Danny Meadow Mouse Becomes Worried

Danny Meadow Mouse limped around through the dear Old Briar-patch, where he had lived with Peter Rabbit ever since he had squirmed out of the claws of Hooty the Owl and dropped there, right at the feet of Peter Rabbit. Danny limped because he was still lame and sore from Hooty's terrible claws, but he didn't let himself think much about that, because he was so thankful to be alive at all. So he limped around in the Old Briar-patch, picking up seed which had fallen on the snow, and sometimes pulling down a few of the red berries which cling all winter to the wild rose bushes. The seeds in these were very nice indeed, and Danny always felt especially good after a meal of them.

Danny Meadow Mouse had grown very fond of Peter Rabbit, for Peter had been very, very good to him. Danny felt that he never, never could repay all of Peter's kindness. It had been very good of Peter to offer to share the Old Briar-patch with Danny, because Danny was so far from his own home that it would not be safe for him to try to get back there. But Peter had done more than that. He had taken care of Danny, such good care, during the first few days after Danny's escape from Hooty the Owl. He had brought good things to eat while Danny was too weak and sore to get things for himself. Oh, Peter had been very good indeed to him!

But now, as Danny limped around, he was not happy. No, sir, he was not happy. The truth is, Danny Meadow Mouse was worried. It was a different kind of worry from any he had known before. You see, for the first time in his life, Danny was worrying about someone else. He was worrying about Peter Rabbit. Peter had been gone from the Old Briar-patch a whole night and a whole day. He often was gone all night, but never all day too. Danny was sure that something had happened to Peter. He thought of how he had begged Peter not to go up to Farmer Brown's young peach orchard. He had felt in his bones that it was not safe, that something dreadful would happen to Peter. How Peter had laughed at him and bravely started off! Why hadn't he come home?

As he limped around, Danny talked to himself:

"Why cannot people be content
With all the good things that are sent,
And mind their own affairs at home
Instead of going forth to roam?"

It was now the second night since Peter Rabbit had gone away. Danny Meadow Mouse couldn't sleep at all. Round and round through the Old Briar-patch he limped, and finally sat down at the edge of it to wait and watch. At last, just as jolly, round, red Mr. Sun sent his first long rays of light across the Green Meadows, Danny saw something crawling towards the Old Briar-patch. He rubbed his eyes and looked again. It was--no, it couldn't be--yes, it was Peter Rabbit! But what was the matter with him? Always before Peter had come home lipperty-lipperty-lipperty-lip, but now he was crawling, actually crawling! Danny Meadow Mouse didn't know what to make of it.

Nearer and nearer came Peter. Something was following him. No, Peter was dragging something after him. At last Peter started to crawl along one of his little private paths into the Old Briar-patch. The thing dragging behind caught in the brambles, and Peter fell headlong in the snow, too tired and worn out to move. Then Danny saw what the trouble was. A wire was fast to one of Peter's long hind legs, and to the other end of the wire was fastened part of a stake. Peter had been caught in a snare! Danny hurried over to Peter and tears stood in his eyes.

"Poor Peter Rabbit! Oh, I'm so sorry, Peter!" he whispered.

Day 123

1. Read chapter 18 of *The Adventures of Danny Meadow Mouse.*
2. Tell someone what happened in this chapter.

CHAPTER XVIII Danny Meadow Mouse Returns a Kindness

There Peter Rabbit lay. He had dragged that piece of stake a long way, a very long way, indeed. But now he could drag it no farther, for it had caught in the bramble bushes. So Peter just dropped on the snow and cried. Yes, sir, he cried! You see he was so tired and worn out and frightened, and his leg was so stiff and sore and hurt him so! And then it was so dreadful to actually get home and be stopped right on your very own doorstep. So Peter just lay there and cried. Just supposing old Granny Fox should come poking around and find Peter caught that way! All she would have to do would be to get hold of that hateful stake caught in the bramble bushes and pull Peter out where she could get him. Do you wonder that Peter cried?

By and by he became aware that someone was wiping away his tears. It was Danny Meadow Mouse. And Danny was singing in a funny little voice. Pretty soon Peter stopped crying and listened, and this is what he heard:

"Isn't any use to cry!
  Not a bit! Not a bit!
Wipe your eyes and wipe 'em dry!
  Use your wit! Use your wit!
Just remember that tomorrow
Never brings a single sorrow.
Yesterday has gone forever
And to-morrow gets here never.
Chase your worries all away;
Nothing's worse than just to-day."

Peter smiled in spite of himself.

"That's right! That's right! Smile away, Peter Rabbit. Smile away! Your troubles, sir, are all to-day. And between you and me, I don't believe they are so bad as you think they are. Now you lie still just where you are, while I go see what can be done."

With that off whisked Danny Meadow Mouse as spry as you please, in spite of his lame leg, and in a few minutes Peter knew by little twitches of the wire on his leg that Danny was doing something at the other end. He was. Danny Meadow Mouse had set out to gnaw that piece of stake all to splinters. So there he sat and gnawed and gnawed and gnawed. Jolly, round, red Mr. Sun climbed higher and higher in the sky, and Danny Meadow Mouse grew hungry, but still he kept right on gnawing at that bothersome stake.

By and by, happening to look across the snow-covered Green Meadows, he saw something that made his heart jump. It was Farmer Brown's boy coming straight over towards the dear Old Briar-patch.

Danny didn't say a word to Peter Rabbit, but gnawed faster than ever.

Farmer Brown's boy was almost there when Danny stopped gnawing. There was only a tiny bit of the stake left now, and Danny hurried to tell Peter Rabbit that there was nothing to stop him now from going to his most secret retreat in the very heart of the Old

Briar-patch. While Peter slowly dragged his way along, Danny trotted behind to see that the wire did not catch on the bushes.

They had safely reached Peter Rabbit's secretest retreat when Farmer Brown's boy came up to the edge of the dear Old Briar-patch.

"So this is where that rabbit that killed our peach tree lives!" said he. "We'll try a few snares and put you out of mischief."

And for the rest of the afternoon Farmer Brown's boy was very busy around the edge of the Old Briar-patch.

Day 124

1. Read chapter 19 of *The Adventures of Danny Meadow Mouse*.
2. Tell someone what happened in the chapter.

CHAPTER XIX Peter Rabbit and Danny Meadow Mouse Live High

Peter Rabbit sat in his secretest place in the dear Old Briar-patch with one of his long hind legs all swelled up and terribly sore because of the fine wire fast around it and cutting into it. He could hear Farmer Brown's boy going around on the edge of the dear Old Briar-patch and stopping every little while to do something. In spite of his pain, Peter was curious. Finally he called Danny Meadow Mouse.

"Danny, you are small and can keep out of sight easier than I can. Go as near as ever you dare to Farmer Brown's boy and find out what he is doing," said Peter Rabbit.

So Danny Meadow Mouse crept out as near to Farmer Brown's boy as ever he dared and studied and studied to make out what Farmer Brown's boy was doing. By and by he returned to Peter Rabbit.

"I don't know what he's doing, Peter, but he's putting something in every one of your private little paths leading into the Briar-patch from the Green Meadows."

"Ha!" said Peter Rabbit.

"There are little loops of that queer stuff you've got hanging to your leg, Peter," continued Danny Meadow Mouse.

"Just so!" said Peter Rabbit.

"And he's put cabbage leaves and pieces of apple all around," said Danny.

"We must be careful!" said Peter Rabbit.

Peter's leg was in a very bad way, indeed, and Peter suffered a great deal of pain. The worst of it was, he didn't know how to get off the wire that was cutting into it so. He had tried to cut the wire with his big teeth, but he couldn't do it. Danny Meadow Mouse had tried and tried to gnaw the wire, but it wasn't the least bit of use. But Danny wasn't easily discouraged, and he kept working and working at it. Once he thought he felt it slip a little. He said nothing, but kept right on working. Pretty soon he was sure that it slipped. He went right on working harder than ever. By and by he had it so loose that he slipped it right off of Peter's leg, and Peter didn't know anything about it. You see, that cruel wire snare had been so tight that Peter didn't have any feeling except of pain left in his leg, and so when Danny Meadow Mouse pulled the cruel wire snare off, Peter didn't know it until Danny held it up in front of him.

My, how thankful Peter was, and how he did thank Danny Meadow Mouse! But Danny said that it was nothing at all, just nothing at all, and that he owed more than that to Peter Rabbit for being so good to him and letting him live in the dear Old Briar-patch.

It was a long time before Peter could hop as he used to, but after the first day he managed to get around. He found that Farmer Brown's boy had spread those miserable wire snares in every one of his private little paths. But Peter knew what they were now. He showed Danny Meadow Mouse how he, because he was so small, could safely run about among the snares and steal all the cabbage leaves and apples which Farmer Brown's boy had put there for bait.

Danny Meadow Mouse thought this great fun and a great joke on Farmer Brown's boy. So every day he stole the bait, and he and Peter Rabbit lived high while Peter's leg was getting well. And all the time Farmer Brown's boy wondered why he couldn't catch Peter Rabbit.

Day 125

1. Read chapter 20 of *The Adventures of Danny Meadow Mouse*.
2. Tell someone what happened in this chapter.

CHAPTER XX Timid Danny Meadow Mouse

Danny Meadow Mouse is timid. Everybody says so, and what everybody says ought to be so. But just as anybody can make a mistake sometimes, so can everybody. Still, in this case, it is quite likely that everybody is right. Danny Meadow Mouse is timid. Ask Peter Rabbit. Ask Sammy Jay. Ask Striped Chipmunk. They will all tell you the same thing. Sammy Jay might even tell you that Danny is afraid of his own shadow, or that he tries to run away from his own tail. Of course this isn't true. Sammy Jay likes to say mean things. It isn't fair to Danny Meadow Mouse to believe what Sammy Jay says.

But the fact is Danny certainly is timid. More than this, he isn't ashamed of it--not the least little bit.

"You see, it's this way," said Danny, as he sat on his doorstep one sunny morning talking to his friend, old Mr. Toad. "If I weren't afraid, I wouldn't be all the time watching out, and if I weren't all the time watching out, I wouldn't have any more chance than that foolish red ant running across in front of you."

Old Mr. Toad looked where Danny was pointing, and his tongue darted out and back again so quickly that Danny wasn't sure that he saw it at all, but when he looked for the ant it was nowhere to be seen, and there was a satisfied twinkle in Mr. Toad's eyes. There was an answering twinkle in Danny's own eyes as he continued.

"No, sir," said he, "I wouldn't stand a particle more chance than that foolish ant did. Now if I were big and strong, like Old Man Coyote, or had swift wings, like Skimmer the Swallow, or were so homely and ugly-looking that no one wanted me, like--like--" Danny hesitated and then finished rather lamely, "like some folks I know, I suppose I wouldn't be afraid."

Old Mr. Toad looked up sharply when Danny mentioned homely and ugly-looking people, but Danny was gazing far out across the Green Meadows and looked so innocent that Mr. Toad concluded that he couldn't have had him in mind.

"Well," said he, thoughtfully scratching his nose, "I suppose you may be right, but for my part fear seems a very foolish thing. Now, I don't know what it is. I mind my own business, and no one ever bothers me. I should think it would be a very uncomfortable feeling."

"It is," replied Danny, "but, as I said before, it is a very good thing to keep one on guard when there are as many watching for one as there are for me. Now there's Mr. Blacksnake and--"

"Where?" exclaimed old Mr. Toad, turning as pale as a toad can turn, and looking uneasily and anxiously in every direction.

Danny turned his head to hide a smile. If old Mr. Toad wasn't showing fear, no one ever did. "Oh," said he, "I didn't mean that he is anywhere around here now. What I was going to say was that there is Mr. Blacksnake and Granny Fox and Reddy Fox and Redtail the Hawk and Hooty the Owl and others I might name, always watching for a chance to make a dinner from poor little me. Do you wonder that I am afraid most of the time?"

"No," replied old Mr. Toad. "No, I don't wonder that you are afraid. It must be dreadful to feel hungry eyes are watching for you every minute of the day and night, too."

"Oh, it's not so bad," replied Danny. "It's rather exciting. Besides, it keeps my wits sharp all the time. I am afraid I should find life very dull indeed if, like you, I feared nothing and nobody. By the way, see how queerly that grass is moving over there. It looks as if Mr. Blacksnake--Why, Mr. Toad, where are you going in such a hurry?"

"I've just remembered an important engagement with my cousin, Grandfather Frog, at the Smiling Pool," shouted old Mr. Toad over his shoulder, as he hurried so that he fell over his own feet.

Danny chuckled as he sat alone on his doorstep. "Oh, no, old Mr. Toad doesn't know what fear is!" said he. "Funny how some people won't admit what everybody can see for themselves. Now, I am afraid, and I'm willing to say so."

Day 126

1. Read chapter 21 of *The Adventures of Danny Meadow Mouse.*
2. Tell someone about this chapter.

CHAPTER XXI An Exciting Day for Danny Meadow Mouse

Danny Meadow Mouse started along one of his private little paths very early one morning. He was on his way to get a supply of a certain kind of grass seed of which he is very fond. He had been thinking about that seed for some time and waiting for it to get ripe. Now it was just right, as he had found out the day before by a visit to the place where this particular grass grew. The only trouble was it grew a long way from Danny's home, and to reach it he had to cross an open place where the grass was so short that he couldn't make a path under it.

"I feel it in my bones that this is going to be an exciting day," said Danny to himself as he trotted along. "I suppose that if I were really wise, I would stay nearer home and do without that nice seed. But nothing is really worth having unless it is worth working for, and that seed will taste all the better if I have hard work getting it."

So he trotted along his private little path, his ears wide open, and his eyes wide open, and his little nose carefully testing every Merry Little Breeze who happened along for any scent of danger which it might carry. Most of all he depended upon his ears, for the grass was so tall that he couldn't see over it, even when he sat up. He had gone only a little way when he thought he heard a queer rustling behind him. He stopped to listen. There it was again, and it certainly was right in the path behind him! He didn't need to be told who was making it. There was only one who could make such a sound as that--Mr. Blacksnake.

Now Danny can run very fast along his private little paths, but he knew that Mr. Blacksnake could run faster. "If my legs can't save me, my wits must," thought Danny as he started to run as fast as ever he could. "I must reach that fallen old hollow fence-post."

He was almost out of breath when he reached the post and scurried into the open end. He knew by the sound of the rustling that Mr. Blacksnake was right at his heels. Now the old post was hollow its whole length, but halfway there was an old knot-hole just big enough for Danny to squeeze through. Mr. Blacksnake didn't know anything about that hole; and because it was dark inside the old post, he didn't see Danny pop through it. Danny ran back along the top of the log and was just in time to see the tip of Mr. Blacksnake's tail disappear inside. Then what do you think Danny did? Why, he followed Mr. Blacksnake right into the old post, but in doing it he didn't make the least little bit of noise.

Mr. Blacksnake kept right on through the old post and out the other end, for he was sure that that was the way Danny had gone. He kept right on along the little path. Now Danny knew that he wouldn't go very far before he found out that he had been fooled, and of course he would come back. So Danny waited only long enough to get his breath and then ran back along the path to where another little path branched off. For just a minute he paused.

"If Mr. Blacksnake follows me, he will be sure to think that of course I have taken this other little path," thought Danny, "so I won't do it."

Then he ran harder than ever, until he came to a place where two little paths branched off, one to the right and one to the left. He took the latter and scampered on, sure that by this time Mr. Blacksnake would be so badly fooled that he would give up the chase. And Danny was right.

"Brains are better far than speed
As wise men long ago agreed,"

said Danny, as he trotted on his way for the grass seed he liked so well. "I felt it in my bones that this would be an exciting day. I wonder what next."

Day 127

1. Read chapter 22 of *The Adventures of Danny Meadow Mouse*.
2. Tell someone what happened in the chapter.

CHAPTER XXII What Happened Next to Danny Meadow Mouse

Danny is so used to narrow escapes that he doesn't waste any time thinking about them. He didn't this time. "He who tries to look two ways at once is pretty sure to see nothing," says Danny, and he knew that if he thought too much about the things that had already happened, he couldn't keep a sharp watch for the things that might happen.

Nothing more happened as he hurried along his private little path to the edge of a great patch of grass so short that he couldn't hide under it. He had to cross this, and all the way he would be in plain sight of anyone who happened to be near. Very cautiously he peeped out and looked this way and looked that way, not forgetting to look up in the sky. He could see no one anywhere. Drawing a long breath, Danny started across the open place as fast as his short legs could take him.

Now all the time, Redtail the Hawk had been sitting in a tree some distance away, sitting so still that he looked like a part of the tree itself. That is why Danny hadn't seen him. But Redtail saw Danny the instant he started across the open place, for Redtail's eyes are very keen, and he can see a great distance. With a satisfied chuckle, he spread his broad wings and started after Danny.

Just about halfway to the safety of the long grass on the other side, Danny gave a hurried look behind him, and his heart seemed to jump right into his mouth, for there was Redtail with his cruel claws already set to seize him! Danny gave a frightened squeak, for he thought that surely this time he would be caught. But he didn't mean to give up without trying to escape. Three jumps ahead of him was a queer-looking thing. He didn't know what it was, but if there was a hole in it he might yet fool Redtail.

One jump! Would he be able to reach it? Two jumps! There was a hole in it! Three jumps! With another frightened squeak, Danny dived into the opening just in time. And what do you think he was in? Why, an old tomato can Farmer Brown's boy had once used to carry bait in when he went fishing at the Smiling Pool. He had dropped it there on his way home.

Redtail screamed with rage and disappointment as he struck the old can with his great claws. He had been sure, very sure of Danny Meadow Mouse this time! He tried to pick the can up, but he couldn't get hold of it. It just rolled away from him every time, try as he would. Finally, in disgust, he gave up and flew back to the tree from which he had first seen Danny.

Of course Danny had been terribly frightened when the can rolled, and by the noise the claws of Redtail made when they struck his queer hiding place. But he wisely decided that the best thing he could do was to stay there for a while. And it was very fortunate that he did so, as he was very soon to find out.

Day 128

1. Read chapter 23 of *The Adventures of Danny Meadow Mouse*.
2. Tell someone what happened in this chapter.

CHAPTER XXIII Reddy Fox Grows Curious

Danny Meadow Mouse had sat perfectly still for a long time inside the old tomato can in which he had found a refuge from Redtail the Hawk. He didn't dare so much as put his head out for a look around, lest Redtail should be circling overhead ready to pounce on him.

"If I stay here long enough, he'll get tired and go away, if he hasn't already," thought Danny. "This has been a pretty exciting morning so far, and I find that I am a little tired. I may as well take a nap while I am waiting to make sure that the way is clear."

With that Danny curled up in the old tomato can. But it wasn't meant that Danny should have that nap. He had closed his eyes, but his ears were still open, and presently he heard soft footsteps drawing near. His eyes flew open, and he forgot all about sleep, you may be sure, for those footsteps sounded familiar. They sounded to Danny very, very much like the footsteps of--whom do you think? Why, Reddy Fox! Danny's heart began to beat faster as he listened. Could it be? He didn't dare peep out. Presently a little whiff of scent blew into the old tomato can. Then Danny knew--it was Reddy Fox.

"Oh, dear! I hope he doesn't find that I am in here!" thought Danny. "I wonder what under the sun has brought him up here just now."

If the truth were to be known, it was curiosity that had brought Reddy up there. Reddy had been hunting for his breakfast some distance away on the Green Meadows when Redtail the Hawk had tried so hard to catch Danny Meadow Mouse. Reddy's sharp eyes had seen Redtail the minute he left the tree in pursuit of Danny, and he had known by the way Redtail flew that he saw something he wanted to catch. He had watched Redtail swoop down and had heard his scream of rage when he missed Danny because Danny had dodged into the old tomato can. He had seen Redtail strike and strike again at something on the ground, and finally fly off in disgust with empty claws.

"Now, I wonder what it was Redtail was after and why he didn't get it," thought Reddy. "He acts terribly put out and disappointed. I believe I'll go over there and find out."

Off he started at a smart trot towards the patch of short grass where he had seen Redtail the Hawk striking at something on the ground. As he drew near, he crept very softly until he reached the very edge of the open patch. There he stopped and looked sharply all over it. There was nothing to be seen but an old tomato can. Reddy had seen it many times before.

"Now what under the sun could Redtail have been after here?" thought Reddy. "The grass isn't long enough for a grasshopper to hide in, and yet Redtail didn't get what he was after. It's very queer. It certainly is very queer."

He trotted out and began to run back and forth with his nose to the ground, hoping that his nose would tell him what his eyes couldn't. Back and forth, back and forth he ran, and then suddenly he stopped.

"Ha!" exclaimed Reddy. He had found the scent left by Danny Meadow Mouse when he ran across towards the old tomato can. Right up to the old can Reddy's nose led him. He hopped over the old can, but on the other side he could find no scent of Danny Meadow Mouse. In a flash he understood, and a gleam of satisfaction shone in his yellow eyes as he turned back to the old can. He knew that Danny must be hiding in there.

"I've got you this time!" he snarled, as he sniffed at the opening in the end of the can.

Day 129

1. Read chapter 24 of *The Adventures of Danny Meadow Mouse*.
2. Tell someone what happened in the whole book!

CHAPTER XXIV Reddy Fox Loses His Temper

Reddy Fox had caught Danny Meadow Mouse, and yet he hadn't caught him. He had found Danny hiding in the old tomato can, and it didn't enter Reddy's head that he couldn't get Danny out when he wanted to. He was in no hurry. He had had a pretty good breakfast of grasshoppers, and so he thought he would torment Danny a while before gobbling him up. He lay down so that he could peep in at the open end of the old can and see Danny trying to make himself as small as possible at the other end. Reddy grinned until he showed all his long teeth. Reddy always is a bully, especially when his victim is a great deal smaller and weaker than himself.

"I've got you this time, Mr. Smarty, haven't I?" taunted Reddy.

Danny didn't say anything.

"You think you've been very clever because you have fooled me two or three times, don't you? Well, this time I've got you where your tricks won't work," continued Reddy, "so what are you going to do about it?"

Danny didn't answer. The fact is, he was too frightened to answer. Besides, he didn't know what he could do. So he just kept still, but his bright eyes never once left Reddy's cruel face. For all his fright, Danny was doing some hard thinking. He had been in tight places before and had learned never to give up hope. Something might happen to frighten Reddy away. Anyway, Reddy had to get him out of that old can before he would admit that he was really caught.

For a long time Reddy lay there licking his chops and saying all the things he could think of to frighten poor Danny Meadow Mouse. At last he grew tired of this and made up his mind that it was time to end it and Danny Meadow Mouse at the same time. He thrust his sharp nose in at the opening in the end of the old can, but the opening was too small for him to get more than his nose in, and he only scratched it on the sharp edges without so much as touching Danny.

"I'll pull you out," said Reddy and thrust in one black paw.

Danny promptly bit it so hard that Reddy yelped with pain and pulled it out in a hurry. Presently he tried again with the other paw. Danny bit this one harder still, and Reddy danced with pain and anger. Then he lost his temper completely, a very foolish thing to do, as it always is. He hit the old can, and away it rolled with Danny Meadow Mouse inside. This seemed to make Reddy angrier than ever. He sprang after it and hit it again. Then he batted it first this way and then that way, growing angrier and angrier. And all the time Danny Meadow Mouse managed to keep inside, although he got a terrible shaking up.

Back and forth across the patch of short grass Reddy knocked the old can, and he was in such a rage that he didn't notice where he was knocking it to. Finally he sent it spinning into the long grass on the far side of the open patch, close to one of Danny's private little paths. Like a flash Danny was out and scurrying along the little path. He dodged into another and presently into a third, which brought him to a tangle of barbed wire left there by Farmer Brown when he had built a new fence. Under this he was safe.

"Phew!" exclaimed Danny, breathing very hard. "That was the narrowest escape yet! But I guess I'll get that special grass seed I started out for, after all."

And he did, while to this day Reddy Fox wonders how Danny got out of the old tomato can without his knowing it.

And so you see what temper does
  For those who give it rein;
It cheats them of the very thing
  They seek so hard to gain.

Day 130

1. Write a book report.
2. Write on a page the title of the book, the author, the characters (who the story was about), what happened to them and your favorite part. Then you can add a picture.
3. You could give this to a parent to add to your portfolio.

Day 131

1. Synonyms are words that mean the same thing. An example would be that the words big and large mean the same thing. They are synonyms. Can you think of synonyms for the following words? (Answers)

angry begin awful shut under choose simple correct say soil

Day 132

1. Antonyms are words that mean the opposite. An example would be that the words big and small mean the opposite. They are antonyms. Can you think of antonyms for the following words? (Answers)

day question more forget bent difficult push none real quiet

Day 133

1. Remember word families? When you can read one word in the family, you can read them all. When you come across a word you don't know, look for familiar pieces in the word.
2. Think of as many words as you can that end with each of the given endings. All of your words will rhyme! (Answers)
3. Here's my example. If I give you AT, you can think of bat, cat, fat, hat, mat, Nat, sat, vat, etc.

4. Now it's your turn. Come up with as many words as you can for each word family.

    __ET   __ IN   __AD   __OP   __UT

Day 134

1. Can you put these groups of words in order? (Answers)
2. Here's one ordered list as an example:

    good better best

    Group 1: muddy   muddiest   muddier

    Group 2: saddest   sadder   sad

    Group 3: more beautiful   most beautiful   beautiful

    Group 4: friendlier   friendly   friendliest

    Group 5: slimy   slimiest   slimier

    Group 6: most interesting   interesting   more interesting

Day 135

1. <u>Homophones</u> are words that sound the same but are spelled differently.
2. Remember <u>synonyms</u> and <u>antonyms</u>? Which pair of words is which? (Answers)
3. This activity continues onto the next page.

enter/exit   deer/dear   ant/aunt

bother/annoy   conclusion/ending   create/destroy blue/blew   connect/join   trade/swap

listen/ignore   right/write   shiny/dull

Day 136

1. Read chapter 1 of *Buster Bear* by Thornton Burgess. I hope this book makes you laugh.
2. Tell someone what happened in this chapter.

I BUSTER BEAR GOES FISHING

Buster Bear yawned as he lay on his comfortable bed of leaves and watched the first early morning sunbeams creeping through the Green Forest to chase out the Black Shadows. Once more he yawned, and slowly got to his feet and shook himself. Then he walked over to a big pine-tree, stood up on his hind legs, reached as high up on the trunk of the tree as he could, and scratched the bark with his great claws. After that he yawned until it seemed as if his jaws would crack, and then sat down to think what he wanted for breakfast.

While he sat there, trying to make up his mind what would taste best, he was listening to the sounds that told of the waking of all the little people who live in the Green Forest. He heard Sammy Jay way off in the distance screaming, "Thief! Thief!" and grinned. "I wonder," thought Buster, "if some one has stolen Sammy's breakfast, or if he has stolen the breakfast of some one else. Probably he is the thief himself."

He heard Chatterer the Red Squirrel scolding as fast as he could make his tongue go and working himself into a terrible rage. "Must be that Chatterer got out of bed the wrong way this morning," thought he.

He heard Blacky the Crow cawing at the top of his lungs, and he knew by the sound that Blacky was getting into mischief of some kind. He heard the sweet voices of happy little singers, and they were good to hear. But most of all he listened to a merry, low, silvery laugh that never stopped but went on and on, until he just felt as if he must laugh too. It was the voice of the Laughing Brook. And as Buster listened it suddenly came to him just what he wanted for breakfast.

"I'm going fishing," said he in his deep grumbly-rumbly voice to no one in particular. "Yes, Sir, I'm going fishing. I want some fat trout for my breakfast."

He shuffled along over to the Laughing Brook, and straight to a little pool of which he knew, and as he drew near he took the greatest care not to make the teeniest, weeniest bit of noise. Now it just happened that early as he was, some one was before Buster Bear. When he came in sight of the little pool, who should he see but another fisherman there, who had already caught a fine fat trout. Who was it? Why, Little Joe Otter to be sure. He was just climbing up the bank with the fat trout in his mouth. Buster Bear's own mouth watered as he saw it. Little Joe sat down on the bank and prepared to enjoy his breakfast. He hadn't seen Buster Bear, and he didn't know that he or any one else was anywhere near.

Buster Bear tiptoed up very softly until he was right behind Little Joe Otter. "Woof, woof!" said he in his deepest, most grumbly-rumbly voice. "That's a very fine looking trout. I wouldn't mind if I had it myself."

Little Joe Otter gave a frightened squeal and without even turning to see who was speaking dropped his fish and dived headfirst into the Laughing Brook. Buster Bear sprang forward and with one of his big paws caught the fat trout just as it was slipping back into the water.

"Here's your trout, Mr. Otter," said he, as Little Joe put his head out of water to see who had frightened him so. "Come and get it."

But Little Joe wouldn't. The fact is, he was afraid to. He snarled at Buster Bear and called him a thief and everything bad he could think of. Buster didn't seem to mind. He chuckled as if he thought it all a great joke and repeated his invitation to Little Joe to come and get his fish. But Little Joe just turned his back and went off down the Laughing Brook in a great rage.

"It's too bad to waste such a fine fish," said Buster thoughtfully. "I wonder what I'd better do with it." And while he was wondering, he ate it all up. Then he started down the Laughing Brook to try to catch some for himself.

Day 137

1. Read chapter 2 of *Buster Bear* by Thornton Burgess.
2. Tell someone what happened in the chapter.

II LITTLE JOE OTTER GETS EVEN WITH BUSTER BEAR

Little Joe Otter was in a terrible rage. It was a bad beginning for a beautiful day and Little Joe knew it. But who wouldn't be in a rage if his breakfast was taken from him just as he was about to eat it? Anyway, that is what Little Joe told Billy Mink. Perhaps he didn't tell it quite exactly as it was, but you know he was very badly frightened at the time.

"I was sitting on the bank of the Laughing Brook beside one of the little pools," he told Billy Mink, "and was just going to eat a fat trout I had caught, when who should come along but that great big bully, Buster Bear. He took that fat trout away from me and ate it just as if it belonged to him! I hate him! If I live long enough I'm going to get even with him!"

Of course that wasn't nice talk and anything but a nice spirit, but Little Joe Otter's temper is sometimes pretty short, especially when he is hungry, and this time he had had no breakfast, you know.

Buster Bear hadn't actually taken the fish away from Little Joe. But looking at the matter as Little Joe did, it amounted to the same thing. You see, Buster knew perfectly well when he invited Little Joe to come back and get it that Little Joe wouldn't dare do anything of the kind.

"Where is he now?" asked Billy Mink.

"He's somewhere up the Laughing Brook. I wish he'd fall in and get drowned!" snapped Little Joe.

Billy Mink just had to laugh. The idea of great big Buster Bear getting drowned in the Laughing Brook was too funny. There wasn't water enough in it anywhere except down in the Smiling Pool, and that was on the Green Meadows, where Buster had never been known to go. "Let's go see what he is doing," said Billy Mink.

At first Little Joe didn't want to, but at last his curiosity got the better of his fear, and he agreed. So the two little brown-coated scamps turned down the Laughing Brook, taking the greatest care to keep out of sight themselves. They had gone only a little way when Billy Mink whispered: "Sh-h! There he is."

Sure enough, there was Buster Bear sitting close beside a little pool and looking into it very intently.

"What's he doing?" asked Little Joe Otter, as Buster Bear sat for the longest time without moving.

Just then one of Buster's big paws went into the water as quick as a flash and scooped out a trout that had ventured too near.

"He's fishing!" exclaimed Billy Mink.

And that is just what Buster Bear was doing, and it was very plain to see that he was having great fun. When he had eaten the trout he had caught, he moved along to the next little pool.

"They are our fish!" said Little Joe fiercely. "He has no business catching our fish!"

"I don't see how we are going to stop him," said Billy Mink.

"I do!" cried Little Joe, into whose head an idea had just popped. "I'm going to drive all the fish out of the little pools and muddy the water all up. Then we'll see how many fish he will get! Just you watch me get even with Buster Bear."

Little Joe slipped swiftly into the water and swam straight to the little pool that Buster Bear would try next. He frightened the fish so that they fled in every direction. Then he stirred up the mud until the water was so dirty that Buster couldn't have seen a fish right under his nose. He did the same thing in the next pool and the next. Buster Bear's fishing was spoiled for that day.

Day 138

1. Read chapter 3 of *Buster Bear* by Thornton Burgess.
2. Tell someone about this chapter.

III BUSTER BEAR IS GREATLY PUZZLED

Buster Bear hadn't enjoyed himself so much since he came to the Green Forest to live. His fun began when he surprised Little Joe Otter on the bank of a little pool in the Laughing Brook and Little Joe was so frightened that he dropped a fat trout he had just caught. It had seemed like a great joke to Buster Bear, and he had chuckled over it all the time he was eating the fat trout. When he had finished it, he started on to do some fishing himself.

Presently he came to another little pool. He stole up to it very, very softly, so as not to frighten the fish. Then he sat down close to the edge of it and didn't move. Buster learned a long time ago that a fisherman must be patient unless, like Little Joe Otter, he is just as much at home in the water as the fish themselves, and can swim fast enough to catch them by chasing them. So he didn't move so much as an eye lash. He was so still that he looked almost like the stump of an old tree. Perhaps that is what the fish thought he was, for pretty soon, two or three swam right in close to where he was sitting. Now Buster Bear may be big and clumsy looking, but there isn't anything that can move much quicker than one of those big paws of his when he wants it to. One of them moved now, and quicker than a wink had scooped one of those foolish fish out on to the bank.

Buster's little eyes twinkled, and he smacked his lips as he moved on to the next little pool, for he knew that it was of no use to stay longer at the first one. The fish were so frightened that they wouldn't come back for a long, long time. At the next little pool the same thing happened. By this time Buster Bear was in fine spirits. It was fun to catch the fish, and it was still more fun to eat them. What finer breakfast could any one have than fresh-caught trout? No wonder he felt good! But it takes more than three trout to fill Buster Bear's stomach, so he kept on to the next little pool.

But this little pool, instead of being beautiful and clear so that Buster could see right to the bottom of it and so tell if there were any fish there, was so muddy that he couldn't see into it at all. It looked as if some one had just stirred up all the mud at the bottom.

"Huh!" said Buster Bear. "It's of no use to try to fish here. I would just waste my time. I'll try the next pool."

So he went on to the next little pool. He found this just as muddy as the other. Then he went on to another, and this was no better. Buster sat down and scratched his head. It was puzzling. Yes, Sir, it was puzzling. He looked this way and he looked that way suspiciously, but there was no one to be seen. Everything was still save for the laughter of the Laughing Brook. Somehow, it seemed to Buster as if the Brook were laughing at him.

"It's very curious," muttered Buster, "very curious indeed. It looks as if my fishing is spoiled for to-day. I don't understand it at all. It's lucky I caught what I did. It looks as if somebody is trying to--ha!" A sudden thought had popped into his head. Then he began to chuckle and finally to laugh. "I do believe that scamp Joe Otter is trying to get even with me for eating that fat trout!"

And then, because Buster Bear always enjoys a good joke even when it is on himself, he laughed until he had to hold his sides, which is a whole lot better than going off in a rage as Little Joe Otter had done. "You're pretty smart, Mr. Otter! You're pretty smart, but there are other people who are smart too," said Buster Bear, and still chuckling, he went off to think up a plan to get the best of Little Joe Otter.

Day 139

1. Read chapter 4 of *Buster Bear* by Thornton Burgess.
2. Tell someone about this chapter.

IV LITTLE JOE OTTER SUPPLIES BUSTER BEAR WITH A BREAKFAST

Getting even just for spite
  Doesn't always pay.
Fact is, it is very apt
  To work the other way.

That is just how it came about that Little Joe Otter furnished Buster Bear with the best breakfast he had had for a long time. He didn't mean to do it. Oh, my, no! The truth is, he thought all the time that he was preventing Buster Bear from getting a breakfast. You see he wasn't well enough acquainted with Buster to know that Buster is quite as smart as he is, and perhaps a little bit smarter. Spite and selfishness were at the bottom of it. You see Little Joe and Billy Mink had had all the fishing in the Laughing Brook to themselves so long that they thought no one else had any right to fish there. To be sure Bobby Coon caught a few little fish there, but they didn't mind Bobby. Farmer Brown's boy fished there too, sometimes, and this always made Little Joe and Billy Mink very angry, but they were so afraid of him that they didn't dare do anything about it. But when they discovered that Buster Bear was a fisherman, they made up their minds that something had got to be done. At least, Little Joe did.

"He'll try it again to-morrow morning," said Little Joe. "I'll keep watch, and as soon as I see him coming, I'll drive out all the fish, just as I did to-day. I guess that'll teach him to let our fish alone."

So the next morning Little Joe hid before daylight close by the little pool where Buster Bear had given him such a fright. Sure enough, just as the Jolly Sunbeams began to creep through the Green Forest, he saw Buster Bear coming straight over to the little pool. Little Joe slipped into the water and chased all the fish out of the little pool, and stirred up the mud on the bottom so that the water was so muddy that the bottom couldn't be seen at all. Then he hurried down to the next little pool and did the same thing.

Now Buster Bear is very smart. You know he had guessed the day before who had spoiled his fishing. So this morning he only went far enough to make sure that if Little Joe were watching for him, as he was sure he would be, he would see him coming. Then, instead of keeping on to the little pool, he hurried to a place way down the Laughing Brook, where the water was very shallow, hardly over his feet, and there he sat chuckling to himself. Things happened just as he had expected. The frightened fish Little Joe chased out of the little pools up above swam down the Laughing Brook, because, you know, Little Joe was behind them, and there was nowhere else for them to go. When they came to the place where Buster was waiting, all he had to do was to scoop them out on to the bank. It was great fun. It didn't take Buster long to catch all the fish he could eat. Then he saved a nice fat trout and waited.

By and by along came Little Joe Otter, chuckling to think how he had spoiled Buster Bear's fishing. He was so intent on looking behind him to see if Buster was coming that he didn't see Buster waiting there until he spoke.

"I'm much obliged for the fine breakfast you have given me," said Buster in his deepest, most grumbly-rumbly voice. "I've saved a fat trout for you to make up for the one I ate yesterday. I hope we'll go fishing together often."

Then he went off laughing fit to kill himself. Little Joe couldn't find a word to say. He was so surprised and angry that he went off by himself and sulked. And Billy Mink, who had been watching, ate the fat trout.

Day 140

1. Read chapter 5 of *Buster Bear* by Thornton Burgess.
2. Tell someone about this chapter.

V GRANDFATHER FROG'S COMMON-SENSE

There is nothing quite like common sense to smooth out troubles. People who have plenty of just plain common sense are often thought to be very wise. Their neighbors look up to them and are forever running to them for advice, and they are very much respected. That is the way with Grandfather Frog. He is very old and very wise. Anyway, that is what his neighbors think. The truth is, he simply has a lot of common sense, which after all is the very best kind of wisdom.

Now when Little Joe Otter found that Buster Bear had been too smart for him and that instead of spoiling Buster's fishing in the Laughing Brook he had really made it easier for Buster to catch all the fish he wanted, Little Joe went off down to the Smiling Pool in a great rage.

Billy Mink stopped long enough to eat the fat fish Buster had left on the bank and then he too went down to the Smiling Pool.

When Little Joe Otter and Billy Mink reached the Smiling Pool, they climbed up on the Big Rock, and there Little Joe sulked and sulked, until finally Grandfather Frog asked what the matter was. Little Joe wouldn't tell, but Billy Mink told the whole story. When he told how Buster had been too smart for Little Joe, it tickled him so that Billy had to laugh in spite of himself. So did Grandfather Frog. So did Jerry Muskrat, who had been listening. Of course this made Little Joe angrier than ever. He said a lot of unkind things about Buster Bear and about Billy Mink and Grandfather Frog and Jerry Muskrat, because they had laughed at the smartness of Buster.

"He's nothing but a great big bully and thief!" declared Little Joe.

"Chug-a-rum! He may be a bully, because great big people are very apt to be bullies, and though I haven't seen him, I guess Buster Bear is big enough from all I have heard, but I don't see how he is a thief," said Grandfather Frog.

"Didn't he catch my fish and eat them?" snapped Little Joe. "Doesn't that make him a thief?"

"They were no more your fish than mine," protested Billy Mink.

"Well, our fish, then! He stole our fish, if you like that any better. That makes him just as much a thief, doesn't it?" growled Little Joe.

Grandfather Frog looked up at jolly, round, bright Mr. Sun and slowly winked one of his great, goggly eyes. "There comes a foolish green fly," said he. "Who does he belong to?"

"Nobody!" snapped Little Joe. "What have foolish green flies got to do with my--I mean our fish?"

"Nothing, nothing at all," replied Grandfather Frog mildly. "I was just hoping that he would come near enough for me to snap him up; then he would belong to me. As long as he doesn't, he doesn't belong to any one. I suppose that if Buster Bear should happen along and catch him, he would be stealing from me, according to Little Joe."

"Of course not! What a silly idea! You're getting foolish in your old age," retorted Little Joe.

"Can you tell me the difference between the fish that you haven't caught and the foolish green flies that I haven't caught?" asked Grandfather Frog.

Little Joe couldn't find a word to say.

"You take my advice, Little Joe Otter," continued Grandfather Frog, "and always make friends with those who are bigger and stronger and smarter than you are. You'll find it pays."

Day 141

1. Read chapter 6 of *Buster Bear* by Thornton Burgess.
2. Tell someone about this chapter.

VI LITTLE JOE OTTER TAKES GRANDFATHER FROG'S ADVICE

Who makes an enemy a friend,
To fear and worry puts an end.

Little Joe Otter found that out when he took Grandfather Frog's advice. He wouldn't have admitted that he was afraid of Buster Bear. No one ever likes to admit being afraid, least of all Little Joe Otter. And really Little Joe has a great deal of courage. Very few of the little people of the Green Forest or the Green Meadows would willingly quarrel with him, for Little Joe is a great fighter when he has to fight. As for all those who live in or along the Laughing Brook or in the Smiling Pool, they let Little Joe have his own way in everything.

Now having one's own way too much is a bad thing. It is apt to make one selfish and thoughtless of other people and very hard to get along with. Little Joe Otter had his way too much. Grandfather Frog knew it and shook his head very soberly when Little Joe had been disrespectful to him.

"Too bad. Too bad! Too bad! Chug-a-rum! It is too bad that such a fine young fellow as Little Joe should spoil a good disposition by such selfish heedlessness. Too bad," said he.

So, though he didn't let on that it was so, Grandfather Frog really was delighted when he heard how Buster Bear had been too smart for Little Joe Otter. It tickled him so that he had hard work to keep a straight face. But he did and was as grave and solemn as you please as he advised Little Joe always to make friends with any one who was bigger and stronger and smarter than he. That was good common sense advice, but Little Joe just sniffed and went off declaring that he would get even with Buster Bear yet. Now Little Joe is good-natured and full of fun as a rule, and after he had reached home and his temper had cooled off a little, he began to see the joke on himself,--how when he had worked so hard to frighten the fish in the little pools of the Laughing Brook so that Buster Bear should not catch any, he had all the time been driving them right into Buster's paws. By and by he grinned. It was a little sheepish grin at first, but at last it grew into a laugh.

"I believe," said Little Joe as he wiped tears of laughter from his eyes, "that Grandfather Frog is right, and that the best thing I can do is to make friends with Buster Bear. I'll try it to-morrow morning."

So very early the next morning Little Joe Otter went to the best fishing pool he knew of in the Laughing Brook, and there he caught the biggest trout he could find. It was so big and fat that it made Little Joe's mouth water, for you know fat trout are his favorite food. But he didn't take so much as one bite. Instead he carefully laid it on an old log where Buster Bear would be sure to see it if he should come along that way. Then he hid near by, where he could watch. Buster was late that morning. It seemed to Little Joe that he never would come. Once he nearly lost the fish. He had turned his head for just a minute, and when he looked back again, the trout was nowhere to be seen. Buster couldn't have stolen up and taken it, because such a big fellow couldn't possibly have gotten out of sight again.

Little Joe darted over to the log and looked on the other side. There was the fat trout, and there also was Little Joe's smallest cousin, Shadow the Weasel, who is a great thief and altogether bad. Little Joe sprang at him angrily, but Shadow was too quick and darted away. Little Joe put the fish back on the log and waited. This time he didn't take his eyes off it. At last, when he was almost ready to give up, he saw Buster Bear shuffling along towards the Laughing Brook. Suddenly Buster stopped and sniffed. One of the Merry Little Breezes had carried the scent of that fat trout over to him. Then he came straight over to where the fish lay, his nose wrinkling, and his eyes twinkling with pleasure.

"Now I wonder who was so thoughtful as to leave this fine breakfast ready for me," said he out loud.

"Me," said Little Joe in a rather faint voice. "I caught it especially for you."

"Thank you," replied Buster, and his eyes twinkled more than ever. "I think we are going to be friends."

"I--I hope so," replied Little Joe.

Day 142

1. Read chapter 7 of *Buster Bear* by Thornton Burgess.
2. Tell someone about this chapter.

VII FARMER BROWN'S BOY HAS NO LUCK AT ALL

Farmer Brown's boy tramped through the Green Forest, whistling merrily. He always whistles when he feels light-hearted, and he always feels light-hearted when he goes fishing. You see, he is just as fond of fishing as is Little Joe Otter or Billy Mink or Buster Bear. And now he was making his way through the Green Forest to the Laughing Brook, sure that by the time he had followed it down to the Smiling Pool he would have a fine lot of trout to take home. He knew every pool in the Laughing Brook where the trout love to hide, did Farmer Brown's boy, and it was just the kind of a morning when the trout should be hungry. So he whistled as he tramped along, and his whistle was good to hear.

When he reached the first little pool he baited his hook very carefully and then, taking the greatest care to keep out of sight of any trout that might be in the little pool, he began to fish. Now Farmer Brown's boy learned a long time ago that to be a successful fisherman one must have a great deal of patience, so though he didn't get a bite right away as he had expected to, he wasn't the least bit discouraged. He kept very quiet and fished and fished, patiently waiting for a foolish trout to take his hook. But he didn't get so much as a nibble. "Either the trout have lost their appetite or they have grown very wise," muttered Farmer Brown's boy, as after a long time he moved on to the next little pool.

There the same thing happened. He was very patient, very, very patient, but his patience brought no reward, not so much as the faintest kind of a nibble. Farmer Brown's boy trudged on to the next pool, and there was a puzzled frown on his freckled face. Such a thing never had happened before. He didn't know what to make of it. All the night before he had dreamed about the delicious dinner of fried trout he would have the next day, and now--well, if he didn't catch some trout pretty soon, that splendid dinner would never be anything but a dream.

"If I didn't know that nobody else comes fishing here, I should think that somebody had been here this very morning and caught all the fish or else frightened them so that they are all in hiding," said he, as he trudged on to the next little pool. "I never had such bad luck in all my life before. Hello! What's this?"

There, on the bank beside the little pool, were the heads of three trout. Farmer Brown's boy scowled down at them more puzzled than ever. "Somebody has been fishing here, and they have had better luck than I have," thought he. He looked up the Laughing Brook and down the Laughing Brook and this way and that way, but no one was to be seen. Then he picked up one of the little heads and looked at it sharply. "It wasn't cut off with a knife; it was bitten off!" he exclaimed. "I wonder now if Billy Mink is the scamp who has spoiled my fun."

Thereafter he kept a sharp lookout for signs of Billy Mink, but though he found two or three more trout heads, he saw no other signs and he caught no fish. This puzzled him more than ever. It didn't seem possible that such a little fellow as Billy Mink could have caught or frightened all the fish or have eaten so many. Besides, he didn't remember ever having known Billy to leave heads around that way. Billy sometimes catches more fish than he can eat, but then he usually hides them. The farther he went down the Laughing Brook, the more puzzled Farmer Brown's boy grew. It made him feel very queer. He would have felt still more queer if he had known that all the time two other fishermen who had been before him were watching him and chuckling to themselves. They were Little Joe Otter and Buster Bear.

Day 143

1. Read chapter 8 of *Buster Bear* by Thornton Burgess.
2. Tell someone about this chapter.

VIII FARMER BROWN'S BOY FEELS HIS HAIR RISE

'Twas just a sudden odd surprise
Made Farmer Brown's boy's hair to rise.

That's a funny thing for hair to do--rise up all of a sudden--isn't it? But that is just what the hair on Farmer Brown's boy's head did the day he went fishing in the Laughing Brook and had no luck at all. There are just two things that make hair rise--anger and fear. Anger sometimes makes the hair on the back and neck of Bowser the Hound and of some other little people bristle and stand up, and you know the hair on the tail of Black Pussy stands on end until her tail looks twice as big as it really is. Both anger and fear make it do that. But there is only one thing that can make the hair on the head of Farmer Brown's boy rise, and as it isn't anger, of course it must be fear.

It never had happened before. You see, there isn't much of anything that Farmer Brown's boy is really afraid of. Perhaps he wouldn't have been afraid this time if it hadn't been for the surprise of what he found. You see when he had found the heads of those trout on the bank he knew right away that some one else had been fishing, and that was why he couldn't catch any; but it didn't seem possible that little Billy Mink could have eaten all those trout, and Farmer Brown's boy didn't once think of Little Joe Otter, and so he was very, very much puzzled.

He was turning it all over in his mind and studying what it could mean, when he came to a little muddy place on the bank of the Laughing Brook, and there he saw something that made his eyes look as if they would pop right out of his head, and it was right then that he felt his hair rise. Anyway, that is what he said when he told about it afterward. What was it he saw? What do you think? Why, it was a footprint in the soft mud. Yes, Sir, that's what it was, and all it was. But it was the biggest footprint Farmer Brown's boy ever had seen, and it looked as if it had been made only a few minutes before. It was the footprint of Buster Bear.

Now Farmer Brown's boy didn't know that Buster Bear had come down to the Green Forest to live. He never had heard of a Bear being in the Green Forest. And so he was so surprised that he had hard work to believe his own eyes, and he had a queer feeling all over,--a little chilly feeling, although it was a warm day. Somehow, he didn't feel like meeting Buster Bear. If he had had his terrible gun with him, it might have been different. But he didn't, and so he suddenly made up his mind that he didn't want to fish any more that day. He had a funny feeling, too, that he was being watched, although he couldn't see any one. He was being watched. Little Joe Otter and Buster Bear were watching him and taking the greatest care to keep out of his sight.

All the way home through the Green Forest, Farmer Brown's boy kept looking behind him, and he didn't draw a long breath until he reached the edge of the Green Forest. He hadn't run, but he had wanted to.

"Huh!" said Buster Bear to Little Joe Otter, "I believe he was afraid!"

And Buster Bear was just exactly right.

Day 144

1. Read chapter 9 of *Buster Bear* by Thornton Burgess.
2. Tell someone about this chapter.

IX LITTLE JOE OTTER HAS GREAT NEWS TO TELL

Little Joe Otter was fairly bursting with excitement. He could hardly contain himself. He felt that he had the greatest news to tell since Peter Rabbit had first found the tracks of Buster Bear in the Green Forest. He couldn't keep it to himself a minute longer than he had to. So he hurried to the Smiling Pool, where he was sure he would find Billy Mink and Jerry Muskrat and Grandfather Frog and Spotty the Turtle, and he hoped that perhaps some of the little people who live in the Green Forest might be there too. Sure enough, Peter Rabbit was there on one side of the Smiling Pool, making faces at Reddy Fox, who was on the other side, which, of course, was not at all nice of Peter. Mr. and Mrs. Redwing were there, and Blacky the Crow was sitting in the Big Hickory-tree.

Little Joe Otter swam straight to the Big Rock and climbed up to the very highest part. He looked so excited, and his eyes sparkled so, that every one knew right away that something had happened.

"Hi!" cried Billy Mink. "Look at Little Joe Otter! It must be that for once he has been smarter than Buster Bear."

Little Joe made a good-natured face at Billy Mink and shook his head. "No, Billy," said he, "you are wrong, altogether wrong. I don't believe anybody can be smarter than Buster Bear."

Reddy Fox rolled his lips back in an unpleasant grin. "Don't be too sure of that!" he snapped. "I'm not through with him yet."

"Boaster! Boaster!" cried Peter Rabbit.

Reddy glared across the Smiling Pool at Peter. "I'm not through with you either, Peter Rabbit!" he snarled. "You'll find it out one of these fine days!"

"Reddy, Reddy, smart and sly, Couldn't catch a buzzing fly!" taunted Peter.

"Chug-a-rum!" said Grandfather Frog in his deepest, gruffest voice. "We know all about that. What we want to know is what Little Joe Otter has got on his mind."

"It's news--great news!" cried Little Joe.

"We can tell better how great it is when we hear what it is," replied Grandfather Frog testily. "What is it?"

Little Joe Otter looked around at all the eager faces watching him, and then in the slowest, most provoking way, he drawled: "Farmer Brown's boy is afraid of Buster Bear." For a minute no one said a word. Then Blacky the Crow leaned down from his perch in the Big Hickory-tree and looked very hard at Little Joe as he said: "I don't believe it. I don't believe a word of it. Farmer Brown's boy isn't afraid of any one who lives in the Green Forest or on the Green Meadows or in the Smiling Pool, and you know it. We are all afraid of him."

Little Joe glared back at Blacky. "I don't care whether you believe it or not; it's true," he retorted. Then he told how early that very morning he and Buster Bear had been fishing together in the Laughing Brook, and how Farmer Brown's boy had been fishing there too, and hadn't caught a single trout because they had all been caught or frightened before he got there. Then he told how Farmer Brown's boy had found a footprint of Buster Bear in the soft mud, and how he had stopped fishing right away and started for home, looking behind him with fear in his eyes all the way.

"Now tell me that he isn't afraid!" concluded Little Joe. "For once he knows just how we feel when he comes prowling around where we are. Isn't that great news? Now we'll get even with him!"

"I'll believe it when I see it for myself!" snapped Blacky the Crow.

Day 145

1. Read chapter 10 of *Buster Bear* by Thornton Burgess.
2. Tell someone about this chapter.

X BUSTER BEAR BECOMES A HERO

The news that Little Joe Otter told at the Smiling Pool,--how Farmer Brown's boy had run away from Buster Bear without even seeing him,--soon spread all over the Green Meadows and through the Green Forest, until every one who lives there knew about it. Of course, Peter Rabbit helped spread it. Trust Peter for that! But everybody else helped too. You see, they had all been afraid of Farmer Brown's boy for so long that they were tickled almost to pieces at the very thought of having some one in the Green Forest who could make Farmer Brown's boy feel fear as they had felt it. And so it was that Buster Bear became a hero right away to most of them.

A few doubted Little Joe's story. One of them was Blacky the Crow. Another was Reddy Fox. Blacky doubted because he knew Farmer Brown's boy so well that he couldn't imagine him afraid. Reddy doubted because he didn't want to believe. You see, he was jealous of Buster Bear, and at the same time he was afraid of him. So Reddy pretended not to believe a word of what Little Joe Otter had said, and he agreed with Blacky that only by seeing Farmer Brown's boy afraid could he ever be made to believe it. But nearly everybody else believed it, and there was great rejoicing. Most of them were afraid of Buster, very much afraid of him, because he was so big and strong. But they were still more afraid of Farmer Brown's boy, because they didn't know him or understand him, and because in the past he had tried to catch some of them in traps and had hunted some of them with his terrible gun.

So now they were very proud to think that one of their own number actually had frightened him, and they began to look on Buster Bear as a real hero. They tried in ever so many ways to show him how friendly they felt and went quite out of their way to do him favors. Whenever they met one another, all they could talk about was the smartness and the greatness of Buster Bear.

"Now I guess Farmer Brown's boy will keep away from the Green Forest, and we won't have to be all the time watching out for him," said Bobby Coon, as he washed his dinner in the Laughing Brook, for you know he is very neat and particular.

"And he won't dare set any more traps for me," gloated Billy Mink.

"Ah wish Brer Bear would go up to Farmer Brown's henhouse and scare Farmer Brown's boy so that he would keep away from there. It would be a favor to me which Ah cert'nly would appreciate," said Unc' Billy Possum when he heard the news.

"Let's all go together and tell Buster Bear how much obliged we are for what he has done," proposed Jerry Muskrat.

"That's a splendid idea!" cried Little Joe Otter. "We'll do it right away."

"Caw, caw caw!" broke in Blacky the Crow. "I say, let's wait and see for ourselves if it is all true."

"Of course it's true!" snapped Little Joe Otter. "Don't you believe I'm telling the truth?"

"Certainly, certainly. Of course no one doubts your word," replied Blacky, with the utmost politeness. "But you say yourself that Farmer Brown's boy didn't see Buster Bear, but only his footprint. Perhaps he didn't know whose it was, and if he had he wouldn't have been afraid. Now I've got a plan by which we can see for ourselves if he really is afraid of Buster Bear."

"What is it?" asked Sammy Jay eagerly.

Blacky the Crow shook his head and winked. "That's telling," said he. "I want to think it over. If you meet me at the Big Hickory-tree at sun-up to-morrow morning, and get everybody else to come that you can, perhaps I will tell you."

Day 146

1. Read chapter 11 of *Buster Bear* by Thornton Burgess.
2. Tell someone what happened in the chapter.

XI BLACKY THE CROW TELLS HIS PLAN

Blacky is a dreamer!
Blacky is a schemer!
His voice is strong;
When things go wrong
Blacky is a screamer!

It's a fact. Blacky the Crow is forever dreaming and scheming and almost always it is of mischief. He is one of the smartest and cleverest of all the little people of the Green Meadows and the Green Forest, and all the others know it. Blacky likes excitement. He wants something going on. The more exciting it is, the better he likes it. Then he has a chance to use that harsh voice of his, and how he does use it!

So now, as he sat in the top of the Big Hickory-tree beside the Smiling Pool and looked down on all the little people gathered there, he was very happy. In the first place he felt very important, and you know Blacky dearly loves to feel important. They had all come at his invitation to listen to a plan for seeing for themselves if it were really true that Farmer Brown's boy was afraid of Buster Bear.

On the Big Rock in the Smiling Pool sat Little Joe Otter, Billy Mink, and Jerry Muskrat. On his big, green lily-pad sat Grandfather Frog. On another lily-pad sat Spotty the Turtle. On the bank on one side of the Smiling Pool were Peter Rabbit, Jumper the Hare, Danny Meadow Mouse, Johnny Chuck, Jimmy Skunk, Unc' Billy Possum, Striped Chipmunk and Old Mr. Toad. On the other side of the Smiling Pool were Reddy Fox, Digger the Badger, and Bobby Coon. In the Big Hickory-tree were Chatterer the Red Squirrel, Happy Jack the Gray Squirrel, and Sammy Jay.

Blacky waited until he was sure that no one else was coming. Then he cleared his throat very loudly and began to speak. "Friends," said he.

Everybody grinned, for Blacky has played so many sharp tricks that no one is really his friend unless it is that other mischief-maker, Sammy Jay, who, you know, is Blacky's cousin. But no one said anything, and Blacky went on.

"Little Joe Otter has told us how he saw Farmer Brown's boy hurry home when he found the footprint of Buster Bear on the edge of the Laughing Brook, and how all the way he kept looking behind him, as if he were afraid. Perhaps he was, and then again perhaps he wasn't. Perhaps he had something else on his mind. You have made a hero of Buster Bear, because you believe Little Joe's story. Now I don't say that I don't believe it, but I do say that I will be a lot more sure that Farmer Brown's boy is afraid of Buster when I see him run away myself. Now here is my plan: "To-morrow morning, very early, Sammy Jay and I will make a great fuss near the edge of the Green Forest. Farmer Brown's boy has a lot of curiosity, and he will be sure to come over to see what it is all about. Then we will lead him to where Buster Bear is. If he runs away, I will be the first to admit that Buster Bear is as great a hero as some of you seem to think he is. It is a very simple plan, and if you will all hide where you can watch, you will be able to see for yourselves if Little Joe Otter is right. Now what do you say?"

Right away everybody began to talk at the same time. It was such a simple plan that everybody agreed to it. And it promised to be so exciting that everybody promised to be there, that is, everybody but Grandfather Frog and Spotty the Turtle, who didn't care to go so far away from the Smiling Pool. So it was agreed that Blacky should try his plan the very next morning.

Day 147

1. Read chapter 12 of *Buster Bear* by Thornton Burgess.
2. Tell someone what happened in the chapter.

XII FARMER BROWN'S BOY AND BUSTER BEAR GROW CURIOUS

Ever since it was light enough to see at all, Blacky the Crow had been sitting in the top of the tallest tree on the edge of the Green Forest nearest to Farmer Brown's house, and never for an instant had he taken his eyes from Farmer Brown's back door. What was he watching for? Why, for Farmer Brown's boy to come out on his way to milk the cows.

Meanwhile, Sammy Jay was slipping silently through the Green Forest, looking for Buster Bear, so that when the time came he could let his cousin, Blacky the Crow, know just where Buster was.

By and by the back door of Farmer Brown's house opened, and out stepped Farmer Brown's boy. In each hand he carried a milk pail. Right away Blacky began to scream at the top of his lungs. "Caw, caw, caw!" shouted Blacky. "Caw, caw, caw!" And all the time he flew about among the trees near the edge of the Green Forest as if so excited that he couldn't keep still. Farmer Brown's boy looked over there as if he wondered what all that fuss was about, as indeed he did, but he didn't start to go over and see. No, Sir, he started straight for the barn.

Blacky didn't know what to make of it. You see, smart as he is and shrewd as he is, Blacky doesn't know anything about the meaning of duty, for he never has to work excepting to get enough to eat. So, when Farmer Brown's boy started for the barn instead of for the Green Forest, Blacky didn't know what to make of it. He screamed harder and louder than ever, until his voice grew so hoarse he couldn't scream any more, but Farmer Brown's boy kept right on to the barn.

"I'd like to know what you're making such a fuss about, Mr. Crow, but I've got to feed the cows and milk them first," said he.

Now all this time the other little people of the Green Forest and the Green Meadows had been hiding where they could see all that went on. When Farmer Brown's boy disappeared in the barn, Chatterer the Red Squirrel snickered right out loud. "Ha, ha, ha! This is a great plan of yours, Blacky! Ha, ha, ha!" he shouted. Blacky couldn't find a word to say. He just hung his head, which is something Blacky seldom does.

"Perhaps if we wait until he comes out again, he will come over here," said Sammy Jay, who had joined Blacky. So it was decided to wait. It seemed as if Farmer Brown's boy never would come out, but at last he did. Blacky and Sammy Jay at once began to scream and make all the fuss they could. Farmer Brown's boy took the two pails of milk into the house, then out he came and started straight for the Green Forest. He was so curious to know what it all meant that he couldn't wait another minute.

Now there was some one else with a great deal of curiosity also. He had heard the screaming of Blacky the Crow and Sammy Jay, and he had listened until he couldn't stand it another minute. He just had to know what it was all about. So at the same time Farmer Brown's boy started for the Green Forest, this other listener started towards the place where Blacky and Sammy were making such a racket. He walked very softly so as not to make a sound. It was Buster Bear.

Day 148

1. Read chapter 13 of *Buster Bear* by Thornton Burgess.
2. Tell someone what happened in the chapter.

XIII FARMER BROWN'S BOY AND BUSTER BEAR MEET

If you should meet with Buster Bear
  While walking through the wood,
What would you do? Now tell me true,
  I'd run the best I could.

That is what Farmer Brown's boy did when he met Buster Bear, and a lot of the little people of the Green Forest and some from the Green Meadows saw him. When Farmer Brown's boy came hurrying home from the Laughing Brook without any fish one day and told about the great footprint he had seen in a muddy place on the bank deep in the Green Forest, and had said his was sure that it was the footprint of a Bear, he had been laughed at. Farmer Brown had laughed and laughed.

"Why," said he, "there hasn't been a Bear in the Green Forest for years and years and years, not since my own grandfather was a little boy, and that, you know, was a long, long, long time ago. If you want to find Mr. Bear, you will have to go to the Great Woods. I don't know who made that footprint, but it certainly couldn't have been a Bear. I think you must have imagined it."

Then he had laughed some more, all of which goes to show how easy it is to be mistaken, and how foolish it is to laugh at things you really don't know about. Buster Bear had come to live in the Green Forest, and Farmer Brown's boy had seen his footprint. But Farmer Brown laughed so much and made fun of him so much, that at last his boy began to think that he must have been mistaken after all. So when he heard Blacky the Crow and Sammy

Jay making a great fuss near the edge of the Green Forest, he never once thought of Buster Bear, as he started over to see what was going on.

When Blacky and Sammy saw him coming, they moved a little farther in to the Green Forest, still screaming in the most excited way. They felt sure that Farmer Brown's boy would follow them, and they meant to lead him to where Sammy had seen Buster Bear that morning. Then they would find out for sure if what Little Joe Otter had said was true, that Farmer Brown's boy really was afraid of Buster Bear.

Now all around, behind trees and stumps, and under thick branches, and even in tree tops, were other little people watching with round, wide-open eyes to see what would happen. It was very exciting, the most exciting thing they could remember. You see, they had come to believe that Farmer Brown's boy wasn't afraid of anybody or anything, and as most of them were very much afraid of him, they had hard work to believe that he would really be afraid of even such a great, big, strong fellow as Buster Bear. Every one was so busy watching Farmer Brown's boy that no one saw Buster coming from the other direction.

You see, Buster walked very softly. Big as he is, he can walk without making the teeniest, weeniest sound. And that is how it happened that no one saw him or heard him until just as Farmer Brown's boy stepped out from behind one side of a thick little hemlock-tree, Buster Bear stepped out from behind the other side of that same little tree, and there they were face to face! Then everybody held their breath, even Blacky the Crow and Sammy Jay. For just a little minute it was so still there in the Green Forest that not the least little sound could be heard. What was going to happen?

Day 149

1. Read chapter 14 of *Buster Bear* by Thornton Burgess.
2. Tell someone what happened in the chapter.

XIV A SURPRISING THING HAPPENS

Blacky the Crow and Sammy Jay, looking down from the top of a tall tree, held their breath. Happy Jack the Gray Squirrel and his cousin, Chatterer the Red Squirrel, looking down from another tree, held their breath. Unc' Billy Possum, sticking his head out from a hollow tree, held his breath. Bobby Coon, looking through a hole in a hollow stump in which he was hiding, held his breath. Reddy Fox, lying flat down behind a heap of brush, held his breath. Peter Rabbit, sitting bolt upright under a thick hemlock branch, with eyes and ears wide open, held his breath. And all the other little people who happened to be where they could see did the same thing.

You see, it was the most exciting moment ever was in the Green Forest. Farmer Brown's boy had just stepped out from behind one side of a little hemlock-tree and Buster Bear had just stepped out from behind the opposite side of the little hemlock-tree and neither had known that the other was anywhere near. For a whole minute they stood there face to face, gazing into each other's eyes, while everybody watched and waited, and it seemed as if the whole Green Forest was holding its breath.

Then something happened. Yes, Sir, something happened. Farmer Brown's boy opened his mouth and yelled! It was such a sudden yell and such a loud yell that it startled Chatterer so that he nearly fell from his place in the tree, and it made Reddy Fox jump to his feet ready to run. And that yell was a yell of fright. There was no doubt about it, for with the yell Farmer Brown's boy turned and ran for home, as no one ever had seen him run before. He ran just as Peter Rabbit runs when he has got to reach the dear Old Briar-patch before Reddy Fox can catch him, which, you know, is as fast as he can run. Once he stumbled and fell, but he scrambled to his feet in a twinkling, and away he went without once turning his head to see if Buster Bear was after him. There wasn't any doubt that he was afraid, very much afraid.

Everybody leaned forward to watch him. "What did I tell you? Didn't I say that he was afraid of Buster Bear?" cried Little Joe Otter, dancing about with excitement.

"You were right, Little Joe! I'm sorry that I doubted it. See him go! Caw, caw, caw!" shrieked Blacky the Crow.

For a minute or two everybody forgot about Buster Bear. Then there was a great crash which made everybody turn to look the other way. What do you think they saw? Why, Buster Bear was running away too, and he was running twice as fast as Farmer Brown's boy! He bumped into trees and crashed through bushes and jumped over logs, and in almost no time at all he was out of sight. Altogether it was the most surprising thing that the little people of the Green Forest ever had seen.

Sammy Jay looked at Blacky the Crow, and Blacky looked at Chatterer, and Chatterer looked at Happy Jack, and Happy Jack looked at Peter Rabbit, and Peter looked at Unc' Billy Possum, and Unc' Billy looked at Bobby Coon, and Bobby looked at Johnny Chuck, and Johnny looked at Reddy Fox, and Reddy looked at Jimmy Skunk, and Jimmy looked at Billy Mink, and Billy looked at Little Joe Otter, and for a minute nobody could say a word. Then Little Joe gave a funny little gasp.

"Why, why-e-e!" said he, "I believe Buster Bear is afraid too!" Unc' Billy Possum chuckled. "Ah believe yo' are right again, Brer Otter," said he. "It cert'nly does look so. If Brer Bear isn't scared, he must have remembered something impo'tant and has gone to attend to it in a powerful hurry."

Then everybody began to laugh.

Day 150

1. Read chapter 15 of *Buster Bear* by Thornton Burgess.
2. Tell someone what happened in the chapter.

XV BUSTER BEAR IS A FALLEN HERO

A fallen hero is some one to whom every one has looked up as very brave and then proves to be less brave than he was supposed to be. That was the way with Buster Bear. When Little Joe Otter had told how Farmer Brown's boy had been afraid at the mere sight of one of Buster Bear's big footprints, they had at once made a hero of Buster. At least some of them had. As this was the first time, the very first time, that they had ever known any one who lives in the Green Forest to make Farmer Brown's boy run away, they looked on Buster Bear with a great deal of respect and were very proud of him.

But now they had seen Buster Bear and Farmer Brown's boy meet face to face; and while it was true that Farmer Brown's boy had run away as fast as ever he could, it was also true that Buster Bear had done the same thing. He had run even faster than Farmer Brown's boy, and had hidden in the most lonely place he could find in the very deepest part of the Green Forest. It was hard to believe, but it was true. And right away everybody lost a great deal of the respect for Buster which they had felt. It is always that way. They began to say unkind things about him. They said them among themselves, and some of them even said them to Buster when they met him, or said them so that he would hear them.

Of course Blacky the Crow and Sammy Jay, who, because they can fly, have nothing to fear from Buster, and who always delight in making other people uncomfortable, never let a chance go by to tell Buster and everybody else within hearing what they thought of him. They delighted in flying about through the Green Forest until they had found Buster Bear and then from the safety of the tree tops screaming at him.

"Buster Bear is big and strong;
His teeth are big; his claws are long;
In spite of these he runs away
And hides himself the livelong day!"

A dozen times a day Buster would hear them screaming this. He would grind his teeth and glare up at them, but that was all he could do. He couldn't get at them. He just had to stand it and do nothing. But when impudent little Chatterer the Red Squirrel shouted the same thing from a place just out of reach in a big pine-tree, Buster could stand it no longer. He gave a deep, angry growl that made little shivers run over Chatterer, and then suddenly he started up that tree after Chatterer. With a frightened little shriek Chatterer scampered to the top of the tree. He hadn't known that Buster could climb. But Buster is a splendid climber, especially when the tree is big and stout as this one was, and now he went up after Chatterer, growling angrily.

How Chatterer did wish that he had kept his tongue still! He ran to the very top of the tree, so frightened that his teeth chattered, and when he looked down and saw Buster's great mouth coming nearer and nearer, he nearly tumbled down with terror. The worst of it was there wasn't another tree near enough for him to jump to. He was in trouble this time, was Chatterer, sure enough! And there was no one to help him.

Day 151

1. Read chapter 16 of *Buster Bear* by Thornton Burgess.
2. Tell someone what happened in the chapter.

XVI CHATTERER THE RED SQUIRREL JUMPS FOR HIS LIFE

It isn't very often that Chatterer the Red Squirrel knows fear. That is one reason that he is so often impudent and saucy. But once in a while a great fear takes possession of him, as when he knows that Shadow the Weasel is looking for him. You see, he knows that Shadow can go wherever he can go. There are very few of the little people of the Green Forest and the Green Meadows who do not know fear at some time or other, but it comes to Chatterer as seldom as to any one, because he is very sure of himself and his ability to hide or run away from danger.

But now as he clung to a little branch near the top of a tall pine-tree in the Green Forest and looked down at the big sharp teeth of Buster Bear drawing nearer and nearer, and listened to the deep, angry growls that made his hair stand on end, Chatterer was too frightened to think. If only he had kept his tongue still instead of saying hateful things to Buster Bear! If only he had known that Buster could climb a tree! If only he had chosen a tree near enough to other trees for him to jump across! But he had said hateful things, he had chosen to sit in a tree which stood quite by itself, and Buster Bear could climb! Chatterer was in the worst kind of trouble, and there was no one to blame but himself. That is usually the case with those who get into trouble.

Nearer and nearer came Buster Bear, and deeper and angrier sounded his voice. Chatterer gave a little frightened gasp and looked this way and looked that way. What should he do? What could he do! The ground seemed a terrible distance below. If only he had wings like Sammy Jay! But he hadn't.

"Gr-r-r-r!" growled Buster Bear. "I'll teach you manners! I'll teach you to treat your betters with respect! I'll swallow you whole, that's what I'll do. Gr-r-r-r!"

"Oh!" cried Chatterer.

"Gr-r-r-r! I'll eat you all up to the last hair on your tail!" growled Buster, scrambling a little nearer.

"Oh! Oh!" cried Chatterer, and ran out to the very tip of the little branch to which he had been clinging. Now if Chatterer had only known it, Buster Bear couldn't reach him way up there, because the tree was too small at the top for such a big fellow as Buster. But

Chatterer didn't think of that. He gave one more frightened look down at those big teeth, then he shut his eyes and jumped--jumped straight out for the far-away ground.

It was a long, long, long way down to the ground, and it certainly looked as if such a little fellow as Chatterer must be killed. But Chatterer had learned from Old Mother Nature that she had given him certain things to help him at just such times, and one of them is the power to spread himself very flat. He did it now. He spread his arms and legs out just as far as he could, and that kept him from falling as fast and as hard as he otherwise would have done, because being spread out so flat that way, the air held him up a little. And then there was his tail, that funny little tail he is so fond of jerking when he scolds. This helped him too. It helped him keep his balance and keep from turning over and over.

Down, down, down he sailed and landed on his feet. Of course, he hit the ground pretty hard, and for just a second he quite lost his breath. But it was only for a second, and then he was scurrying off as fast as a frightened Squirrel could. Buster Bear watched him and grinned.

"I didn't catch him that time," he growled, "but I guess I gave him a good fright and taught him a lesson."

Day 152

1. Read chapter 17 of *Buster Bear* by Thornton Burgess.
2. Tell someone what happened in the chapter.

XVII BUSTER BEAR GOES BERRYING

Buster Bear is a great hand to talk to himself when he thinks no one is around to overhear. It's a habit. However, it isn't a bad habit unless it is carried too far. Any habit becomes bad, if it is carried too far. Suppose you had a secret, a real secret, something that nobody else knew and that you didn't want anybody else to know. And suppose you had the habit of talking to yourself. You might, without thinking, you know, tell that secret out loud to yourself, and some one might, just might happen to overhear! Then there wouldn't be any secret. That is the way that a habit which isn't bad in itself can become bad when it is carried too far.

Now Buster Bear had lived by himself in the Great Woods so long that this habit of talking to himself had grown and grown. He did it just to keep from being lonesome. Of course, when he came down to the Green Forest to live, he brought all his habits with him. That is one thing about habits,--you always take them with you wherever you go. So Buster brought this habit of talking to himself down to the Green Forest, where he had many more neighbors than he had in the Great Woods.

"Let me see, let me see, what is there to tempt my appetite?" said Buster in his deep, grumbly-rumbly voice. "I find my appetite isn't what it ought to be. I need a change. Yes, Sir, I need a change. There is something I ought to have at this time of year, and I haven't got it. There is something that I used to have and don't have now. Ha! I know! I need some fresh fruit. That's it--fresh fruit! It must be about berry time now, and I'd forgotten all about it. My, my, my, how good some berries would taste! Now if I were back up there in the Great Woods I could have all I could eat. Um-m-m-m! Makes my mouth water just to think of it. There ought to be some up in the Old Pasture. There ought to be a lot of 'em up there. If I wasn't afraid that some one would see me, I'd go up there."

Buster sighed. Then he sighed again. The more he thought about those berries he felt sure were growing in the Old Pasture, the more he wanted some. It seemed to him that never in all his life had he wanted berries as he did now. He wandered about uneasily. He was hungry--hungry for berries and nothing else. By and by he began talking to himself again.

"If I wasn't afraid of being seen, I'd go up to the Old Pasture this very minute. Seems as if I could taste those berries." He licked his lips hungrily as he spoke. Then his face brightened. "I know what I'll do! I'll go up there at the very first peep of day to-morrow. I can eat all I want and get back to the Green Forest before there is any danger that Farmer Brown's boy or any one else I'm afraid of will see me. That's just what I'll do. My, I wish tomorrow morning would hurry up and come."

Now though Buster didn't know it, some one had been listening, and that some one was none other than Sammy Jay. When at last Buster lay down for a nap, Sammy flew away, chuckling to himself. "I believe I'll visit the Old Pasture to-morrow morning myself," thought he. "I have an idea that something interesting may happen if Buster doesn't change his mind."

Sammy was on the lookout very early the next morning. The first Jolly Little Sunbeams had only reached the Green Meadows and had not started to creep into the Green Forest, when he saw a big, dark form steal out of the Green Forest where it joins the Old Pasture. It moved very swiftly and silently, as if in a great hurry. Sammy knew who it was: it was Buster Bear, and he was going berrying. Sammy waited a little until he could see better. Then he too started for the Old Pasture.

Day 153

1. Read chapter 18 of *Buster Bear* by Thornton Burgess.
2. Tell someone what happened in the chapter.

XVIII SOMEBODY ELSE GOES BERRYING

Isn't it funny how two people will often think of the same thing at the same time, and neither one know that the other is thinking of it? That is just what happened the day that Buster Bear first thought of going berrying. While he was walking around in the Green Forest, talking to himself about how hungry he was for some berries and how sure he was that there must be some up in the Old Pasture, some one else was thinking about berries and about the Old Pasture too.

"Will you make me a berry pie if I will get the berries tomorrow?" asked Farmer Brown's boy of his mother.

Of course Mrs. Brown promised that she would, and so that night Farmer Brown's boy went to bed very early that he might get up early in the morning, and all night long he dreamed of berries and berry pies. He was awake even before jolly, round, red Mr. Sun thought it was time to get up, and he was all ready to start for the Old Pasture when the first Jolly Little Sunbeams came dancing across the Green Meadows. He carried a big tin pail, and in the bottom of it, wrapped up in a piece of paper, was a lunch, for he meant to stay until he filled that pail, if it took all day.

Now the Old Pasture is very large. It lies at the foot of the Big Mountain, and even extends a little way up on the Big Mountain. There is room in it for many people to pick berries all day without even seeing each other, unless they roam about a great deal. You see, the bushes grow very thick there, and you cannot see very far in any direction. Jolly, round, red Mr. Sun had climbed a little way up in the sky by the time Farmer Brown's boy reached the Old Pasture, and was smiling down on all the Great World, and all the Great World seemed to be smiling back. Farmer Brown's boy started to whistle, and then he stopped.

"If I whistle," thought he, "everybody will know just where I am, and will keep out of sight, and I never can get acquainted with folks if they keep out of sight."

You see, Farmer Brown's boy was just beginning to understand something that Peter Rabbit and the other little people of the Green Meadows and the Green Forest learned almost as soon as they learned to walk,--that if you don't want to be seen, you mustn't be heard. So he didn't whistle as he felt like doing, and he tried not to make a bit of noise as he followed an old cow-path towards a place where he knew the berries grew thick and oh, so big, and all the time he kept his eyes wide open, and he kept his ears open too.

That is how he happened to hear a little cry, a very faint little cry. If he had been whistling, he wouldn't have heard it at all. He stopped to listen. He never had heard a cry just like it before. At first he couldn't make out just what it was or where it came from. But one thing he was sure of, and that was that it was a cry of fright. He stood perfectly still and listened with all his might. There it was again--"Help! Help! Help"--and it was very faint and sounded terribly frightened. He waited a minute or two, but heard nothing more. Then he put down his pail and began a hurried look here, there, and everywhere. He was sure that it had come from somewhere on the ground, so he peered behind bushes and peeped behind logs and stones, and then just as he had about given up hope of finding where it came from, he went around a little turn in the old cow-path, and there right in front of him was little Mr. Gartersnake, and what do you think he was doing? Well, I don't like to tell you, but he was trying to swallow one of the children of Stickytoes the Tree Toad. Of course Farmer Brown's Boy didn't let him. He made little Mr. Gartersnake set Master Stickytoes free and held Mr. Gartersnake until Master Stickytoes was safely out of reach.

Day 154

1. Read chapter 19 of *Buster Bear* by Thornton Burgess.
2. Tell someone what happened in the chapter.

XIX BUSTER BEAR HAS A FINE TIME

Buster Bear was having the finest time he had had since he came down from the Great Woods to live in the Green Forest. To be sure, he wasn't in the Green Forest now, but he wasn't far from it. He was in the Old Pasture, one edge of which touches one edge of the Green Forest. And where do you think he was, in the Old Pasture? Why, right in the middle of the biggest patch of the biggest blueberries he ever had seen in all his life! Now if there is any one thing that Buster Bear had rather have above another, it is all the berries he can eat, unless it be honey. Nothing can quite equal honey in Buster's mind. But next to honey give him berries. He isn't particular what kind of berries. Raspberries, blackberries, or blueberries, either kind, will make him perfectly happy.

"Um-m-m, my, my, but these are good!" he mumbled in his deep grumbly-rumbly voice, as he sat on his haunches stripping off the berries greedily. His little eyes twinkled with enjoyment, and he didn't mind at all if now and then he got leaves, and some green berries in his mouth with the big ripe berries. He didn't try to get them out. Oh, my, no! He just chomped them all up together and patted his stomach from sheer delight. Now Buster had reached the Old Pasture just as jolly, round, red Mr. Sun had crept out of bed, and he had fully made up his mind that he would be back in the Green Forest before Mr. Sun had climbed very far up in the blue, blue sky. You see, big as he is and strong as he is, Buster Bear is very shy and bashful, and he has no desire to meet Farmer Brown, or Farmer Brown's boy, or any other of those two-legged creatures called men. It seems funny but he actually is afraid of them. And he had a feeling that he was a great deal more likely to meet one of them in the Old Pasture than deep in the Green Forest.

So when he started to look for berries, he made up his mind that he would eat what he could in a great hurry and get back to the Green Forest before Farmer Brown's boy was more than out of bed. But when he found those berries he was so hungry that he forgot his fears and everything else. They tasted so good that he just had to eat and eat and eat. Now you know that Buster is a very big fellow, and it takes a lot to fill him up. He kept eating and eating and eating, and the more he ate the more he wanted. You know how it is. So he wandered from one patch of berries to another in the Old Pasture, and never once thought of the time. Somehow, time is the hardest thing in the world to remember, when you are having a good time.

Jolly, round, red Mr. Sun climbed higher and higher in the blue, blue sky. He looked down on all the Great World and saw all that was going on. He saw Buster Bear in the Old

Pasture, and smiled as he saw what a perfectly glorious time Buster was having. And he saw something else in the Old Pasture that made his smile still broader. He saw Farmer Brown's boy filling a great tin pail with blueberries, and he knew that Farmer Brown's boy didn't know that Buster Bear was anywhere about, and he knew that Buster Bear didn't know that Farmer Brown's boy was anywhere about, and somehow he felt very sure that he would see something funny happen if they should chance to meet.

"Um-m-m, um-m-m," mumbled Buster Bear with his mouth full, as he moved along to another patch of berries. And then he gave a little gasp of surprise and delight. Right in front of him was a shiny thing just full of the finest, biggest, bluest berries! There were no leaves or green ones there. Buster blinked his greedy little eyes rapidly and looked again. No, he wasn't dreaming. They were real berries, and all he had got to do was to help himself. Buster looked sharply at the shiny thing that held the berries. It seemed perfectly harmless. He reached out a big paw and pushed it gently. It tipped over and spilled out a lot of the berries. Yes, it was perfectly harmless. Buster gave a little sigh of pure happiness. He would eat those berries to the last one, and then he would go home to the Green Forest.

Day 155

1. Read chapter 20 of *Buster Bear* by Thornton Burgess.
2. Answer the questions at the end of the chapter.
3. Tell someone what happened in the chapter.

XX BUSTER BEAR CARRIES OFF THE PAIL OF FARMER BROWN'S BOY

The question is, did Buster Bear steal Farmer Brown's boy's pail? To steal is to take something which belongs to some one else. There is no doubt that he stole the berries that were in the pail when he found it, for he deliberately ate them. He knew well enough that some one must have picked them--for whoever heard of blueberries growing in tin pails? So there is no doubt that when Buster took them, he stole them. But with the pail it was different. He took the pail, but he didn't mean to take it. In fact, he didn't want that pail at all.

You see it was this way: When Buster found that big tin pail brimming full of delicious berries in the shade of that big bush in the Old Pasture, he didn't stop to think whether or

286

not he had a right to them. Buster is so fond of berries that from the very second that his greedy little eyes saw that pailful, he forgot everything but the feast that was waiting for him right under his very nose. He didn't think anything about the right or wrong of helping himself. There before him were more berries than he had ever seen together at one time in all his life, and all he had to do was to eat and eat and eat. And that is just what he did do. Of course he upset the pail, but he didn't mind a little thing like that. When he had gobbled up all the berries that rolled out, he thrust his nose into the pail to get all that were left in it. Just then he heard a little noise, as if some one were coming. He threw up his head to listen, and somehow, he never did know just how, the handle of the pail slipped back over his ears and caught there.

This was bad enough, but to make matters worse, just at that very minute he heard a shrill, angry voice shout, "Hi, there! Get out of there!" He didn't need to be told whose voice that was. It was the voice of Farmer Brown's boy. Right then and there Buster Bear nearly had a fit. There was that awful pail fast over his head so that he couldn't see a thing. Of course, that meant that he couldn't run away, which was the thing of all things he most wanted to do, for big as he is and strong as he is, Buster is very shy and bashful when human beings are around. He growled and whined and squealed. He tried to back out of the pail and couldn't. He tried to shake it off and couldn't. He tried to pull it off, but somehow he couldn't get hold of it. Then there was another yell. If Buster hadn't been so frightened himself, he might have recognized that second yell as one of fright, for that is what it was. You see Farmer Brown's boy had just discovered Buster Bear. When he had yelled the first time, he had supposed that it was one of the young cattle who live in the Old Pasture all summer, but when he saw Buster, he was just as badly frightened as Buster himself. In fact, he was too surprised and frightened even to run. After that second yell he just stood still and stared.

Buster clawed at that awful thing on his head more frantically than ever. Suddenly it slipped off, so that he could see. He gave one frightened look at Farmer Brown's boy, and then with a mighty "Woof!" he started for the Green Forest as fast as his legs could take him, and this was very fast indeed, let me tell you. He didn't stop to pick out a path, but just crashed through the bushes as if they were nothing at all, just nothing at all. But the funniest thing of all is this--he took that pail with him! Yes, Sir, Buster Bear ran away with the big tin pail of Farmer Brown's boy! You see when it slipped off his head, the handle was still around his neck, and there he was running away with a pail hanging from his neck! He didn't want it. He would have given anything to get rid of it. But he took it because he couldn't help it. And that brings us back to the question, did Buster steal Farmer Brown's boy's pail? What do you think?

Day 156

1. Read chapter 21 of *Buster Bear* by Thornton Burgess.
2. Tell someone about this chapter.

XXI SAMMY JAY MAKES THINGS WORSE FOR BUSTER BEAR

"Thief, thief, thief! Thief, thief, thief!" Sammy Jay was screaming at the top of his lungs, as he followed Buster Bear across the Old Pasture towards the Green Forest. Never had he screamed so loud, and never had his voice sounded so excited. The little people of the Green Forest, the Green Meadows, and the Smiling Pool are so used to hearing Sammy cry thief that usually they think very little about it. But every blessed one who heard Sammy this morning stopped whatever he was doing and pricked up his ears to listen.

Sammy's cousin, Blacky the Crow, just happened to be flying along the edge of the Old Pasture, and the minute he heard Sammy's voice, he turned and flew over to see what it was all about. Just as soon as he caught sight of Buster Bear running for the Green Forest as hard as ever he could, he understood what had excited Sammy so. He was so surprised that he almost forgot to keep his wings moving. Buster Bear had what looked to Blacky very much like a tin pail hanging from his neck! No wonder Sammy was excited. Blacky beat his wings fiercely and started after Sammy.

And so they reached the edge of the Green Forest, Buster Bear running as hard as ever he could, Sammy Jay flying just behind him and screaming, "Thief, thief, thief!" at the top of his lungs, and behind him Blacky the Crow, trying to catch up and yelling as loud as he could, "Caw, caw, caw! Come on, everybody! Come on! Come on!"

Poor Buster! It was bad enough to be frightened almost to death as he had been up in the Old Pasture when the pail had caught over his head just as Farmer Brown's boy had yelled at him. Then to have the handle of the pail slip down around his neck so that he couldn't get rid of the pail but had to take it with him as he ran, was making a bad matter worse. Now to have all his neighbors of the Green Forest see him in such a fix and make fun of him, was more than he could stand. He felt humiliated. That is just another way of saying shamed. Yes, Sir, Buster felt that he was shamed in the eyes of his neighbors, and he wanted nothing so much as to get away by himself, where no one could see him, and try to get rid of that dreadful pail. But Buster is so big that it is not easy for him to find a hiding place. So, when he reached the Green Forest, he kept right on to the deepest, darkest, most lonesome part and crept under the thickest hemlock-tree he could find.

But it was of no use. The sharp eyes of Sammy Jay and Blacky the Crow saw him. They actually flew into the very tree under which he was hiding, and how they did scream! Pretty soon Ol' Mistah Buzzard came dropping down out of the blue, blue sky and took a seat on a convenient dead tree, where he could see all that went on. Ol' Mistah Buzzard began to grin as soon as he saw that tin pail on Buster's neck. Then came others,--Redtail the Hawk, Scrapper the Kingbird, Redwing the Blackbird, Drummer the Woodpecker, Welcome Robin, Tommy Tit the Chickadee, Jenny Wren, Redeye the Vireo, and ever so many more. They came from the Old Orchard, the Green Meadows, and even down by the Smiling Pool, for the voices of Sammy Jay and Blacky the Crow carried far, and at the sound of them everybody hurried over, sure that something exciting was going on.

Presently Buster heard light footsteps, and peeping out, he saw Billy Mink and Peter Rabbit and Jumper the Hare and Prickly Porky and Reddy Fox and Jimmy Skunk. Even timid little Whitefoot the Wood Mouse was where he could peer out and see without being seen. Of course, Chatterer the Red Squirrel and Happy Jack the Gray Squirrel were there. There they all sat in a great circle around him, each where he felt safe, but where he could see, and every one of them laughing and making fun of Buster.

"Thief, thief, thief!" screamed Sammy until his throat was sore. The worst of it was Buster knew that everybody knew that it was true. That awful pail was proof of it.

"I wish I never had thought of berries," growled Buster to himself.

Day 157

1. Read chapter 22 of *Buster Bear* by Thornton Burgess.
2. Tell someone about the chapter.

XXII BUSTER BEAR HAS A FIT OF TEMPER

A temper is a bad, bad thing
  When once it gets away.
There's nothing quite at all like it
  To spoil a pleasant day.

Buster Bear was in a terrible temper. Yes, Sir, Buster Bear was having the worst fit of temper ever seen in the Green Forest. And the worst part of it all was that all his neighbors of the Green Forest and a whole lot from the Green Meadows and the Smiling Pool were also there to see it. It is bad enough to give way to temper when you are all alone, and there is no one to watch you, but when you let temper get the best of you right where others see you, oh, dear, dear, it certainly is a sorry sight.

Now ordinarily Buster is one of the most good-natured persons in the world. It takes a great deal to rouse his temper. He isn't one tenth so quick tempered as Chatterer the Red Squirrel, or Sammy Jay, or Reddy Fox. But when his temper is aroused and gets away from him, then watch out! It seemed to Buster that he had had all that he could stand that day and a little more. First had come the fright back there in the Old Pasture. Then the pail had slipped down behind his ears and held fast, so he had run all the way to the Green Forest with it hanging about his neck. This was bad enough, for he knew just how funny he must look, and besides, it was very uncomfortable. But to have Sammy Jay call everybody within hearing to come and see him was more than he could stand. It seemed to Buster as if everybody who lives in the Green Forest, on the Green Meadows, or around the Smiling Brook, was sitting around his hiding place, laughing and making fun of him. It was more than any self-respecting Bear could stand.

With a roar of anger Buster Bear charged out of his hiding place. He rushed this way and that way! He roared with all his might! He was very terrible to see. Those who could fly, flew. Those who could climb, climbed. And those who were swift of foot, ran. A few who could neither fly nor climb nor run fast, hid and lay shaking and trembling for fear that Buster would find them. In less time than it takes to tell about it, Buster was alone. At least, he couldn't see any one.

Then he vented his temper on the tin pail. He cuffed at it and pulled at it, all the time growling angrily. He lay down and clawed at it with his hind feet. At last the handle broke, and he was free! He shook himself.

Then he jumped on the helpless pail. With a blow of a big paw he sent it clattering against a tree. He tried to bite it. Then he once more fell to knocking it this way and that way, until it was pounded flat, and no one would ever have guessed that it had once been a pail.

Then, and not till then, did Buster recover his usual good nature. Little by little, as he thought it all over, a look of shame crept into his face. "I--I guess it wasn't the fault of that thing. I ought to have known enough to keep my head out of it," he said slowly and thoughtfully.

"You got no more than you deserve for stealing Farmer Brown's boy's berries," said Sammy Jay, who had come back and was looking on from the top of a tree. "You ought to know by this time that no good comes of stealing."

Buster Bear looked up and grinned, and there was a twinkle in his eyes. "You ought to know, Sammy Jay," said he. "I hope you'll always remember it."

"Thief, thief, thief!" screamed Sammy, and flew away.

Day 158

1. Read chapter 23 of *Buster Bear* by Thornton Burgess.
2. Tell someone the story of the whole book.
3. How would you describe Buster Bear? Write a list of words that tell about him. What does he look like? What does he act like? Is he funny? Is he grumpy?

XXIII FARMER BROWN'S BOY LUNCHES ON BERRIES

When things go wrong in spite of you
To smile's the best thing you can do--
To smile and say, "I'm mighty glad
They are no worse; they're not so bad!"

That is what Farmer Brown's boy said when he found that Buster Bear had stolen the berries he had worked so hard to pick and then had run off with the pail. You see, Farmer Brown's boy is learning to be something of a philosopher, one of those people who accept bad things cheerfully and right away see how they are better than they might have been. When he had first heard some one in the bushes where he had hidden his pail of berries, he had been very sure that it was one of the cows or young cattle who live in the Old Pasture during the summer. He had been afraid that they might stupidly kick over the pail and spill the berries, and he had hurried to drive whoever it was away. It hadn't entered his head that it could be anybody who would eat those berries.

When he had yelled and Buster Bear had suddenly appeared, struggling to get off the pail which had caught over his head, Farmer Brown's boy had been too frightened to even move. Then he had seen Buster tear away through the brush even more frightened than he was, and right away his courage had begun to come back.

"If he is so afraid of me, I guess I needn't be afraid of him," said he. "I've lost my berries, but it is worth it to find out that he is afraid of me. There are plenty more on the bushes, and all I've got to do is to pick them. It might be worse."

He walked over to the place where the pail had been, and then he remembered that when Buster ran away he had carried the pail with him, hanging about his neck. He whistled. It was a comical little whistle of chagrin as he realized that he had nothing in which to put more berries, even if he picked them. "It's worse than I thought," cried he. "That bear has cheated me out of that berry pie my mother promised me." Then he began to laugh, as he thought of how funny Buster Bear had looked with the pail about his neck, and then because, you know he is learning to be a philosopher, he once more repeated, "It might have been worse. Yes, indeed, it might have been worse. That bear might have tried to eat me instead of the berries. I guess I'll go eat that lunch I left back by the spring, and then I'll go home. I can pick berries some other day."

Chuckling happily over Buster Bear's great fright, Farmer Brown's boy tramped back to the spring where he had left two thick sandwiches on a flat stone when he started to save his pail of berries. "My, but those sandwiches will taste good," thought he. "I'm glad they are big and thick. I never was hungrier in my life. Hello!" This he exclaimed right out loud, for he had just come in sight of the flat stone where the sandwiches should have been, and they were not there. No, Sir, there wasn't so much as a crumb left of those two thick sandwiches. You see, Old Man Coyote had found them and gobbled them up while Farmer Brown's boy was away.

But Farmer Brown's boy didn't know anything about Old Man Coyote. He rubbed his eyes and stared everywhere, even up in the trees, as if he thought those sandwiches might be hanging up there. They had disappeared as completely as if they never had been, and Old Man Coyote had taken care to leave no trace of his visit. Farmer Brown's boy gaped foolishly this way and that way. Then, instead of growing angry, a slow smile stole over his freckled face. "I guess some one else was hungry too," he muttered. "Wonder who it was? Guess this Old Pasture is no place for me to-day. I'll fill up on berries and then I'll go home."

So Farmer Brown's boy made his lunch on blueberries and then rather sheepishly he started for home to tell of all the strange things that had happened to him in the Old Pasture. Two or three times, as he trudged along, he stopped to scratch his head thoughtfully. "I guess," said he at last, "that I'm not so smart as I thought I was, and I've got a lot to learn yet."

This is the end of the adventures of Buster Bear in this book because--guess why. Because Old Mr. Toad insists that I must write a book about his adventures, and Old Mr. Toad is such a good friend of all of us that I am going to do it. THE END

Day 159

1. Write a book report.
2. Write on a page the title of the book, the author, the characters (who the story was about), what happened to them and your favorite part. Then you can add a picture.
3. You could give this to a parent to add to your portfolio.

Day 160

1. Read the poem out loud.

    All things bright and beautiful,
    All creatures great and small,
    All things wise and wonderful,
    The Lord God made them all.

Each little flower that opens,
Each little bird that sings,
He made their glowing colors,
He made their tiny wings.

The purple-headed mountain,
The river running by,
The sunset, and the morning,
That brighten up the sky;

The cold wind in the winter,
The pleasant summer sun,
The ripe fruits in the garden,
He made them every one.

The tall trees in the greenwood,
The meadows where we play,
The rushes by the water,
We gather every day;

He gave us eyes to see them,
And lips that we might tell
How great is God Almighty,
Who has made all things well.

Day 161

1. Read the poem out loud. This poem is by "anonymous." The author is unknown.
2. Read the poem on Day 160 again.

Work while you work,
Play while you play;

This is the way
To be happy each day.

All that you do,
Do with your might;
Things done by halves
Are never done right.

Day 162

1. Read the poem.
2. Read the poem from Day 160 out loud again.

   Hearts Are Like Doors
   Hearts, like doors, will open with ease,
   To very, very little keys.
   And don't forget that two of these
   Are "Thank you, sir" and "If you please!"

Day 163

1. Read the poem . (Mother Goose rhyme adapted)
2. Read the poem from Day 160 out loud again.

   Monday's child is fair of face,
   Tuesday's child is full of grace:
   Wednesday's child is thoughtful and kind,
   Thursday's child has a sharp mind.
   Friday's child is loving and giving,
   Saturday's child works hard for a living;
   And the child born in Sunday's light,
   Loves the Lord with all his might.

Day 164

1. Read the poem.
2. Read the poem from Day 160 out loud again.

The Months
Thirty days hath September,
April, June, and November;
All the rest have thirty-one,
Except for February alone,
Which has four and twenty-four
Till leap year gives it one day more.

Day 165

1. Read the poem.
2. Read the poem from Day 160 out loud again.

The Goops By Gelett Burgess
The Goops they lick their fingers,
And the Goops they lick their knives,
They spill their broth on the tablecloth —
Oh, they lead disgusting lives!
The Goops they talk while eating,
And loud and fast they chew,
And that is why I'm glad that I
Am not a Goop — are you?

Day 166

1. Read the poem.
2. Read the poem from Day 160 out loud again.

GENEROSITY
> When you have candy, do you go
>> And give your sister half?
> When little brother stubs his toe,
>> Do you look on and laugh?
> The greediest Goop would give away
>> The things he didn't need—
> To share the toys with which you play,
>> That's generous, indeed!

Day 167

1. Read the poem.
2. Read the poem from Day 160 out loud again.

The Little Bird Mother Goose Rhyme
Once I saw a little bird
Come hop, hop, hop;
So I cried, "Little bird,
Will you stop, stop, stop?"
And was going to the window
To say "How do you do?"
But he shook his little tail,
And far away he flew.

Day 168

1. Each day read the chapter or chapter portion. This book is just for fun. It's called, *Answering the Call: The Roma of Macedonia.*
2. It is based on real people and places and events in Macedonia.
3. Every day tell someone about the story and about what you learned from the story.

Chapter 1   An Email from Grandpa Joe

"All done helping Dad clean up breakfast!" Joshua announced as he bounded into the living room. Dad was right behind him.

"I'm off to work. Come and get your hugs!" Dad squatted and held out his arms. Samuel leapt off the couch and flew into his father's arms. Peter didn't wait for him to finish his hug and snuggled his head into his father's side. Dad let go of Samuel and gave Peter a hug.

"Are you going to be my big, happy, two-year-old boy today?" Dad asked Peter.

"Yes, Daddy," Peter answered. Dad gave him a smile big enough to make Peter laugh.

Joshua and Rebecca came to get their hugs as well.

"What are you working on there, Rebecca?" Dad asked his oldest child.

"I'm knitting a sweater for baby Anna for this fall. I'm just getting started. I should be done before the weather gets cooler." Rebecca held up her pink yarn and knitting needles to show how much she had finished so far.

"I'm sure she'll love it," Dad responded putting a hand on Rebecca's shoulder. "Best for last," Dad chuckled as he went over to the couch to give his wife a kiss goodbye.

"Have a great day. I think we'll have big news to tell you when you get home today," Mom told Dad with a twinkle in her eye. Dad smiled and nodded.

"I love hearing all your news at the end of the day. Can't wait to get back home! I love you all." Dad gave a wave as he walked out the door. Mom went back to reading to Samuel and Peter who were cuddled up on either side of her. Rebecca kept working on making a sweater for baby Anna who was sleeping in another room. Joshua sat down at the computer to check the email. The first email he read made his eyes open wide.

"Rebecca come quick!" Rebecca carefully put down her knitting so she wouldn't lose her place. "Hurry! Hurry!" Joshua shouted excitedly.

"Here I am," Rebecca said as she walked over to the computer. Mom looked up from the book and smiled at her two oldest children now gasping over the email.

"Mom, did you know about this?" Rebecca questioned her mom.

"I don't know. Why don't you tell me what you're looking at?" Mom replied with a laugh.

"It's a letter from Grandpa Joe," Joshua began. "He wants to take us on a trip. He's visiting missionaries next week in Macedonia, and he says we're coming with him!"

"Oh yes, I remember him telling me something about that," Mom teased.

"You knew!" Rebecca exclaimed. She turned back to the computer. "We're going to be flying with Grandpa Joe and Grandma Kay to Skopje, the capital city of Macedonia."

"That's *scope-yeh,* not *scop- gee,*" Mom tutored.

"*Scope-yeh,*" Rebecca repeated and then continued. "We'll be staying in the Roma village of Shutka with Lydia and Dan Taylor and their baby daughter Susanna. I remember them! I prayed for them when Susanna was going to be born. I decided I would pray for her every year. She was born the day before my tenth birthday. I'll always remember to pray for her every year in October when we have our birthdays."

"Hey, that's neat," Joshua thought out loud. "I'm going to ask God to give me a special birthday missionary to pray for every year too."

"That's a great idea, Joshua," Mom encouraged. "Would you two like to know some more about your trip?"

"Of course!" the children agreed.

Mom opened a drawer in the desk and pulled out some papers. "These are your plane tickets," she began to explain. "You will leave from the Philadelphia airport on Monday, August 28th, and you'll get there on Tuesday. That means you'll have to sleep on the airplane." Rebecca and Joshua looked at each other and smiled as mom continued. "You'll be there for four days. We'll be able to write back and forth on email while you are there. You can tell us every day all the neat things you are doing. Now, let's look again at that email and make sure we don't miss anything. Then we'll get packing. We've only got a week until the big day!"

Rebecca started reading the email aloud to the others. "We didn't read this last part before. It says, 'It will be hot like here in Pennsylvania so pack your summer clothes. Also, pack a gift for the Taylors, the missionaries we will be staying with. It would be a good idea to bring some chocolates too. In Macedonia you give a gift of chocolate to all the children in any home you visit. We love you all! We'll be seeing you soon! Blessings, Grandpa Joe and Grandma Kay.'"

"Presents," Joshua said out loud tapping his finger on his forehead. "What's something that would be special, something you couldn't get if you're not in America?"

"Something in English," Rebecca chimed in.

"Something in English," Joshua repeated as he started thinking again. He sat up straight suddenly. "How about music?"

"Great idea!" Mom decided immediately. "Worship music might mean the most to them. Joshua, why don't you think about what your favorite worship CD is. We'll look for it when we go shopping to prepare for the trip. Rebecca, do you have an idea for a gift for their baby?"

"Could I make her a hat? I think I could knit it in a week if I get started soon."

"Another great idea," Mom answered. "Why don't you look through our yarn and see if we have something you could use to get started right away."

Joshua went over to the family's CDs and started looking through them. He was trying to decide which he liked best. That would be the one he would buy as a gift for Mr. and Mrs. Taylor.

Rebecca opened a cabinet and pulled out a big bag of yarn. She pulled out a ball of white yarn, a ball of pink yarn and a ball of purple yarn. She squeezed them all trying to decide which she liked best. She was planning for the winter hat she would make for little Susanna.

Mom sat at the desk and took out a pad of paper and a pen. She started making lists. She made one list of the things the children needed to pack. She made another list of the things they needed to buy. At the top of both lists she wrote, "Chocolate."

Day 169

Chapter 2   World Books

"Found it!" Joshua exploded.

"What did you find?" asked Rebecca.

"The CD we should buy for the Taylors," Joshua explained.

"Can I see?" Rebecca walked over to Joshua. He handed her the CD. "Oh, this is a good one. You did a great job picking. Want to see what yarn I picked to use for Susanna's hat?"

"Sure," replied Joshua. Rebecca picked up a purple ball of yarn and tossed it to Joshua. "They'll love it," Joshua said with a smile.

"Thanks," Rebecca said and smiled back at him.

Mom turned around from her work at the desk. "Let's get going on school for today. You two can do your math and reading after lunch. This morning why don't you get out your world books and start working on adding Macedonia to it."

"Yes!" Joshua cheered. He bounced to the book shelf and pulled off a blue three-ring binder. "I'll get yours too," he called over his shoulder to Rebecca. He pulled a red binder off the shelf.

"I'll get some paper." Rebecca walked over to the desk and got out two pieces of plain white paper and two pieces of lined paper. She opened the bottom desk drawer and pulled out a three-hole punch. She carefully lined up the plain paper and placed it in the hole punch. She pressed down. Now each paper had three holes in it. "Joshua, could you go get construction paper from the kids' room?"

"Sure," Joshua said as he scooted out of the living room. He was back in a flash with two pieces of green construction paper.

"I'll put holes in these too," Rebecca said as she took the paper from Joshua. "Now we're all set Mom."

"Good. Now where is Macedonia going to go in your book?" Mom asked in her teacher voice.

Rebecca and Joshua flipped through their binders. Every time they learned about a country they put what they learned in their world books. Each piece of construction paper had the name of a country on it. They kept all the countries in order from A to Z.

"It goes here!" Joshua was the first to find the spot. "It goes in between Holland and Niger."

"Is that right, Rebecca?" Mom asked.

"Yep. He's got it right," Rebecca responded.

"Write Macedonia on your construction paper and put that in your binders to mark the spot where you'll put everything we collect about Macedonia. Do you remember how to spell it?"

Joshua went over to the computer to check the email to make sure he got all the letters in the right place. The kids placed their green papers in their binders.

"We got that done, Mom. Can I get out the atlas?" Rebecca asked.

"I think that would be a good first step," Mom answered.

Joshua was already on the job and got the atlas off the bookshelf. He sat on the floor across from the other boys who were playing a matching game. Joshua started flipping through it. Rebecca sat down next to him. She straightened out her skirt as Joshua looked for Macedonia.

"Here's a map," Joshua announced. "Macedonia is in Europe. That's on the other side of the Atlantic Ocean from us. Macedonia's right above Greece."

Rebecca had an idea. "Let's look online for a map. We can print it out and put it in our notebooks."

Mom spoke up. "Why don't you finish looking through the atlas first. Find a picture of the Macedonian flag and draw it in your binders. Then you can get on the computer to see what you can learn about the country."

"All right, Mom," Rebecca replied. She turned back to Joshua who had already found a picture of the Macedonian flag.

"It looks like a sun!" Joshua shared with Mom. "I have a new idea! We could make this flag out of construction paper. Could we do that, Mom, and put it in our world books?"

"Sure," Mom quickly agreed to the plan. "Anna's waking up so I'm going to go get her and take her and your brothers outside for a bit. You can show me your books when we come back in."

Hearing it was time to go outside, Samuel picked up the game he had started playing and shoved it back on the game shelf. He ran to start getting his shoes on. Peter followed him everywhere he went.

Day 170

Rebecca and Joshua got to work on their flags. They each took a piece of red construction paper. They shared a yellow piece of paper and cut out circles and strips for the sun's rays. They took turns using the glue to put the sun together on the red background.

"Your flag looks the best," Joshua noticed.

"Thanks, Joshua. I think you did a really good job too. You can be first to show Mom when she comes back in."

"Yeah! Thanks! You can show Dad first when he gets home."

"Okay." Rebecca was happy that she would be able to show her flag to Dad first.

"What next?" Joshua asked his big sister.

"What do we know? Let's write what we can on our papers."

They took out pens and their lined papers. They wrote what they knew.

Country: Macedonia
Capital: Skopje
Continent: Europe
Border Countries: Greece, Bulgaria, Serbia, Kosovo, Albania

"I think we're ready to look on the internet now," Rebecca decided. Joshua was the first to the computer and took the seat. "I guess I'll go get another chair from the kitchen," Rebecca said as Joshua started their search.

"Here's the travel website we've looked at before for other countries. It says that the money in Macedonia is called denars. It says the people there speak Macedonian, Albanian, Turkish and Romani. It also says that almost 70% of the people there are Orthodox Christians and 30% are Muslims. What does that all mean, Rebecca?"

"Which part? All those languages just means that there are people in Macedonia who speak all those languages. Macedonian is probably the language that just about everyone knows. 70% Orthodox Christian means that most of the people living in Macedonia call themselves Christians. We can ask Grandpa if those people really worship God or just say they are Christians because they were born in Macedonia. 30% Muslim means that there are many people there who follow the rules of Islam. There's a lot we don't know still. Tomorrow's Friday and Grandma Kay and Grandpa Joe will be here for dinner. We can ask them then."

"What should we put in our books?" Joshua asked.

"Let's write the basics for now," Rebecca started writing and Joshua copied her list into his notebook.

Language: Macedonian
Religion: Orthodox Christian, Muslim
Money: the denar

"We still don't know anything about the Roma," Joshua realized. "I'm going to search the Roma now. We're going to be staying in a Roma village." Joshua started his search. He found out that the Roma are from India.

"That means they will have dark skin like people from India," Rebecca pointed out.

"This article talks about the Roma being poor and being discriminated against," Joshua told Rebecca.

"Maybe that's why the Taylors picked them to share the Gospel with."

"Maybe," Joshua said and smiled at his sister. "I hope we get to tell someone about Jesus when we are there."

"It's hard when you don't speak the language, but the Bible does say that we can share about God by how we live. So we'll have to try and live like Jesus so they can see Him in us. Can we do it?" Rebecca challenged her brother with a smile.

"Yeah, we can do it. Please help us do it, God," Joshua prayed.

Day 171

Chapter 3   The Big Day

Friday arrived and Grandpa Joe and Grandma Kay came for dinner as usual. Rebecca and Joshua had lots of questions for them.

Rebecca remembered to ask if the Macedonians really worshipped God.

Grandpa answered. "There are several churches in Macedonia where God is worshipped, but most Macedonians don't really know God. They say they are Christians out of tradition."

Joshua was next to ask. "Grandpa, do the Roma call themselves Christians?"

"Almost all the Roma in Macedonia call themselves Muslim," Grandpa told them.

Samuel and Peter had questions too. Samuel wanted to know if the missionaries in Macedonia lived in huts. Peter wanted to know if they had ice cream in Macedonia. The answer to Samuel's question was no. The answer to Peter's question was yes.

"Grandpa Joe," Rebecca said and waited for his attention. "The Roma don't have their own country. They left India and split up and live in lots of different countries now, right?"

"That's right, Rebecca," Grandpa Joe encouraged. "You've been doing your research."

Rebecca continued her question. "Are there Roma in America? Do they have Roma in the Congo where you were a missionary?"

"Well, Rebecca," Grandpa began. "The Roma mostly live in Europe where Macedonia is. The Congo is in Africa, which of course you know because your mother grew up there.

There aren't many Roma in Africa except in the countries closest to Europe. There are Roma in America, though."

Joshua had a question this time. "So the Roma just wandered around until they found homes?"

"In a way, yes," Grandpa Joe answered. "For a long time the Roma just wandered the world. Many people don't know that today they mostly stay put. Most people know the Roma as Gypsies, but that's not the nicest word to use. Shutka, the village we are going to, is the largest Roma settlement in the world. That means more Roma live in one place there than anywhere else. There are about forty thousand Roma in Shutka."

"Shootka," Joshua repeated to himself.

The night ended with cake for dessert. Grandpa Joe and Grandma Kay got seven hugs each and said goodnight.

Saturday. Sunday. The weekend flew by. The shopping list was checked off. The packing list was checked off. Everything was ready for the big day.

Monday morning came and the house was buzzing. Baby Anna slept through the excitement. Grandma Kay was the first through the door. Grandpa Joe followed with a loud call, "We're here!"

The suitcases were all set by the door. The family gathered around. Dad prayed for everyone's health and safety. He prayed that Rebecca and Joshua would be a blessing to the Taylor family. He praised God for His faithfulness. "Amen," the family chorused when he finished.

Rebecca and Joshua hugged their little brothers and their mom. Dad carried out the suitcases to the car. Mom held her hand over her heart as she watched Rebecca and

Joshua climb into the car with their father and grandparents. It was an hour before Dad returned with an empty car.

"Are Rebecca and Joshua on the airplane now?" Samuel wanted to know.

"I want to see the airplane," Peter started repeating, running to look out the window.

"I don't think they are up in the air yet," Dad said gently. "I couldn't stay with them until they got on the plane. I stayed with them until they got their luggage checked."

"What does 'luggage checked' mean?" Samuel asked.

"That just means they take the suitcases to put them on the plane," Dad explained. "The man at the counter was surprised that Joshua was only eight years old but had traveled overseas before. He acted like an old pro." Dad shook his head, chuckling.

Day 172

"Well, Dad, now what do we do?" Mom asked with a sigh.

"Well, do you think you're up for going out for ice cream?" Dad offered. "Or, would you like me to take the boys and you girls can relax here?"

"Ice cream sounds great," Mom decided.

"Ice cream! Ice cream!" Samuel and Peter called out, jumping around the room. Rebecca and Joshua weren't going to get ice cream, but they were just as excited. They were getting on the plane and settling into their seats. Rebecca sat next to Grandma Kay and Joshua sat on the aisle. Grandma Kay held Grandpa Joe's hand as the plane took off into the sky.

After Rebecca and Joshua were served dinner on the plane, they started talking about what they thought it would be like in Macedonia and what they thought the Roma would look like. Joshua was the first to make a guess. "I think the Roma women will have their heads covered because they are Muslim. A lot of Muslim women cover themselves when they are outside."

Rebecca disagreed. "I think they will look like the pictures we have seen of gypsies. The women will wear long, flowy, colorful skirts and will wear big gold hoop earrings."

"I guess we'll know soon," Joshua said.

"I guess we will," Rebecca replied.

Eight hours passed and while everyone on the plane slept, the plane started to land. Their plane didn't land in Macedonia, though. It landed in Germany, another country in Europe.

"Why did we stop here, Grandma Kay?" Rebecca leaned over and asked her seat neighbor.

"There are no planes that go from America to Macedonia," Grandma Kay explained. "There are planes from Germany to Macedonia though. One more plane ride and we'll be there."

"We get to go on another plane, Joshua," Rebecca told her brother. She knew he would be thrilled. They had been on planes several times before, but planes always excited Joshua.

The grandparents and grandchildren sat together waiting to get on board their next flight.

"Grandpa Joe?" Rebecca turned to her grandfather.

"Yes, Rebecca?" Grandpa Joe looked eager to help.

"Could you teach us some words in Macedonian?"

"Well, I do know a little. I try and learn as much of the languages as I can in the countries I visit. And I've had to travel to lots of countries for my job at the missions agency. Here are two good ones to know. The first is *zdravo*, rhymes with bravo. That's how you say hello. You try and say it."

The kids tried to sound like Grandpa Joe. They said *zdravo* to each other and shook hands like they were really meeting each other and saying hello.

"What's the second one, Grandpa Joe?" Joshua asked eagerly.

"To say thank you to someone you say *fala*. Like "Deck the halls with boughs of holly, fa la..." Grandpa Joe started to sing to teach the kids how the word sounds and to help them remember it.

Rebecca got out her notebook she had packed and took notes.

"Do the Roma speak Macedonian?" Joshua asked his grandfather.

"They know the language," Grandpa Joe began, "but in their homes they speak Romani, a whole other language."

"Can you teach us some Romani?" Rebecca asked.

"No, I haven't learned any of their language. The Taylors will be happy to teach you though."

"Okay," Joshua said and got out his notebook too. They wrote in what they had learned about the Roma.

People group: Roma
Origin: India
Religion: Muslim
Language: Romani

The family boarded their flight to Macedonia. Rebecca and Joshua looked around and wondered how many of the people were from Macedonia and going home and how many people were visiting like them. They sat quietly looking out the window as they took off from Germany and landed in Skopje, Macedonia.

Day 173

Chapter 4   The Arrival

The children weren't phased when they exited the airplane down a ladder onto the runway. They had done that before. They were surprised though to see how small the airport was. There were only two rooms. In the first room they got their passports stamped to show they were allowed to be in the country. In the second room they picked up their suitcases.

"Are there really only two rooms in the airport, Grandpa Joe?" Rebecca asked.

"No, there are four. Two coming and two going. These two rooms are for the people arriving in Macedonia. They have two rooms for the people leaving Macedonia too."

Rebecca and Joshua giggled quietly to each other.

"I don't see anyone with really dark skin," Joshua noticed.

"The Roma are poorer than most other people in the country," Grandma Kay instructed. "They would have less money to be able to travel by airplane than others."

Rebecca understood and nodded.

"I don't think I see any Roma, but I think I see Americans," Joshua blurted out when they walked out of the airport. "Is that Mr. and Mrs. Taylor waving at us?"

Grandma Kay answered, "Yes, it is. And that's Susanna laughing at her parents waving their arms."

Dan and Lydia Taylor wore big smiles. They were younger than Rebecca and Joshua's parents. Susanna was ten months old and liked to laugh. The Taylors knew Grandpa Joe and Grandma Kay. That's what they called them too. Everyone at the Answering the Call missions agency called them Grandpa Joe and Grandma Kay. Everyone loved them and they loved everybody.

Joshua and Rebecca sat behind Susanna in the van. They wanted her to get to know them so she would play with them. Grandpa Joe sat up front with Mr. Taylor.

Eventually, the van stopped at a red light. Little children ran up to the van on both sides. They held out their hands and put on sad faces.

"What are they doing, Grandma Kay?" Joshua asked.

"Those are Roma children begging for money," Grandma Kay answered.

Mr. Taylor rolled down his window and said something to the boy on his side. The boy started washing the side window where the baby was. The girl on the other side ran to the front of the car and rubbed a rag on the headlights. The boy ran back to Mr. Taylor's window. He gave him a few coins. The boy smiled and started talking to Mr. Taylor. Soon the light changed and the boy waved as the van drove off.

"Was that Macedonian?" Rebecca asked Mr. Taylor.

"No, that was Romani," Mr. Taylor said. "That's why he was excited to stay and talk to me instead of trying to get money from other cars."

"Why were they begging?" Joshua asked Mrs. Taylor.

"Their parents probably don't have jobs. They send their children out to get money," she explained.

"Are all Roma poor?" Joshua questioned Mrs. Taylor again.

"No, they aren't all poor. But, in general, no matter what country they live in, they tend to be poorer than other people. They often aren't given jobs. Many of them haven't been to school or only went to school until they were about thirteen years old."

Rebecca and Joshua looked at each other. They knew they would be in school until they were adults.

"Look, Rebecca! A horse and cart!" Joshua exclaimed.

"They decorated the horse with red tassels," Rebecca pointed out. "What's on the back of the cart?"

"Those are empty plastic bottles," Mrs. Taylor answered her. "They collect them from trash dumpsters and sell them to those who recycle bottles."
Rebecca looked thoughtful.

The van passed lines of stores. The things being sold were piled out on the sidewalk in front of the stores. People dodged the traffic to cross the street between to the two rows of shops.

"Are those Roma women?" Joshua wanted to know. "The ones with their heads covered with scarves. They are Muslims, right?"

"They are Muslim women, but they are Albanian," Mrs. Taylor informed him. "The Roma are mostly Muslim, but they don't cover themselves like these women. We're about to drive through a Roma area. Everyone you see there will be Roma."

Joshua and Rebecca focused their attention out their windows. The van turned and they went up a hill. The houses suddenly looked different. They were small and cramped. They were built right up against the street with no yard. There were several bright blue ones.

They saw some little children running around wearing nothing at all. They saw a grandma squatting up against a wall. Her hair was wrapped up in a white scarf. She was wearing a purple and black velvety-looking skirt. On her feet were black slippers. They saw a woman standing in the street holding a hose. She seemed to be cleaning the street. The water rushed down the hill. There was a man sitting on a carton behind a cardboard box set up as a table. He was selling candy from his little stand. They all had black hair and dark skin like they were very, very tan.

"They don't really look like we thought, huh?" Joshua whispered to his sister.

"They are sort of dressed normal," Rebecca responded. "Some of the women are wearing long skirts and gold earrings though. But, no, it's not really what I expected."

At the end of the winding street the Roma neighborhood ended. They drove past lines of tall apartment buildings which looked like big blocks of cement.

"That Roma neighborhood wasn't very big," Rebecca remarked.

"That was actually a pretty good sized community," Mrs. Taylor corrected. "The Roma are scattered everywhere. That's what makes Shutka, our neighborhood, special. There are more Roma all together there than anywhere else in the whole world even though some other countries have millions more Roma than Macedonia. In just a minute we'll be there. See if you can tell when we've arrived in Shutka. By the way, the word Shutka means trash."

"Trash?!" Rebecca and Joshua exclaimed unbelieving.

Day 174

Chapter 5   Shutka

"We're here, aren't we?" Joshua was the first to notice they had entered Shutka. Mrs. Taylor had given them a big clue. He figured it out by the mounds of trash lining the road. Dogs roamed through the garbage for their lunches. Across the street from the trash piles were three enormous houses.

"I thought the Roma were poor?" Rebecca questioned no one in particular.

"Many are poor, Rebecca," Mrs. Taylor explained. "But, there are many Roma who live in other countries where they can make more money. They come back to Shutka and build these big homes. Many of them are empty. Because this is the biggest group of Roma in the world, many Roma in other countries have family here and like to come here to hold their celebrations like weddings. They may live in their home for a month each summer or two and that's all. It impresses others, though, to have a big home, even if they don't live in it."

"Seems like a waste of money," Rebecca decided.

"Well, Rebecca," Mr. Taylor responded this time. "The Roma don't live for God the way we do. They spend money on many things that we think are foolish. One of the most important things to them are their celebrations. They spend more money than they have on their parties. But it's important to them. It makes their lives worth it. That's why we're here. To show them there's something better to live for. God can give their lives importance and meaning.

"When you minister to people, you need to remember where they are coming from. You can't just tell them it's silly to spend money on big parties. We need to work within their culture. We need to show them that they have a reason to celebrate in Jesus."

"Thanks for teaching my grandkids, Dan," Grandpa Joe said with appreciation. "They are eager to learn from you about the Roma and about missions. I think they're eager to play with Susanna too. I hope they will be an encouragement to you while we're here."

"Guests are always an encouragement to us," Mrs. Taylor said and smiled at the children. "When we get to tell someone new about the job we are doing here, it reminds us of the importance of the work. It gets us excited to keep going."

"Then we're extra glad we're here," said Grandma Kay.

The van was moving very slowly now down bumpy roads. There were huge holes in the road making the van dip and bump as it slowly plodded along. Rebecca thought their car was going to be hit as another car squeezed past them on the narrow street. There was no room to pull over to let someone pass. The houses were right up against the street. They splashed through a big puddle. A teenage girl in jeans and a tee shirt was hosing the little cement area next to her home. The water ran out into the street.

"That's the second woman we've seen with a hose," Rebecca told Joshua. "We should find out why." Joshua nodded.

"Later we'll ask," he added. Rebecca nodded. The van was slowing down. Mr. Taylor pulled the van off the road into the dirt.

"Here's our stop," he called to his passengers.

Another huge house stood before them. It was three floors high. There was a fence around it with a cement "yard" in front of the house.

"Don't get too excited," Mrs. Taylor commented. "We live on half of the first floor. The rest isn't ours. We share it with our landlord's family."

Mrs. Taylor was the first to the door behind her husband. He opened the door and slipped off his shoes. Mrs. Taylor did the same. "Welcome," she said and gestured for the rest to enter.

Everyone followed suit and took off their shoes at the door. They walked down a narrow hallway covered with a blue rug. They saw the bathroom on one side of the hall. They walked into the room on the other side. Inside was a dining table, a desk, a couch, coffee table, cabinets and a green rug on the floor.

"Why don't I give you the full tour now?" Mrs. Taylor sparkled as she began showing her home. The first room was open to the kitchen which was more like a narrow hallway. The house had one more door. "This is Susanna's room," Mrs. Taylor said as she came into the room. There was a crib, a bookcase, a box of toys, a wardrobe, a soft chair and another rug. Along two walls were mats. "Those will be your beds," Mrs. Taylor told Rebecca and Joshua.

"Perfect!" exclaimed Joshua. "It'll be like camping!"

"Good," Mrs. Taylor said gently.

Day 175

Grandma Kay was sitting at the desk when the children came out of the other room. "I'm writing your family an email to let them know we arrived. Why don't you each write something as well?"

Rebecca let Joshua go first. Joshua wrote about the plane. Rebecca wrote about the Taylors' house. Rebecca checked their email before she got out of the computer chair. "There's a message from mom and dad," she reported. She read it out loud. She clicked on "reply" and wrote, "We love you too," before clicking on "send."

Mr. Taylor spoke up. "We'd like to take you for a little walk. We'd like you to meet someone too. You have an invitation to join a party tomorrow. We need to introduce you to the host family. They are neighbors of ours. They are very excited you will be at their celebration."

"What kind of party is it?" Rebecca asked right away.

"An engagement party," Mr. Taylor answered. "I don't think there is anything like it in America. You'll find out soon enough what it's like." Mr. Taylor let out a little laugh.

Mr. Taylor led the way again this time out the door. The group of Americans started walking down the street.

"Rebecca, look!" Joshua tugged on Rebecca's dress with excitement. "Do you see?"

Rebecca looked ahead down the street. A gaggle of geese were being walked down the street by an elderly man with a long walking stick. The loud honking carried over the other street noises. A car rumbled past. Huge bags of onions were tied to its roof. Music from a stereo blasted from someone's house.

When the group got to a street crowded with stores, Grandpa Joe asked to go to the exchange office. "That's the money store," he told the kids. "I'm going to buy denars, Macedonian money, with my dollars from America." When he came out of the store, he showed Rebecca and Joshua the money he got. The bills had 10, 50, 100 and 1000 written on them.

"1000!" Joshua shouted.

"Ssh! Don't tell everyone how much money I got," Grandpa Joe corrected. "1000 is only the same as twenty dollars anyway."

They walked on past a small convenient store, a music store and a butcher shop. Mr. Taylor led the others into one of the shops. There was one young man behind a counter. Under the window was a stove. Hamburgers, hot dogs and French fries were cooking. There was little room to stand so Rebecca, Joshua and Grandma Kay went back outside to wait. The men soon returned with a bag of food and drinks.

"We're going to head back home to eat," Grandpa Joe directed.

Rebecca and Joshua took in the sights on the walk home. They saw little kids running around in their underwear carrying bottles of water which they dumped out on each other. Mr. Taylor warned the children to stay away from all the stray dogs they saw. They also had to avoid all the puddles in the street.

"Why are the streets always wet?" Rebecca asked Mrs. Taylor, who was pushing Susanna in a stroller.

"They like to keep things really clean," Mrs. Taylor explained. "They clean in front of their homes with water every day."

When they had almost reached the Taylors' home, they were greeted by a neighbor.

"This is the family that is holding the engagement party tomorrow," Mr. Taylor informed everyone. Rebecca and Joshua shook the woman's hand. The neighbor kissed Mrs. Taylor on both cheeks.

While walking the rest of the way to the house, Mrs. Taylor told everyone that the neighbors had invited them to the party.

"The party will be tomorrow from four in the afternoon until around midnight," Mrs. Taylor said. "Your bodies will think that's ten in the morning until six in the evening. It's six hours earlier in America than here. Maybe that will help you stay awake for the party. But I don't think we'll stay until midnight."

Rebecca whispered to Joshua to change his watch to read six hours later. It was one in the afternoon in America. They changed their watches to say it was seven in the evening.

Back home they ate their hot dog sandwiches. The hot dogs were on huge buns and had French fries on top of them covered in ketchup and mayonnaise. After Susanna was asleep the kids had a time of prayer with their grandparents and the Taylors. The Taylors went into Susanna's room to sleep. Grandma Kay and Grandpa Joe slept on the couch which pulled open into a bed. Rebecca and Joshua curled up on the foam mats covered with shiny, smooth material. They went to sleep to the sounds of music and dogs barking.

Day 176

Chapter 6   What's For Dinner?

There was excitement on the Taylors' street the next day. Several families were preparing for the party. Mrs. Taylor went with her neighbors to get her hair done at a hair salon. She came back with her hair in curls on top of her head. Susanna stared at her. She wasn't sure who it was at first. Mrs. Taylor announced they were all going to another neighbor's house for dinner at three o'clock.

At three Rebecca and Joshua followed the Taylors over to their neighbors with their notebooks in hand. They entered through a metal gate and walked across the cement area in front of the house. Rebecca stayed close to Grandma Kay. She was worried about being pecked by the three chickens milling around on the cement walkway in front of the house.

A woman dressed in a long black skirt and yellow t-shirt came out from the house. She stood next to a string of peppers that were shaped like bananas hanging on the outside wall of the house. She shook hands with everyone. Joshua remembered to say, "Zdravo." Mrs. Taylor kissed the woman on both cheeks. Everyone kicked off their shoes outside the entrance. They stepped into the home onto a thin red rug. Every inch of the floor was covered with rugs.

The woman took everyone into the house's other room, which had a tablecloth spread on the floor. A younger woman stopped placing plates on the tablecloth to come over and greet the guests. A boy, smaller than Peter, hung onto her pant leg. Grandma Kay handed the boy the chocolate bar she remembered to bring.

"This is Erika," Mrs. Taylor introduced the young woman. "She is a believer. So is her husband, who's not here right now. His name is Adam. We can go ahead and sit down at the plates."

Mrs. Taylor sat down, and Erika brought a plastic rattle over for Susanna to hold. Rebecca stayed next to Grandma Kay and Joshua sat with Grandpa Joe and Mr. Taylor on the other side of the spread. The older woman who had greeted them sat down with Mrs. Taylor and began inquiring about the guests.

Erika finished setting out plates and glasses and started bringing out the food. She brought out enough small loaves of bread for everyone to have their own loaf. She brought out a salad of tomatoes and cucumbers with grated cheese covering the top. She brought out a pot of food that looked mysterious to Rebecca and Joshua.

"What is that?" Rebecca asked her grandmother.

"Let's ask," Grandma Kay answered in a whisper. She looked at the older woman and pointed to the pot. "What's in there?" she asked with a big smile.

The older woman responded eagerly and began demonstrating with her hands how the dish is prepared. Mrs. Taylor translated.

"The dish is called *sarma*. Ground beef is cooked on the stove top with onion and seasonings. Then it is mixed with rice. You take a handful of the mixture and roll it up in a leaf of pickled cabbage. The rolls are then put in the pot, covered with water and boiled."

"Sounds delicious," Grandma Kay said.

Adam came in the room with his father. They greeted everyone with a handshake. Adam asked Grandpa Joe in English with a strong accent, "How are you?"

"Just fine," Grandpa Joe said slowly and clearly.

"Welcome to our home," Adam said, again in English.

"Thank you," responded Grandpa Joe.

The Taylors explained that Adam was a young leader in the church started in Shutka. They shared Adam's testimony with the group of Americans as well. Adam had an uncle in the church and had been to his house to visit his cousin at times when there were Bible study groups in his home. He sometimes listened to the discussions and was interested. But he decided that he was young and wanted to just live and have fun and could study religion when he was older. Soon after he had a dream where he saw Jesus come to him and tell him to follow Him. Adam decided to give his life to following Christ.

Day 177

"Wow," thought Rebecca. "Did Erika have a dream about Jesus too?" she asked.

"No, Adam told Erika about Jesus and she decided it sounded good," explained Mr. Taylor. "They were soon to be married when Adam gave his life to Christ. She followed him in his decision. There are others in the church though who came to Jesus through dreams. There are others who were healed miraculously and then believed. One woman was healed of cancer. God can work around the fact that there are few missionaries here to evangelize and to disciple the people here."

"God is good!" Grandma Kay exclaimed.

"God certainly knows how to take care of His children," Grandpa Joe added. "How do their families feel about them being Christians?"

Mr. Taylor relayed the question to Adam and then translated his answer. "At first they threatened me that bad things would happen if I became a Christian. Sometimes it was very hard to go against them. Now though they accept me and don't give me a hard time. My family celebrates Muslim holidays and observes Muslim traditions which can be hard. The money I earn goes to the family and they use it to celebrate these Muslim holidays, and Erika has to work to cook and clean to prepare for those holidays. Things like that are hard. Our son knows how to pray, but sometimes we catch him copying the Muslim prayers where you bow with your head to the ground."

"Please," Erika said with a gesture to let everyone know to start eating.

"I'll pray," Grandpa Joe offered. "Thank you, Father God, for this food, for your constant provision for all our needs, for your love and grace, for calling us Your children. Please bless this family and use them to bless this community to the glory of the name of Jesus. Amen."

"*Ameen*," chorused Erika and Adam.

"Ameen, that is how they say amen," Grandpa Joe told his grandchildren.

Rebecca started writing in her notebook.

Muslims sometimes become Christians through dreams and healings.

Food:
Sarma, ground meat and rice rolled into a cabbage leaf and boiled
Salad, cucumber and tomato in chunks with grated cheese on top
A whole loaf of bread for each person!

As the family began eating Erika brought in a bottle of what the kids thought was soda. She poured each person a glass full. Joshua picked up his glass and started to drink. Immediately his face scrunched up, and he quickly covered his mouth with his hand. He swallowed with a grimace.

"What is that?" Joshua asked his grandfather. Adam's family laughed when they saw him. They knew it was an unusual taste for Americans but that some really liked it too.

"Was it sour?" he asked chuckling.

"I'm not sure if it was sour, but it sure wasn't sweet! I thought it was soda."

"Well, it is soda," Grandpa Joe told Joshua. "Original soda. It's soda water. We like to call it bubble water. It's soda without the sugar or flavoring. They drink it a lot here. People like it."

"I guess people can get used to anything," Joshua added.

"I'm not so sure I want to try it, let alone drink enough to get used to it," decided Rebecca.

"Try it once, and I'll let you write Mom and Dad about what it's like," prodded Joshua.

"No, thank you," replied Rebecca. "You can tell them. I already know what it's like. I saw your face! I think I'll start with the salad. That's mostly recognizable."

The family ate and made sure Erika and Adam's mother knew how good the meal was.

Rebecca took one last look around their home before they left. She wanted to remember everything from the vases of plastic flowers everywhere to the old black and white photographs on the wall.

Day 178

Chapter 7   The Party

Mrs. Taylor came out of the room to oohs and aahs. "How do you like my penguin pants?" she asked her amazed audience.

Her "penguin pants" were shimmery white pants that ballooned out and came down to her ankles. The bottom of the pants were trimmed with silver sequins. She also wore a white blouse with very wide sleeves. The blouse was trimmed with silver thread. Over it all she wore a long blue vest reaching close to the floor. The vest was embroidered in silver with pictures of birds and flowers. Her hair done up on top of her head in curls completed the fantastic look.

"I love the pants!" Rebecca piped up. "Is everyone going to be dressed like you?"

"Not everyone. Only the women will dress this fancy. The men just wear regular clothes but try and look nice. The married women will wear some sort of get up like this one, but they are all different. The unmarried girls won't wear them. They won't receive an outfit like this until they are getting married themselves."

"I can't wait to see what everyone else looks like," Joshua whispered to his sister. "Is it time to go?" he questioned the group.

"It's about time," Mr. Taylor answered. "And don't worry, you all will look just fine in your regular clothes. People wear what they have. They know you don't have clothes like these."

Rebecca noticed Mrs. Taylor slip on special sandals while they were leaving the house. They were covered in blue sequins. Mr. Taylor pushed the stroller this time while the gang walked to the party. Rebecca thought it was funny to see someone dressed up so fancy walking through rocky, muddy streets.

The children noticed more and more people. Some were dressed like Mrs. Taylor. "They must be going where we're headed," they thought and gave each other sideways glances.

The group turned the corner and saw a mass of people standing around two huge speakers which towered above them. Between the two speakers was a band of teenagers playing drums, keyboards and guitars. One held a microphone and sang in Romani.

"Here we are," Mr. Taylor told the group. "It's going to be louder when we get to the other side of those speakers. It will be hard to talk to each other. Any questions before we go over there?"

"Yeah, what do we do?" Joshua asked with wide eyes.

"Just stay together." Mr. Taylor told him with an encouraging smile. "Here we go!"

The troupe walked in single file past the crowds of onlookers. It was certainly loud on the other side of the speakers! Rebecca couldn't help but hold her ears. Grandma Kay took hold of one of her elbows. Grandpa Joe held onto Joshua. Mrs. Taylor came and gestured to Grandma Kay with her head to come with her. She nodded and the three ladies walked out into the middle of the street to join the other women already dancing. The dance was a long line of women and girls holding hands. They walked in a certain rhythm: forward, backward, side to side. Rebecca couldn't get the hang of it and kept stepping on Mrs. Taylor's feet and bumping into Grandma Kay. Everyone smiled at her though.

There were other girls in the circle. Some were younger than Rebecca. Two of them wore dresses that looked like little wedding gowns. There was one older girl in a real white wedding gown.

Mr. Taylor and the other men and boys stood off to the side and watched. Mr. Taylor yelled in Joshua's ear to tell him the girl in the wedding dress was the girl who was engaged. She was 18 years old and met her husband-to-be just this past week.

After awhile Grandma Kay and Rebecca joined the boys for a break. Mrs. Taylor eventually joined them, after almost two hours. The music stopped after about three hours of playing without a break.

"Is the party over?" Rebecca asked Mrs. Taylor. "Everyone is leaving."

"No, that was just part one. Now we eat!" Mrs. Taylor answered and rubbed Rebecca's back. "The people are just going home to change their clothes. They will be back. The women will change into evening gowns. I'm going to change too. Let's head home."

An hour later the Taylors and their American guests were back on the same street with the band and other guests. There were now long wooden tables set up in the street. Mrs. Taylor was wearing a dress she had used as a bridesmaid in her brother's wedding several years before.

Rebecca and Joshua had gotten more used to the loud music by now. They sat next to each other at one of the tables. Grandpa Joe and Grandma Kay sat on either side of them. Grandma Kay poured drinks for the kids. On each table were bottles of soda pop. The children didn't recognize any of the bottle labels. Their soda was yellow. They later learned it was pear flavored.

Soon waiters brought out plates of food. The plates had salad made of thinly shredded cabbage and sliced cucumber, beef that looked like sausage, and a scoop of beef stew next to mashed potatoes. Rebecca liked the salad. Joshua liked the stew. Neither were too sure about "the meat sticks" which is what they called them. The next day they learned they were called *kebaps*.

A man with a microphone went around to each table and person by person collected the gift of money offered to the bride-to-be. The man took the money and then announced over the speakers who the person was and how much money he gave. The children couldn't believe it!

The children went home with their grandparents before the cake was served. It was after ten at night; they were tired. The party ended with more dancing and finished after midnight. Rebecca and Joshua were long asleep before then.

Day 179

Chapter 8   A Visit to the City

When Joshua woke up to the bright sun shining through the curtains, he saw Rebecca already dressed and reading something.

"What is that?" Joshua asked.

"It's a note from Mom and Dad. I found it in the bottom of my suitcase. There are pictures from Peter and Samuel. You must have some too hidden in the bottom of your suitcase."

Joshua dug down to the bottom of his suitcase and pulled up a pile of papers.

"These are so fun. Let's ask to write an email to tell them thanks."

Rebecca and Joshua quietly opened their door out into the main room. The grownups were all awake and sipping tea or juice.

The kids showed off their letters and pictures and got permission to write an email.

"What do we get to do today?" Joshua asked eagerly.

"Well, we do have something planned. How about a bus trip into the city?"

"Yes! I've never been on a bus!" Joshua jumped up as if they would leave that moment.

"Well, good," Mr. Taylor laughed. "Your grandpa and I will stay home and get some work done. Mrs. Taylor will give the rest of you a bit of a tour."

Mrs. Taylor picked up where Mr. Taylor stopped. "We should get going in about half an hour. We'll eat breakfast and then walk up the hill to the bus stop. I have bread ready for our breakfast so we can eat as soon as everyone's ready."

The family gathered and blessed the food and began to pass the fresh bread around the table. They were rolls shaped like crescent moons and filled with jam.

After breakfast the men volunteered to clear the table. Grandma Kay and Mrs. Taylor got kisses as everyone headed for the door. Susanna got to ride in a backpack. She giggled from her perch.

The group walked up hill to the bus stop at the end of the street. There was no way of knowing it was a bus stop. There were no signs, benches or other markers. There were two men waiting there as well.

The first bus that came zoomed past without stopping. Mrs. Taylor let them know that bus wasn't the number they needed. The next bus slowed to a stop with a loud screech. Mrs. Taylor ushered the kids and Grandma Kay in first and then followed. She paid the driver and joined the others in a row of seats along the wall of the bus. Mrs. Taylor handed Grandma Kay a ticket.

"May I please hold my ticket?" Rebecca asked.

"You don't get a ticket. Kids get to ride free. You won't have to pay for a couple of years yet."

Rebecca looked around at everyone else holding their ticket. She hoped she really didn't need one as Mrs. Taylor explained that sometimes policemen got on the buses to check for tickets.

Each time as a stop neared people stood and made their way to the doors. They had to hold onto the seatbacks to keep from falling. At each stop several people would get off and others would get on.

The children watched the people on the bus. They watched the teenagers and the old men. They smiled at the other children, who didn't smile back but stared instead.
Finally Mrs. Taylor said their stop was next.

"It's too dangerous to stand up before the bus stops. There are others standing so the driver will stop for them to get off. When the bus stops, head for that door there." Mrs. Taylor pointed to the middle set of doors. The bus had three sets.

The bus screeched and stopped and Mrs. Taylor acted as mother hen and kept everyone together and got them out the door.

"The drivers aren't very patient here. I got you out first to make sure they didn't close the doors on any of you. It happens sometimes."

Rebecca's eyes were wide thinking about getting shut into the bus with her family already on the outside. She was thankful for Mrs. Taylor's knowledge and experience.

The kids had been so focused on the bus that they hadn't noticed the tower looming up next to them. Joshua was the first to notice.

"Can we go up there?" He pointed to the walls of an old stone fortress which sat on a hill in downtown Skopje.

"That's exactly where we are going."

The children felt like soldiers marching across the drawbridge. They stopped to look down into the moat which no longer had any water in it. The children ran their fingers along the stone wall as they passed through the huge gate.

"You are free to run ahead if you like, kids. We're going to head down this path here." Mrs. Taylor pointed along a walkway.

The kids ran until they reached a circular tower.

"Let's go ask if we can go inside," Joshua said.

Rebecca was the first to turn around and dart back to the adults.

"Excuse me, Mrs. Taylor," Rebecca started when she got their attention. "Can we go in that tower down there?"

"You can go in carefully. Stay inside though. You can walk right out through the doorways in the tower out onto a ledge, but don't. There are no railings to protect you from accidentally falling. From inside the tower you can look out over city."

"Should we wait for you, Grandma?"

"Yes, why don't you."

"Okay." Rebecca smiled at her Grandma and thought about how neat it was they were here together all the way in Macedonia.

"Joshua!" Rebecca called to her brother. "Let's go along these stepping stones."

The pair counted as they skipped from stone to stone up to the wall. Joshua thought of a question and turned back leaping from stone to stone.

"What are those little windows for in the wall? They are hard to see out of, but I know I've seen pictures of castles with those same things."

"They aren't for looking out. That's why they are so small," answered Mrs. Taylor. "They are called arrow slits. They are for shooting out arrows. They are small so arrows can't shoot back in. This fortress is nearly 1500 years old. Over the years it's been rebuilt and added to. Let's go up in here first and look out over the city."

Everyone walked up the few steps into the circular tower. There were three open doorways where they could look out. The kids looked out of each one wondering what it looked like more than 1000 years ago. It must have been very different from what they could see now. Out one doorway they could see the tall downtown buildings. Out another window they saw the Vardar River. Through the third window they saw red roofs crowded together and counted seven tall skinny towers popping up above the houses.

"Each one of those things you see sticking up is a minaret. A minaret is part of a mosque," Mrs. Taylor explained when she noticed the children looking in their direction. "Do you know what a mosque is?"

"It's where Muslims worship their god." Rebecca knew the answer. "It seems like a lot of mosques," she sadly noted.

"There are new ones being built. And new churches being built, but not many that glorify God. There's a lot of work to be done here."

Mrs. Taylor saw the kid's glum faces.

"But nothing is impossible for our God!" Mrs. Taylor turned the children to face her. "He can do all things. You can make a big difference too. Pray for Macedonia every day. Pray for our family too and for more workers to come and share the good news about Jesus!"

Rebecca and Joshua nodded, "We will."

"Good. Let's do some more exploring."

Grandma Kay put her arm around Rebecca as they walked down the stairs of the tower. They walked all around the fortress and finally back out across the drawbridge.

The tour continued with a picnic lunch on Mount Vodno. On the top of the mountain was an enormous cross that was lit at night. They spread their picnic blanket out halfway up the mountain in the middle of a pine forest. Susanna was happy for the chance to crawl around and play.

The bus home was more crowded than the way there. Several people stood to make room for the children and women to sit down. Grandma Kay was thankful for her seat. She thought to pray for the city as she watched it go by out her window.

The group made it home in time for Susanna to take a nap. Grandma Kay thought a nap sounded like a good idea too. Rebecca and Joshua talked about the morning as they wrote down all they could remember in their notebooks.

Day 180

1. What did you learn about Macedonia? the Roma? missionaries?

Chapter 9   True Missionaries

After dinner that evening everyone enjoyed sitting around and hearing the Taylors' stories about their first arriving and learning the language. They talked about the friends they had made and the heartbreaks they had already experienced.

Once Susanna was in bed Mr. Taylor announced a surprise for his wife. "We're going to get to go on a date, sweetheart."

"Really?" Mrs. Taylor looked at Grandpa Joe and Grandma Kay.

"Really. We set it up already. I'm ready to go when you are."

"I'll change in a flash!" Mrs. Taylor was gone and back as fast as she promised. "Thank you so much for giving us this time. We haven't been on a date since Susanna was born."

"It's no trouble for us. We enjoy quiet evenings. And we get to spend time with our wonderful grandchildren." Rebecca and Joshua couldn't help but smile at Grandpa Joe's comment.

"Have a great time," Grandma Kay said as she walked the couple to the door. "We'll be okay."

Mrs. Taylor waved as the two walked up the hill to catch the bus downtown.

Grandpa Joe turned his attention to the children. "Now, there are a few things I'd like to do while they are gone. We could do some cleaning, like the top of the fridge and things like that. We could also wrap the presents we brought for them. And, we could write them a letter to thank them for welcoming us into their home. Let's pray for them now and then decide how to get the rest of those things done."

"May I please clean?" Rebecca asked, not waiting until after prayer.

"We'll decide in a bit, okay?" Grandpa Joe reminded her.

Rebecca nodded and sat on the floor with Joshua near her grandparents. The group prayed for the Taylors and for the country and for the Roma. There was a lot to pray for. They all really wanted to see the Roma of Macedonia following Jesus as their Lord. They prayed for more workers to join the Taylors who wanted to serve God more than anything else.

When the group said their "Amens", Grandpa Joe took the first job assignment. "I think I would like to write the thank you letter. Rebecca would like to clean. Grandma?" Grandpa Joe looked at his bride asking what she would like to do.

"I'll take wrapping," Grandma answered and looked to Joshua. "What do you think you would like to do?"

"Well, Mrs. Taylor said today that we could help a lot by praying. Could I write prayer requests for the Taylors on an email and send it to our family and the friends we write emails to?"

"That's a wonderful idea." Grandpa Joe put his hand on Joshua's shoulder. "Let's all get to work."

The team divided up and got to work in the kitchen and living room. Susanna slept in the other room. The kids were asleep by the time the Taylors tiptoed into the room.

"Thank you so much," Mrs. Taylor said and gave Grandma Kay a hug. "We had a wonderful time."

The next morning started early for Rebecca and Grandma Kay. The two of them snuck out together to walk to the little store around the corner. They bought eggs, bread, cheese and juice to make breakfast for everyone. Once they got to work in the kitchen preparing everything, it didn't take Mrs. Taylor long to figure out their surprise.

"What a treat. What are you making?" Mrs. Taylor saw the ingredients they had out.

"Scrambled eggs with cheese and cinnamon toast. Nothing fancy." Grandma Kay winked at Mrs. Taylor. "You go ahead and take some extra time reading your Bible this morning.

Mrs. Taylor gave Grandma Kay a squeeze and went back into the living room.

The family enjoyed the breakfast feast and talked about the plan for their last day together. Grandpa Joe addressed everyone at the table.

"Today I'm going to spend as much time as I can talking and praying with Mr. and Mrs. Taylor. Grandma Kay would like to spend some time with Mrs. Taylor as well. Can you two play with Susanna this morning? It's okay if she wants to be with her mom sometimes, too."

"Of course," Joshua responded.

"We'll be so happy to play with her all day! She's so cute and fun to be with." Rebecca started making faces at Susanna in her high chair.

"Great. And I hear Grandma Kay and Rebecca are going to be making our dinner today as well. That will be a big help so Mrs. Taylor can be with me to talk about everything on their minds. Let's all pray together before we start the day."

Grandpa Joe prayed for everyone. By now they were feeling very much like one big family.

Grandpa Joe, Mr. Taylor and their wives sat around in the living room talking and laughing and asking and answering questions while the kids played as quietly as they could in the other room.

The day passed quickly and happily. The family opened their presents and were excited by the thoughtfulness of their guests. While Susanna took her nap, the children joined the adults for a time of prayer. Then Grandma Kay and Rebecca cooked a simple dinner of chicken and vegetables. The kids emailed home one more time and told their parents they were excited to be seeing them in another day.

Grandma Kay suggested that they all should get their clothes ready for the next day and get everything packed up completely. They had to leave for the airport at four the next morning. Rebecca and Joshua organized their things for the trip the next day. Joshua asked Rebecca why their mom had packed a couple of long sleeved shirts that they never wore. Rebecca thought that Mom had just wanted to make sure they were prepared. Joshua thought it was strange and wondered.

Mr. Taylor listened in as the children were talking.

"Do you remember, Rebecca, how we were going to show people Jesus by how we lived? I'm not sure anyone noticed our lights," Joshua said, a bit discouraged.

Mr. Taylor piped in. "You children certainly do shine Christ's light. You have been a big encouragement to us and a big help. Our neighbors have been wondering why you are here and what you have been doing. When we tell them, they can't understand why you would come all this way when you aren't even our family. That gives us a chance to share about God's love and how they can be part of God's family. Anyone who is truly following Jesus will always make an impact where they are, even if they can't speak a word."

"We did do it, Rebecca!" Rebecca smiled at her happy brother.

"Thanks for encouraging us," Rebecca thanked Mr. Taylor. "We really wanted to share the gospel with someone. We know we would need to learn the language in order to really explain to someone about Jesus. But we're happy to show people love and make people curious to learn about God."

"You two are true missionaries," Mr. Taylor declared.

Answers

Day 1
> 5. to get him out of the nest so he could teach him to fly

Day 2
> 4. Farmer Green's cat

Day 12
> 4. a snowman

Day 23
> 2. They were told by their mother not to go. He was disobeying.

Day 24
> 2. He had lost them in the garden and Mr. McGreggor uses them to make a scarecrow.

Day 25
> 2. a place to sit on her eggs

Day 26
> 2. a wolf
> 3. He wants to eat the eggs.

Day 27
> 2. He doesn't live there.
> 3. No, he's got a long way to go to get home.

Day 30
> 2. His tail broke in two.

Day 31
> 2. Solomon Owl

Day 33
> 2. He thinks he's going to eat him.

Day 35
> 3. No, he put a bag over his head.

Day 36
> 3. Farmer Green's chicken house

Day 40
> 2. It's stuck inside him. He's hitting himself against trees trying to break it up.

Day 45
> 3. "to decide which is in the right" Solomon was deciding who was right when two animals argued.

Day 53
> 2. It's too hot to move.
> 3. The season for roses is over and they have wilted and died. Maybe they are growing in other areas where it is warmer.
> 4. She's under water.

Day 55
> 2. weather and whether

Day 58
2. Work time is for working and not playing.
3. twit- twee…
Day 59
2. Your cheerful attitude can bring joy to someone.
Day 60
2. He's good at loving his mother.
Day 61
2. put her things away
3. The sheep are taken to a river or pond and thrown in to be washed. Then they are dried before they are sheared.
Day 62
2. She fed them and visited them often and stayed still and quiet near them.
3. Share and are don't rhyme.
Day 63
2. It can be more fun to work and to be productive than to play.
Day 67
2. the girl, her daughter
Day 68
2. cut by thorns
Day 69
2. Pretty isn't looking good but doing something worthwhile.
Day 71
2. He dropped his glasses in a pot of purple dye.
Day 72
2. He wasn't dressed properly.
Day 75
3. her brother, Austin
Day 76
3. greet each other in the street
Day 92
2. He said he had a member for the club. It was sly because the bird had a red wing and hid his head under his wing so it looked red. Sly means sneaky, tricky.
Day 102
They are all filled in with O. This shows three different ways OO can be read.
Day 103
Examples: bed, Ned, Ted, red, led; pig, big, rig, dig; can, ban, man, ran; pot, hot, not, rot; run, bun, nun, pun
Day 131
Examples: angry, mad; begin, start; awful, bad; shut, close; under, below; choose, pick; simple, easy; correct, right; say, speak; soil, dirt

Day 132

Examples: day, night; question, answer; more, less; forget, remember; bent, straight; difficult, easy; push, pull; none, some; real, fake; quiet, loud

Day 133

Examples: pet, get, wet, let; pin, tin, sin, win; bad, dad, pad, mad; pop, mop, top, bop; but, cut, rut, nut

Day 134

The second word begins with "more" or ends with "er." The last word begins with "most" or ends with "est."

Day 135

Synonyms are words that mean the same. Antonyms are words that are the opposite. Homophones are words that sound the same but are spelled differently.

PLEASE consider passing this book along to a family in need
by contacting us at allinonehomeschool@gmail.com.

ABOUT THE EASY PEASY ALL-IN-ONE HOMESCHOOL

The Easy Peasy All-in-One Homeschool is a free, complete online homeschool. There are 180 days of ready-to-go assignments for every level and every subject. It's created for your children to work as independently as you want them to. Preschool through high school is available as well as courses ranging from English, math, science and history to art, music, computer, thinking, physical education and health. A daily Bible lesson is offered as well. The mission of Easy Peasy is to enable those to homeschool who otherwise thought they couldn't.

Look for other books in the EP Reader Series and for more offline materials to come.

Made in the USA
Columbia, SC
17 July 2020